ELISE DOWNING

COASTING

RUNNING AROUND THE COAST OF BRITAIN – LIFE, LOVE AND (VERY) LOOSE PLANS

summersdale

COASTING

An Hachette UK Company
www.hachette.co.uk

Summersdale Publishers Ltd
Part of Octopus Publishing Group Limited
Carmelite House
50 Victoria Embankment
LONDON
EC4Y 0DZ
UK

www.summersdale.com

Printed and bound by CPI Group (UK) Ltd, Croydon, CR0 4YY

ISBN: 978-1-78783-981-6

Substantial discounts on bulk quantities of Summersdale books are available to corporations, professional associations and other organizations. For details contact general enquiries: telephone: +44 (0) 1243 771107 or email: enquiries@summersdale.com.

*For my Pap, who cared about books more
than anybody else I've ever known.*

*(He would have told you off for folding the corners
of this one but don't worry, I don't mind.)*

GREAT BRITAIN

John O'Groats
Tongue
Lossiemouth
Isle of Skye
Isle of Mull
Dundee
Edinburgh
Berwick-upon-Tweed
Isle of Arran
Ayr
Gretna
Sunderland
Whitby
Bridlington
Blackpool
Liverpool
Skegness
Hunstanton
Porthmadog
Fishguard
Aldeburgh
Swansea
Leigh-on-Sea
Bristol
Whitstable
Dartford
Minehead
Folkestone
Portsmouth
Beachy Head
St Ives
Looe
Plymouth
Lulworth Cove
Falmouth

SAFETY BRIEFING

This is a book about muddling through a big adventure without any experience or expertise. It's about having an idea and then setting about making it happen, even when you don't have the foggiest idea what you're doing. For the most part, I think this is a good attitude to have. I'm not sure anybody really knows what they're doing, at least not as much as it probably looks like they do from the outside.

I recently listened to an episode of the *Real Talk Radio* podcast where the guest was talking about their journey to sobriety. They said that "You don't have to be strong enough on day one to get to year ten" and it's a line that really stuck with me. I think we can apply that mentality to a lot of things. You only really need to know enough to get through the first day, or even just to take the first step. The rest of it you can work out along the way, most of the time. If you always waited until you felt 100 per cent ready, I don't think you would ever end up doing anything.

However, my caveat to this is that if you want to spend a lot of time outdoors, then I really would recommend learning how to read a map properly. Not as a nice-to-have, but as an absolute essential – especially if you're going to be alone, in remote places, in bad weather conditions. There are lots of stories over the coming pages that reference my inability to read a map and not only did this make my journey a lot more difficult than it needed to be, it was downright stupid. It all worked out okay for me in the end, and admittedly was the source of a few funny stories along the way, but it so easily could have been disastrous.

Buy a map and a compass and learn how to use them. It's not as hard as you think it'll be. And carry a torch with you at all times too, if there's even the slightest chance that you might end up out after dark.

Safety briefing over. Time to get on with the story.

CHAPTER 1

It was a nondescript Tuesday in early March and I was at work, looking at a road map of Great Britain and trying to work out if we could deliver something to a customer in the Scottish Highlands. I was working for a small company in London, my first job after university, and I had a secret: I hated it.

I loved my colleagues. I loved desk beers at 5 p.m. on a Friday. I loved telling people that I worked for a cool, young startup. But the actual getting up every morning and going to work bit? The thought of doing that every single day *forever more*? I feel awkward saying it because it's such a glaring cliché, but the idea of that felt completely devastating and, frankly, intolerable.

Sitting at my desk that afternoon, my mind started to wander. I found myself wondering if anybody had ever been around the whole coast of Britain before. Not ran, necessarily, just been around by any means – by bike, by car, on foot. I placed that customer's order, finished my shift, took the night bus home to my flat-share and went to bed. When I woke up in the morning, that thought was still there.

Had anybody circumnavigated our whole island before? Had they done it in one go? Had they done it alone?

I thought about the coast of Britain for a few more days after that first inkling of an idea before discussing it with anybody. I did some research and learned that quite a few people had walked and cycled and sailed around, but I couldn't find much about anybody running it at that point. Interesting, I thought.

There planted a tiny seed: perhaps it could be me.

———

For the few months prior I had been dating Greg. It was a completely doomed, very unhealthy, absolute non-starter of a relationship – if we can even call it that – but at the time Greg was my go-to adventure person. I had met him at an adventure festival the year before and we'd followed each other on Twitter afterwards. We were pen pals for a while until I moved to London after graduating, when we started meeting up to spend evenings wandering around Covent Garden holding hands and eating in chain restaurants.

Greg lived a few hours from London and we didn't see each other often, but we would exchange hundreds of messages every day. He had so many huge dreams and plans and ideas, and it was exciting to be around. He shared them in a way that made me feel like perhaps I was allowed to have those sorts of ideas too. I didn't have to just settle for things as they were – I could go out and make something happen. He opened my eyes to the community of people out there going on ridiculous, amazing human-powered journeys. Running over continents, sailing across oceans, cycling around entire planets... It was following these people, people who were just like me, really, that made me wonder if it perhaps wasn't totally out of the question for me to do something like that too.

But being with Greg wasn't all good. In fact, it was mostly pretty terrible. As the months went on, I started to suspect that perhaps the things he was telling me weren't always entirely accurate. Nothing ever quite seemed to add up, whether it was what he'd had for breakfast, where he worked, stories about his family and his friends, the swimming pool that was apparently in his garden, the businesses he said he was doing deals with, the celebrities he was supposedly hanging out with... His version of events never matched up with mine (or with anybody else's, it seemed). At first I just put it down to misunderstandings, but after a while I started to feel like I was going mad. I was living in a fog and I couldn't break through to anything that made sense.

It's confusing to look back on. Our whole relationship was so miserable, but without Greg opening my eyes to all this adventure and possibility, and without the motivation of wanting to impress him (however much I hate to admit that), would I have dared to go and run around a country? Would I have even wanted to? I'm not sure.

Is it worth spending month after month crying on buses, on trains, on friends, in the toilets at work, in the pub, unable to shake that impenetrable feeling of doom and inadequacy and utter confusion, if in the midst of it you make the best decision of your life? Is it worth losing yourself completely for a year, for longer, if it leads to you doing the thing you're most proud of?

I've thought about it a lot, and I'm still not sure. But that's how it was.

———

Greg was the first person I talked to about my idea. I messaged him on the way to work one morning and told him there was something that I was thinking about.

"It's about 5,000 miles," I texted. "Maybe I could do it in a few years? I need to save up, and train, and well, you know, figure out what on earth I'm doing. But perhaps in a few years I could do this thing? What do you think?"

"Set off in November," he replied. "Go then, in six months' time, or you'll never go at all."

Right. Okay then.

Now, memories of Greg live firmly in the Very Negative Experience box. It took a while, but the lid is shut. It's hard, looking back at that time, to sift through all the sadness and pull out any positives. But if I'm trying hard to be objective, this was something that Greg got right. If he hadn't told me to go sooner, and I hadn't so readily agreed, I'm almost certain that I wouldn't be sitting here now writing this story. If I'd waited, allowed time for all that preparation, I never would have gone at all.

Six months – that was long enough, right? I moved out of the too expensive flat I shared with a friend and took a room in a house with six others instead. The savings from this alone would be enough to get me round the coast, I thought. (I was wrong about this it turns out, very wrong, but we can talk about that later.) Six months was plenty long enough to research some kit and look at a few maps. And to learn how to run a long way, perhaps – something I had never done before.

November 1st. It had a ring to it. No matter that I'd be staring right down the barrel of a grim English winter, this was it.

I told my parents next, who seemed a bit bemused. I'm sure they thought that this was just another of my many ridiculous ideas that would never happen. And I can't blame them really. I would call them on pretty much a daily basis to announce yet another new career plan: banker, MI5 agent, social worker, baker, physiotherapist... this was just another one to add to the list.

Next I told my boss, then my best friends. We were in a pub garden at the end of a night out and it just came out. It probably goes down as one of my weirder drunken confessions, and that's saying a lot. They definitely thought it was ridiculous. My brother Chris was the most confused though. He was the sporty one in our family and has been running competitively since he was eight years old. He definitely hadn't seen this coming.

I don't think there was anybody to whom this felt like the natural, obvious next step for me.

You see, I was completely unqualified to be setting off on a 5,000-mile run. Just writing it down, even now after I've actually done the thing, it sounds barbaric. When I tell people about it now, having done it, they immediately get the wrong idea about my athletic abilities. No, really, honestly, I'm not a very good runner, I tell them, and I definitely wasn't then. It sounds like I'm just being modest, but it's the truth.

I had been running for less than three years at the point I decided to run around the country. On New Year's Day 2013, I sat down to write resolutions with my cousin, and one of mine was to run a half marathon. It felt like an unfathomably long way. The thought of running for more than 2 hours without stopping… I couldn't get my head around that being something my legs would ever be able to do.

I was obsessed with the "not stopping" part, which is ironic really given that so much of ultrarunning, and especially adventure running, is all about the stopping. Stop for a picture, for a sandwich, to refill your water, for snacks, for a chat, to read a map, for more snacks. It's just a moving picnic, really. But back then, all my achievements were framed by this idea of not stopping.

I was living in Sweden at the time, studying in Gothenburg on my year abroad, and the temperature hung around –10°C, or lower, for most of the winter. I didn't have any proper running kit and, Scandinavia being as notoriously expensive as it is, I couldn't afford to buy any. I set off for my first run in early January wearing two pairs of old cotton leggings, a sweatshirt from a charity shop, a bulky rain coat and pink knitted gloves. I didn't even have a digital watch, let alone any kind of GPS device. There's a picture of me somewhere running my first 10K race that March, wearing that faded old sweatshirt and squinting through the sweat in my eyes at my analogue watch face to see if I was going to make it home in under the one-hour mark.

From the very beginning running felt hard, but it also felt like a kind of magic. It was the way the impossible could become possible so tangibly, so quickly, before your eyes, with just a little bit of work. I hadn't experienced that before with anything else. I couldn't run a mile, and then I could. I couldn't run 5 km, and then I could. I became obsessed with reading about running, and my ambitions started to far outweigh my talent. Before I'd even finished my first half marathon, the original goal, I was already imagining myself running marathons, even ultramarathons. It's hard to explain: it simultaneously felt utterly ridiculous and completely inevitable.

If only my dedication to doing the training had matched my enthusiasm for reading about it and talking about it. I found myself standing on the start line of the Great Birmingham Run in October having barely run for months. I got around – without stopping, most importantly, of course – and immediately started thinking about running a full marathon. I told people I was doing it to raise money for charity but, really, I think I just wanted to be able to say I'd run a marathon. And I definitely wanted to tell people I'd done it a lot more than I actually wanted to do it, even if that's not a particularly honourable motivation to admit to.

Whatever the reason, I signed up to run the Milton Keynes Marathon the following May, which would be just over a year since I'd made that New Year's resolution, six months on from the first half marathon, and – although I couldn't possibly have predicted it then – 18 months before I set off to run approximately 200 marathons around the coast. Looking back at those timescales, I can see why everybody was a bit confused.

Marathon morning dawned three days after my university dissertation hand-in date. I had spent pretty much a week solid in the library living on Haribo, energy drinks and McDonald's, and I was still a bit hungover from the celebratory night out. I couldn't tell you the last time I'd been for a run. On the drive to the race start we listened to my dad's favourite country CD and "Me and Bobby McGee" came on. Kenny Rogers sang about freedom just being another word for having nothing left to lose, which felt fitting.

To make matters worse, I was dressed as a purple Crayola crayon. My dad, reluctantly having succumbed to my pleas that fancy dress would help us raise more money, was wearing fairy wings and a tutu.

I had never run far enough to discover chafing before then. I didn't understand about fuelling and I attempted to run the whole thing on just water. I walked for a solid 8 miles of the race, sobbing, and a small child in the crowd shouted "Crying crayon" at me. The heckling didn't stop there: as I ran on the closed lane of a dual carriageway (side note: if you don't like dual carriageways and roundabouts, I probably wouldn't recommend the Milton Keynes Marathon), a car of boys yelled "Run fatty run" at me out of the window as they drove past, which felt unnecessary. As I approached the final mile, well over 5 hours after starting, somebody sprinted past me wearing flip-flops.

It wasn't a pleasant experience. Certainly not one that would make you want to abandon everything to go and spend ten months of your life doing nothing but running, that's for sure.

As I started to tell people about this stupid idea to run a lap of the country, I was just waiting for somebody to confront me with the truth. "You fraud," they'd say, "you big, big fraud. You barely managed to finish a marathon! You're the crying crayon! What makes you think you can entertain the idea of doing this thing. Nobody else has done it before, what makes you think it's even possible?"

These days I live in a bubble of people who spend every minute of their free time going on ridiculous runs and climbing mountains in terrible weather and cycling triple-digit distances, but at the time it wasn't something any of my friends were really doing. A few months before my November start date, I saw a Facebook post from Dave Cornthwaite inviting strangers to come camping with him in the woods. Dave is best known for "Expedition1000", his project to complete 25 journeys of 1,000 miles or more via different non-motorised modes of transport. That year, he was having a summer off from adventuring, and wanted to put some faces to the names he saw on his list of Facebook followers. It was the inklings of the community that would grow into the Yes Tribe, now 16,000+ strong.

So, on a breezy Friday night in June, I packed a rucksack with an enormous heavy sleeping bag and an old foam mat, and headed off to spend the night in the woods with a group of perfect strangers. It sounded like a great opportunity to meet some people who might not think I was completely out of my mind. It also, admittedly, sounds like the opening scene of a horror movie. This only fully dawned on me as I stepped onto the platform in Wendover and saw a group of people standing around with packs and camping gear looking not particularly like serial killers – but isn't that how they always get you?

Spoiler: they weren't serial killers.

We hiked up a hill, rolled out our bivvy bags and somebody lit a fire. As we stood around it, drinking warm cans of beer, Dave asked us all to share any adventures we were planning or projects we were working on right now. That's how I'll always remember those early days of the Yes Tribe: a place to share the things that are exciting and scary and that you want to do despite the fact you're completely unqualified – or perhaps they're so appealing *because* of that. As we went around the circle I could hear my heart thudding in my ears, almost deafening me. I was sure they'd laugh me out of the woods. As well as Dave, there were some other bone fide Adventurers with a capital A there, like Sean Conway who had recently become the first person to complete a Land's End to John o' Groats triathlon, running, cycling and swimming the length of the country. Yep, *swimming*. What would they say when they realised I was just an idiot who couldn't even run a marathon without crying, and now I was planning to run around a whole country? It was ridiculous.

It was soon my turn.

"I'm going to run around the coast of the UK. I think it'll take me about ten months. I'm probably going to start in November," I told them. And nobody laughed at me, the opposite in fact, they couldn't have been more encouraging. I obviously hadn't told them about the whole crying crayon incident or the fact I had no idea what I was doing, so that might have helped, but still. Everybody just said nice things and Dave asked how I'd be sharing it. I hadn't really thought about that before, but I went home and made a Facebook page and suddenly it felt like this was a thing. A real thing. A thing that I was doing.

Not everybody had quite so much faith in me.

September came and I was 20 miles into my first ultramarathon with my friend Sophie. We were lost somewhere in Hertfordshire. Sophie was a few metres ahead, and I was straggling behind trying to cry without her noticing. For some reason we hadn't felt the need to do any substantial preparation at all, despite the fact I'd entered the race thinking it would be a good build-up to the coast. My "training" had consisted of a few 5 km jogs and one 16-mile run the week before the race, but I'd read a blog where somebody had talked about running 100 km "with their mind", so I assumed I'd be able to do the same. I was wrong. Sophie, generally being much fitter than me and with a history of competitive sport to fall back on, was pulling this tactic off a lot more successfully. She wasn't crying, for one.

As I limped along, I was texting Greg. The fact that I was running and texting probably tells you everything you need to know about the pace we were moving at. "I can't do it," I told him. "I want to quit. I don't think I can go much further."

"If you pull out of this, I don't think it bodes well for you running around the coast," he replied.

Again, when you finally stop looking at somebody through rose-tinted glasses, it can become hard to sift through all the awful memories of them and pluck out the times that perhaps they were being genuine. But on this one, he probably did have a point. It wasn't the first time I'd heard it, either. A few weeks earlier Sophie's boyfriend had asked why I thought I'd be able to stick at a ten-month run when I couldn't even be bothered to train properly for this one race. It was a valid question, and one to which I didn't really have an answer.

I pulled out at the next checkpoint. It was in a graveyard and I sat sobbing on the ground while a couple got married on the other side of the church. I had so badly wanted to finish that race, to prove a point, but whether you run an ultramarathon with your legs or your head, clearly I wasn't strong enough in either.

I was setting off to run 5,000 miles in less than six weeks. If I couldn't finish this one race, what right did I have to even start that adventure?

———

I had always thought of myself as not much of a crier but in those few weeks before setting off, I seemed to do little else. In the pictures from my work leaving drinks, my face is so wet from tears that it looks almost blurry. I went to Yestival, the festival Dave had set up for the Yes Tribe, which had exploded after a summer of campouts and outdoor activities, and I spent most of my time there crying too. At the end Dave made me stand up on stage and tell everybody what I was planning to do. It suddenly felt very real and truly horrifying.

It was ridiculous. I knew that I was so lucky to be in a position where I could abandon my whole life for ten months on a whim, but it all felt so unknown. I had decided to do this thing, nobody was forcing me, and it should have been exciting but I didn't feel excited at all. I just wanted to change my mind and go back to work and say it was all a big mistake. It would be embarrassing, sure, and my friends would never let me live it down, but perhaps it would be less embarrassing than quitting in a week or a month's time? Better to save face by not even trying, than to give something a go and then have to admit you weren't up to it, surely?

I finished work two weeks before starting the run. I moved out of my shared house in London and took all of my stuff back to my parents', where I was staying until I set off. I think the idea was that I'd spend that time doing any last bits of planning, sorting my kit out, generally just getting ready. In reality, I didn't do anything useful. I didn't know what I was meant to do.

Several times over the preceding months, I had sat in front of a blank page ready to make a plan but, honestly, I didn't know what that actually involved. I had no idea how far I'd be able to cover at that stage, so it seemed pointless to write out an itinerary of any kind. The route wouldn't be an issue either – I just needed to keep the sea to my left, surely. There were no vaccines to get, no foreign languages or new cultures to read up on, no complicated logistics to get to the start line. All I had to do was take a train from my parents' in Northampton to Greenwich, where I was starting. In a bid to have something to post on my new website, I took a map of Great Britain and painstakingly drew a red line around it using Paint, and then made a Facebook event for the first day in case anybody wanted to join me, and that was it. Done.

My mum said, many times, that she preferred it before I had arrived back home. She liked it better when I was still in London and she didn't have to face the reality of quite how disorganised I was. Sitting here, writing this several years later, I can see that she may have had a point. I've since morphed into an aggressive and passionate planner of all things. I plan more for a 5K run in the park now than I did for that whole trip. It makes me feel a bit itchy remembering how haphazard it all was, but I really didn't see what else there was to do.

———

On Sunday 1st of November I took the train to London and waited with my parents outside the National Maritime Museum to see if anybody else was going to show up to run with me. There wasn't anything particularly meaningful about my choice to start there. I just didn't have any attachments to anywhere on the coast itself and figured I'd have to come in to cross the Thames at some point anyway, so may as well start in London. A friend had pointed out that the museum was fitting, with its connection to the sea, and that was it decided.

The plan was to run 17 miles on that first day, from Greenwich to Dartford. A few weeks earlier, I had made a Facebook event inviting people to join me for the send-off. It felt a bit presumptuous to think anybody would be interested, but I'd nervously told people to meet at half past ten to give us plenty of time to get to Dartford before dark and posted my phone number for emergencies (which, looking back, feels like a GDPR breach of my own data).

It was one of the foggiest days I can ever remember. We couldn't see more than a few feet in front of us and for about half an hour I was getting calls from people who were apparently nearby. "We're here to see you off," they were saying, "but where are you?" Sometimes I could hear them they were so close, but we still couldn't see each other. I hadn't expected simply finding the start point to be such a navigational challenge, but perhaps it was a suitable omen for what was to come. Eventually everybody found us and we hung around awkwardly for a while. I thought that I should probably say something, but I wasn't really sure what.

Fairly unceremoniously, we started. Seventeen people ran with me on that first day, plus my friends Mimi and Harriet who had arrived on children's scooters they'd found in Harriet's parents' garage. They lasted about 100 m before giving up and going to the pub – apparently scooting is harder than running.

The rest of us carried on along the Thames path, which was eerily quiet in the fog, heading east past some sewage works, Barking Power Station poking out of the mist on the other side of the river, shopping trolleys bobbing in the water. The time I probably should have spent doing useful preparation of some kind, I had spent baking instead, so we stopped midway for homemade rocky road and flapjacks. Everybody was pleased about this except my dad, who I was making carry the Tupperware boxes like a one-man moving aid station. People peeled off at several points, heading home for roast dinners, or to see friends, or to catch up on chores before work tomorrow. It all felt very normal and I was jealous. I never thought I'd be jealous of somebody doing their laundry on a Sunday afternoon.

The route I had planned followed the Thames to Erith and then took the A206 to Dartford. As this section wasn't technically part of the coast I didn't feel too bad about cutting a corner (as I discovered along the way, I never really did start feeling bad about that. There are lots of route purists out there, but it turns out I'm not one of them). But I think we can say that running alongside a dual carriageway isn't exactly what I'd had in mind when I'd pictured idyllic days by the seaside. My legs hurt too – 17 miles is a long way to run, after all. And my pack, which I was running with for the first time that day, had started to chafe. I laugh now thinking about how much I moaned about that thin red line of friction on my lower back. Little did I know what was to come – a blazing inferno would be lit over the next ten months that no amount of Body Glide could put out.

But I'd done it! Day One of the adventure was over! I was on my way! I was doing this thing! There was no turning back now!

It seemed like a worse idea than ever.

CHAPTER 2

There are lots of incredible places in the world. Beautiful, exotic, beguiling places. Breathtaking backdrops, mesmerising landscapes, irresistible paths, all steeped in history and culture and a sense of wonder. The kind of places you might imagine an adventure beginning.

Then there is Dartford, Kent. Population 109,000, 18 miles as the crow flies from central London, birthplace of 50 per cent of the Rolling Stones. The town has become a victim of the success of nearby Bluewater Shopping Centre, and if I were to describe it in one word it would be this: grey. Yet, despite all those many other amazing places, places just waiting for somebody to come along and explore them, it was Dartford that was my first stop.

Seven of us had run all the way there and we went for a celebratory end-of-day-one lunch in Wetherspoons, because nowhere else seemed to be open, and that night I stayed at the Holiday Inn with my parents. It all felt distinctly unadventurous. The next morning we ate some below-average scrambled eggs from the breakfast buffet and then drove back to the train station, where I'd finished running the day before, to start Day Two. It was still early days and I didn't want to feel like I'd skipped any sections.

―――――――

Before we go any further, I just want to stick a quick disclaimer in here. As I've said, I know how lucky I was to be in a position where I could even entertain the idea of quitting my job to go running for a year, for no reason other than that I wanted to. I was young, I had no responsibilities and if it had all gone wrong, I always had a home to go back to.

Luck is a strange thing to talk about. I often hear people saying, "The harder I work, the luckier I get." That's true, to an extent, but I also feel strongly that it's the underlying safety net of privilege that makes it possible, or at least a lot, lot easier, to take that leap into the unknown and make those scary, "brave" decisions. It is just luck of the draw as to whether you're born with that feeling of safety and security, and I feel very grateful that I was.

My family is by no means particularly well-off. My dad is a gardener and my mum works in a cafe. They live in a pebble-dashed semi in the Midlands, I went to a pretty rubbish state school and almost all of my childhood holidays involved camping trips to Wales in leaking tents. But there is no question of me ever not having a bed to go home to or food to eat when I get there. When I've screwed up by being Bad With Money with a capital B (and W and M) I could call home and ask for a bailout. My dad could only offer that bailout because he's always been very frugal and Good With Money (capital G, W and M), but for a lot of people it isn't possible to be good with money. No matter how careful they are and how many takeaway coffees and avocados they don't buy, there's simply nothing left over to be good with.

With all that in mind, I find it infuriating when people are on these incredible trips, which some people could only dream of, and all they can do is moan about it, hamming up the hard bits. It's meant to be fun! You chose to do this! Enjoy it! Stop complaining! Don't you know how lucky you are?!

And yet – and yet – at times it was *so awful*. Alongside all the good bits, there was a lot of being cold and lonely and scared. I want to tell this story truthfully, warts and all, but please just know that even when I'm moaning about having had wet feet for three months straight, I did, and do, feel very aware of how lucky I was to be there at all. Hard work plays a part, for sure, but chance plays a much bigger one.

———————

Back to Day Two.

I'll admit that it's probably not okay to be throwing tantrums in car parks when you're 23, or any time past your tenth birthday really, but that's what I found myself doing. I only had around 6 miles to run that day, to Gravesend, edging my way along the Thames until, hopefully, I would reach the sea a few days later.

The day before I had only carried a half-full pack, my parents having taken the rest of my stuff ahead in the car before coming back to run with me. Now, in the Dartford station car park, I was attempting to pack my full bag for the first time. I'd chosen my pack for no other reason than it was the one adventurer Anna McNuff had recently used to run the length of New Zealand. She seemed like she knew what she was doing, so I'd shamelessly copy-catted the kit list she'd posted on her blog almost to the letter. I'd never actually run with the pack before that first day though, and I definitely hadn't practised cramming all of my belongings into it.

I'm not going to pretend there was any logic to this strategy at the time, I was just disorganised, nothing more to it. But, I do strongly believe that in this case, ignorance was bliss. Running with a heavy pack is hard. It feels like running through treacle – it weighs you down, ripping your back to shreds. Thank goodness I didn't do any training runs with it and find that out ahead of time.

So it was probably for the greater good that I found myself in that car park trying to stuff my sleeping bag into the top of the bag. It was a two-person job; I pummelled the contents of the bag down while my mum attempted to close the drawstring. It wasn't going well and although it was absolutely not my mum's fault at all, she took the brunt of the blame. And all I could think about was how much I didn't really want to be there.

"I don't want to do it," I shouted – at my mum, at my dad, at nobody in particular. "I just want to go home."

I stomped off across the car park – not really sure where I was heading, to be honest – and right through a patch of stinging nettles. I limped back over, ankles inflamed, ego dented.

"I don't want to do it," I said again, but quieter this time.

"You don't have to, you know," my dad said. "You can just come home with us."

But I couldn't. Dramatically quitting your job and announcing to everybody you know that you're going to go and run around a country when *you aren't even a very good runner* is a fairly odd thing to do in the first place. Admitting defeat on the second day wasn't an option. I love my friends, but they aren't known for being particularly sympathetic to a stupid decision. I would literally never live it down if I went home now.

So, if for no other reason than to save face, I struggled into my backpack (which, in the time I had been throwing my tantrum, my mum had managed to persuade to close) and put one foot in front of the other until I got to Gravesend. My parents ran with me and I complained the entire way – an absolutely joy to be around, as always.

We went for a coffee together and then my mum went off to try and buy me a tennis ball because somebody had told us it was an essential piece of kit, acting like a portable foam roller. She came back with a squeaky dog toy instead – the closest thing she could find, apparently – and then we had to say goodbye. My mum and dad were catching the train back to Dartford, where their car was parked, then they'd drive home and tomorrow they would both be back at work. Back to normal life.

I couldn't quit yet, I had to at least give this a go, but I really did wish that I could just go with them.

I was planning to camp the whole way, for two reasons:

1. I just thought that was what you did on an adventure, and
2. I couldn't afford to do anything else.

Dave had generously offered to loan me his tent for the duration of the trip, a super lightweight one-man Nordisk weighing in at just over 800 g. I spent a decent chunk of money on a sleeping bag that claimed it would keep me warm down to around −2°C, and didn't think much more about it.

After stealing her kit list, I had come to befriend run-across-New-Zealand Anna. I met her for a coffee one evening after work, a few weeks before I was due to set off. She excitedly asked me all about my plans and looked fairly horrified to learn I hadn't really made any, beyond the first day. She took out her laptop and set about helping me map out the first month. She started furiously filling in spreadsheets, looking very efficient, while I sat next to her feeling a bit dazed.

As well as running the length of New Zealand (the tan lines and chafe marks from which she was still sporting), Anna had also spent six months cycling around all 50 states of America, and that's just the tip of the iceberg as far as her impressive-feats CV goes. She is definitely no stranger to an adventure. She told me that, when in doubt about where to sleep, it was a good idea to look for a hill. We saw "Plum Pudding Hill" on the map and Anna suggested that it might be a good place to sleep on the second or third night. I readily agreed without considering that I'd never wild camped by myself before and had what was probably a statistically irrational but nonetheless very real fear of serial killers. It's well known that serial killers like to lurk around on deserted coast paths on the off-chance that one lone runner might come along and decide to camp there once in a blue moon.

Coasting

She also told me to be prepared for all the kindness that was sure to come my way. Strangers who would invite me into their homes, drive miles to bring me snacks, spend hours poring over maps, proudly wanting to help me devise the best route possible for their area. I trusted Anna, of course, but I also didn't believe her. That won't happen in the UK, I thought. This is the kind of thing that happens elsewhere, not on home turf.

But she was right, of course. In fact, it had already begun. Hadn't Dave already loaned me his tent? Wasn't Anna there giving up her evening to help me? It took a few more weeks though for me to recognise that perhaps she knew what she was talking about.

———

One sunny Saturday during the summer before the trip, I was walking on the South Downs with Greg.

Not long after I'd told the world about my big adventure, we'd fallen out about something and not spoken for a several months. There had been an argument, I can't remember what about. The usual, I suppose – me asking when we could spend time together, and being told how difficult and unreasonable I was in response. He had blocked my number and left me wondering what exactly I'd done wrong.

Then we'd bumped into each other at a mutual friend's birthday party and afterwards, he had texted me and told me he still loved me. I must have believed him because there we were, out for a walk and attempting to rekindle things.

We passed Belle Tout, a decommissioned lighthouse converted into a B&B, perched on Beachy Head. It was a beautiful spot, looking out to sea with towering white cliffs stretching out on either side.

"Let's stay here," he'd said, "I'll come and run this section with you and we can stay at the lighthouse."

When I got home, I sat down and worked out roughly when I might arrive there (the most detailed planning I did for the whole thing pre-departure). It would be fairly early on in the trip, some time in late November. When I looked at booking a room, they had a two-night minimum stay. I emailed and told them what I was doing, and asked if there was any chance we could book for just one night.

"This sounds like a fantastic challenge, Elise. We would love to put you up free of charge – please just confirm the date."

I really hadn't expected that, but I was thrilled – like, over-the-moon excited. A free stay in a lighthouse?! I received this email while deep in the pre-trip fear and anxiety phase, and it gave me a tiny glimmer of hope that perhaps this wasn't a completely terrible idea after all.

And it made me think. People who run hotels, B&Bs, hostels – they're just people. Perhaps if I told them what I was doing, maybe over the winter, while they were quiet anyway, they might give me a room for the night. If nothing else it would be a good way to meet some more people, get the word out a little, rather than spending a lonely ten months in a tent by myself. I also hoped that meeting more people might enable me to raise more money for the two charities I'd chosen – Young Minds, a children's mental health charity, and Beyond Food, which supports people who have been impacted by homelessness. Fundraising wasn't the driving force behind my run, or the primary reason I'd chosen to do it, but if me doing this big challenge meant some people felt inclined to donate to causes I thought were important, then I definitely wasn't going to complain about that. Any donations went straight to the charities, they didn't cover any of my costs, and I was keen to do anything I could to encourage people to donate.

I felt uncomfortable asking, but something I slowly started to learn was that, on the whole, people only help you if they want to. I wanted to give people as much space as possible to decide that no, actually, they don't want to help. I only ever sent emails, which could be easily ignored or replied to with a polite "no, sorry", rather than phoning or turning up on a B&B's doorstep and putting them under pressure.

And there was a lot of getting ignored, quite a few "no thank yous", but I was also completely overwhelmed by the people who said yes, and welcomed me in, and made my trip about one hundred times better than it would have been otherwise. More than that, I feel confident that it was those "yeses" that made it happen at all, along with all the other people I ended up staying with – the friends of friends, the families who watched my Facebook videos, the local running clubs.

If I'd been confined to my tent for the whole winter, with the sun setting at four o' clock in the afternoon and the never-ending mud and the constant wet feet and all those serial killers I thought were hiding in the bushes, I have no doubt I would have given up after about 5 miles.

———

The first "yes" came from The Clarendon Royal Hotel in Gravesend. Even before I realised how scared of camping I was, I knew it would be hard to find a spot to camp on those first few nights when I was still running through built-up places as we headed out of London.

So, after hugging my mum and dad goodbye (a sign in itself that this was a momentous day – we really aren't huggers) and picking up some snacks from the supermarket, I headed to the Clarendon for the night. I checked in and the lovely lady on reception asked some questions about what I was doing. I felt a little awkward telling her it was only the second day and that I really hadn't done anything remotely remarkable yet. She pointed me in the direction of my room and then there I was – out on my own, this was it.

It all felt so ridiculously mundane. When you read other people's accounts of adventure, within the first 48 hours they've usually already caught an emergency helicopter, fought off a mountain lion, been initiated into a jungle tribe, nearly drowned and probably suffered a case of mild frostbite too. All I had done was run along some A-roads with a selection of people I already knew, visited several major supermarket chains and eaten a slice of dry cake in Costa Coffee. That night, I had a bath, practised packing and re-packing my rucksack, and couldn't help but ponder that so far this was perhaps the most mild, comfortable, distinctly unadventurous adventure that had ever been.

I had decided not to run around the Hoo Peninsula or the Isle of Sheppey. The former is technically still part of the Thames Estuary for the most part, rather than the coast, and the latter an island, despite being attached to the mainland by a bridge. This meant my next stop as I headed east towards the coast was Rochester. After two and a half days of scrap heaps, graffiti and power stations, I finally found some countryside. I was clearly pretty excited about this because, standing on a grass verge in front of a fairly rubbish-looking field, I decided to record a video. It would end up being the first of many and I can confirm, without any shadow of a doubt, that the hardest thing about writing this book has been having to watch back those video diaries for research purposes. A painful experience all around, but especially that first one. I remember my brother messaging me after I uploaded it to ask why I had a completely different voice on camera. He wasn't wrong.

If you'd asked me beforehand if I'd ever be caught uploading selfie videos to Facebook, the answer would have been a flat "no". The thought was utterly mortifying. I was convinced people would hunt me down and heckle me with rotten tomatoes for being so embarrassing. Maybe it was because I was already veering so far away from anything even slightly resembling a comfort zone, that posting that video was just another drop in the ocean.

Whatever made me do it, on the evening of Day Three I winced a bit, told myself to get over myself, and published the video on Facebook. Ironically, I did get a troll posting something horrible on that first video (quite impressive, really, given that I only had about 100 followers at the time), but that was drowned out by all the nice comments and nobody ever said anything mean again.

Those videos ended up becoming a big part of my trip, however strange that may sound. Talking to the camera for a few minutes was a lot less effort than writing a blog post, and it turns out people are much more likely to watch them. The number of likes on my Facebook page continued to grow. I couldn't believe that anybody was actually interested in what I was doing, and in my mind it was just my mum watching those videos over and over and racking up the numbers, but of course it wasn't. Each of those "likes" represented a person – people who rooted for me every single day, ran with me, donated to my fundraising page, invited me to stay with them, let me hang out with their pets.

One of those people was George. A friend of a friend of a friend, Aaron, had put us in touch. Aaron had stayed with George while cycling from London to Istanbul and, seeing what I was doing, suspected my route might take me past George's front door, gave me his phone number and told me to get in touch. I hesitated but, still in avoiding-camping-at-all-costs-because-I'm-terrified mode, eventually sent George a text message. He said I was more than welcome to stay, and told me he'd pick me up from the town centre after work.

At about 5 p.m. that evening I was waiting in the designated spot when an old Land Rover appeared with George and his brother Bruce in the front seats. I say the front seats – actually, these were the only seats. Bruce had stripped the back ones out so that he could transport sheep around. Bruce jumped into the back and told me to get in the front.

"Don't tell Mum we all came back together," George warned me, "we'll have to pretend he drove separately. Oh, and there's no phone signal at our house, either."

All that fear of serial killers jumping out of bushes and here I was, clearly willingly getting into the car with two. I asked George how he knew Aaron.

Coasting

"I met him in the Co-op," he told me.

It turned out Aaron and George weren't lifelong friends as I'd imagined. Rather, one evening George had popped to the local Co-op and found Aaron in there, at the very beginning of his bike tour. It was getting dark and Aaron hadn't sorted anywhere to camp yet, so George took him back to their house for the night. I get the impression his mum was a little surprised. The next day, George had gone to work and Aaron had hung out at their house for most of the day before eventually pedalling off. This had all happened only a few months earlier, and now George was having every waif and stray passing through Kent on an adventure thrown in his direction. Although, in fairness, that's probably not many people. As I was discovering, Mid Kent isn't exactly the epicentre of the adventure world.

"How do *you* know Aaron?" George returned the question.

"Oh, he just messaged me on Facebook. I don't know him at all..."

Luckily, or I probably wouldn't be here writing this now, Aaron was a trustworthy guy. George's family fed me spaghetti bolognaise, introduced me to their dog, got the OS maps out and helped me plot the best route to the sea and made me up a bed on the sofa for the night.

It had only been 24 hours since I had said goodbye to my parents, and I was still only about 30 miles from London and my old life, but sitting there among somebody else's family, it slowly started to feel more like I had imagined an adventure would.

CHAPTER 3

It took me a week and about 70 miles of running to reach Whitstable, my first real glimpse of the sea. As my mum helpfully pointed out, if I'd picked a different island to run around, the Isle of Wight for instance, I could be finished by now. As it was, I still had the best part of a year and approximately 4,930 miles to go.

I'm going to refer to 5,000 miles a lot over the coming pages and I feel like I probably need to explain how I arrived at that number. If you aren't interested in all of the intricacies of the British coastline, feel free to skip ahead. I thought I just needed to keep the sea to the left and with that I'd be able to easily navigate between ice cream vans and cream tea stops. It turns out it's actually a bit of a minefield.

It's difficult to say exactly how long the coast of Britain is. It's constantly changing, and almost impossible to truly measure. It's dependent on weather, and tides, and what you actually mean by coastline. The official definition is that it's the "line that forms the boundary between the land and the ocean", but you're very rarely going to find yourself precisely toeing this line. For adventure purposes, are you just referring to the closest accessible paths to this waterline? Are you including every nook and cranny of the Western Highlands? What about the mudflats along the east coast? And the islands (there are more than 6,000, 183 of which are inhabited)? Wikipedia will tell you that the coastline of Great Britain is 7,723 miles, although it admits that "no details are provided about how this figure was calculated".

Most people who have walked or cycled the route claim to have travelled somewhere between 4,000 and 7,000 miles around the mainland, not including any islands. That's a pretty sizable bracket. The official England Coast Path is now open and, if you were setting off today, you could join that up with the Wales Coast Path to have a clear idea of distance for at least two of the three countries. Scotland still remains a big unknown though – and is the place where the most decisions have to be made. How much of a purist are you going to be?

As I've already mentioned, I wasn't much of one.

Lots of people doing these kinds of trips are super strict about picking up each day in the exact spot where they took their last footstep, sticking as closely to the route as possible, regardless of what that means in terms of safety or scenery, and meticulously tracking every inch of every mile of every day with GPS. It wasn't really like that for me.

It wasn't something I gave a great deal of thought to before setting off, but quite quickly I realised that I had two priorities that came before sticking as closely to the coast as possible:

1. Running the nicest route
2. Running the safest route

Once those things were taken care of, then I started worrying about how closely I was sticking to the coast – but they always came first. If the route that most closely hugs the coast was a really sketchy A-road with no footpath, I wasn't taking it (well, I tried my best not to after the first few times at least…). Equally when I realised I could do a bit of island hopping and explore Arran, Mull and Skye rather than just following all the squiggles and peninsulas of the Scottish mainland's west coast religiously, I did that too. And when I found myself on the grass verge of a dual carriageway with no option but to risk my life running a mile alongside it or go back and add about 20 miles on, and a car pulled up and offered me a lift? Yeah, I took that ride, skipped that mile, no qualms whatsoever. They felt like the right decisions at the time and I definitely haven't lost any sleep over them since.

Although the all-England path wasn't open when I did it, sections that form it were, like the huge 630-mile South West Coast Path and lots of shorter ones. These official trails were largely amazingly well resourced with plenty of charts and guides giving exact distances from place to place. Using a combination of information from these official trails, accounts from people who had walked the coast, a bit of playing around on Google Maps and some guesswork, I put the figure of 5,000 miles on the whole thing. From there, to work out how long it might take me, I just needed to know how far I could feasibly run each day. This was a tricky part because, as you've probably realised by now, *I had absolutely no bloody idea what I was doing.*

However, something I had done was send "The Email". I've since carried out an informal but comprehensive study on this, and it seems that almost everybody setting out on a first-time Big Adventure sends "The Email". It's a message to somebody more experienced who has done something similar before, often a plea for reassurance masquerading as a request for practical advice. I sent mine to Anna – the same Anna whose kit list I'd stolen and who has dished out wild camping advice already in this story. It was thanks to this email that we came to be friends.

> *Hello Anna,*
> *I hope you're well. I hope you don't mind but I'm getting in touch for some running-long-distances-wearing-a-rucksack advice.*

And on it went. Lots of "I think" and "kind of" and "might"s littered around because clearly something was holding me back from fully committing in writing. Anna replied impressively fast given that she was deep in the New Zealand bush at the time and it usually takes me about five months to email people back at the best of times. She was – as is Anna's trademark – extremely enthusiastic. At no point did she say, "Hold up, you can't run that far, what are you talking about you fool!" Instead it was a big dose of enthusiasm, some practical tips and the suggestion that we Skype next time she had wi-fi. She signed off with:

> *Lastly – it's tough as, but I still BLOODY LOVE running. Incredible adventure and it's what us human beans are made for.*
> *Enjoy basking in the glory of a new-found life direction, and hopefully chat soon!*
> *Axx*

Part of the reason I thought I could do this whole thing in the first place was looking at other people, like Anna, going on these sorts of adventures and realising that they're just another human. If they could do it, why couldn't I? So, just as I stole her kit list, I looked at Anna's daily distances for her New Zealand run and figured I could probably match those as well. She was hoping to average 15–20 miles per day, over much rougher terrain, so I pencilled myself in for 17 miles a day. If my 5,000 miles guess was correct, this would mean I'd be running for ten months.

One piece of advice for if you're planning to copycat somebody else's adventure style: don't choose Anna McNuff, or anybody else clearly born with a degree of athletic pedigree you simply don't possess. Anna's parents are both Olympians, she is an ex-GB rower, and since hanging up her oars she has made a hobby of completing all sorts of endurance challenges. Meanwhile, my main speciality at school was skipping PE. While my brother spent several evenings a week at athletics training, you could find me waiting in the car and whinging to be taken to McDonald's. I had no business thinking that just because Anna could do it, I could do it too, but I also didn't have anything better to go on.

It was a total stab in the dark, but those numbers became fixed in my mind: 5,000 miles, 17 miles per day, 10 months. On hard days, I'd just be thinking, only X more days/miles to go, and those goalposts felt so reassuring. It was, then, probably a self-fulfilling prophecy more than any accurate guesswork when, 301 days later – almost ten months to the day – I crossed the finish line. But still, I liked how nice and neat it was.

Coasting

———

Let's rewind 4,930 miles from the finish line back to Whitstable. (Although, as the crow flies, in that moment I was actually only 50 miles from the finish line. This is one of the quirks of running in a big circle and something that messed with my head constantly during the beginning stages.) I was one week down and that morning I had run from Faversham, nestled inland just south of the Oare Marshes. I hit the coast for the first time a few miles to the west of Whitstable. The sun had come out and it really did feel like A Moment. This was it! I was at the seaside! This is what I'd come to do!

I ran into town late on a Sunday afternoon, and the harbour was busy with families, couples and groups of friends. They were gathered together eating food from fresh seafood stalls under the weak November sunshine, all hanging onto those last few hours of the weekend. I headed up a side road towards the high street and found a cafe where I could sit inside and charge my phone. The first fish and chips of a trip that was dedicated to the British seaside: it felt significant. It's a shame that it was ruined somewhat by the clawing anxiety in my chest owing to the fact that I had no idea where I was going to sleep that night.

I had been lucky so far. Between those emails I'd sent and hospitality from friends and friends of friends, I still hadn't had to pitch my tent. Sunday night in Whitstable was a glaring blank space in the calendar though, and I had been avoiding thinking about it. I assumed that once it got to it I'd just bite the bullet, pitch the tent, and that would be it – what other choice would I have? I half-heartedly looked at the map and saw that the seafront was built-up for miles further on – residential, then holiday parks, then beyond that there were marshes. I'm sure that somebody braver than me would have just found the corner of a field and flung their tent up, but I wasn't that person.

Clearly this was all a ridiculous idea. It just wasn't going to work. I couldn't camp. It didn't matter whether that was because there genuinely weren't any spots or because I was too afraid, the outcome was the same. I had factored into my budget inevitably needing to pay for accommodation occasionally, but I couldn't afford to stay somewhere every single night. Even hostels and bunk houses would have broken my budget, let alone the expensive seaside B&Bs that were often the only option. And there was only so much I could abuse people's kindness. I felt uncomfortable enough about sending my very-easy-to-ignore emails; there was no way I was going to be begging for free rooms any more than that. This was clearly doomed. Perhaps this was why people tend to choose adventures in more wild and remote places where you can easily camp every night with no chance of being found.

I finished my fish and chips and started wandering around some shops to kill time. Maybe I should just give up now and go home? But I'd only just got to the sea, and my legs felt okay, and my pack hadn't totally destroyed my back yet. I didn't want to give up. I had a quick look online to see if any hotels had spaces – I could just take the hit tonight and come up with a better plan tomorrow – but there was hardly anything and it was all so expensive, over £100 a night.

I was about to book one, thinking I had no other option, when I remembered Airbnb. I had a look and there were some rooms available, and much cheaper than the hotels. I messaged a couple of hosts, told them what I was doing and asked if they would be willing to rent the room out so last minute – it was around 5 o'clock at this point and already dark.

Julia replied. The cabin in her garden was available, and I could stay tonight no problem, and no charge. She shared her address and told me to head over when I was ready. I carried on wandering around the supermarket for a while – it felt a bit weird to appear literally 5 minutes later. This marked the beginning of what my mum will happily tell you was her least favourite part of me running around the coast – the fact that whenever I was bored (which was fairly often – you might imagine an adventure to be non-stop action, but actually there's a lot of time to kill), I'd call her and give her an in-depth rundown of everything on the supermarket shelves. She once hung up on me to do the washing-up instead, because apparently that was more interesting.

After I'd spent enough time describing everything in the freezer aisle to my mum, I headed over to Julia's. That night, I slept a deep, grateful sleep. It was the first time in my life where I'd woken up in the morning genuinely not knowing where I would be going to bed, and it had shaken me. The next morning I woke up to a breakfast hamper by the door full of cereal, croissants and orange juice, and when I checked later I saw that, as well as not letting me pay, Julia had donated to my fundraising page.

Letting people help felt so alien to me at the start and rather than getting used to it, the more it happened, the more uncomfortable I felt. I never felt like I really deserved their kindness but I did slowly realise that without it, I wasn't going to get anywhere – financially, physically or emotionally. I just kept trying to remember: people don't offer to do things that they don't want to do. I could give up now, or I could stop getting in my own way and accept that people wanted to help.

CHAPTER 4

One of my earliest childhood memories is a family holiday to Margate. I must have been four or five, and the south of England was having a heatwave. I remember wearing a blue, white and red dress, eating pasta in an Italian restaurant and asking my mum, "Is this the hottest place in the world?"

I set off from Julia's cabin in Whitstable feeling a little more optimistic about things. I followed the coast path for 17 miles past Herne Bay, Reculver and Westgate-on-Sea, and then set foot on Margate beach for the first time since 1997. It was a cloudy Monday afternoon and the clouds were hanging low, making the air wet. Strands of hair had escaped from my plait and frizzed up with the moisture to create a very attractive halo effect. I had been running in just a T-shirt but quickly pulled a fleece and a raincoat from my bag.

Margate no longer felt like the hottest place in the world. I couldn't help but think of all those exotic (read: warm) places where I imagined other people were having adventures.

I was staying with the Warrilows that night. I had met Will at one of the Yes Tribe campouts, and he had got in touch to invite me to stay with his family when I ran through Margate. I made my way to their house as the late-afternoon light began to fade, and was soon sitting inside with Will's parents, a cup of tea and a plate of biscuits in front of me. The Warrilows' house had once been a B&B, back when Margate had been the go-to destination for Londoners wanting a seaside break. Although it was a home now, there were still the long corridors and plenty of bedrooms.

I headed to my room for the night to shower and get changed, wincing slightly as I climbed the stairs. I'd never really run far enough to get injured before, but I guessed that the pinching sensation in my lower legs was the beginning of shin splints. Google told me to kneel down on the floor, heels to bum, and lean back as far as I could to stretch my shins. I was a little dubious – can you really stretch bones? If you can, should you? But I gave it a go nonetheless.

It didn't seem to help much, but it didn't feel any worse either. I headed down for dinner. Over bowls of pasta we talked about my route and where I was heading next. Andrew and Vanessa, Will's parents, immediately started offering out their friends.

"We have a friend in Brighton, he's called Med, he likes cycling," Andrew told me, "I'm sure he'd let you stay for the night."

"And when will you get to Rye? We have some other friends who own a restaurant there, perhaps you could stop by," Vanessa pitched in.

"We know somebody in Southampton too. I'll give you his email address."

Coasting

The six degrees of separation was playing out before my eyes. It was the first time this happened, but was something I would end up experiencing over and over again, a domino effect of kindness. I'd stay the night with one person who'd then put me in touch with their friend, or a colleague, or a family member, or a friend of a friend, and so on and so forth, over and over. Thanks to the Warrilows' connections alone, it looked like my tent would remain unpitched for some time yet.

I felt conflicted though. Was I really doing this properly if I was spending every single night in a warm bed, eating homecooked meals with other people's families? Or, actually, was accepting the hospitality of strangers exactly in the spirit of an adventure? Was it dishonest of me to accept so much from strangers, if they were offering it based on the belief I was taking on some kind of hardship, when actually the days were passing by in relative comfort? Was there a maximum quota of easy runs and warm, dry, lovely nights you can have while still claiming to be doing a big, hard thing? Even if it hadn't crossed anybody else's mind – which I really doubted it had, I was definitely overthinking this – I couldn't shake the feeling of unease.

As I was setting off the next morning, Vanessa handed me a tinfoil-wrapped package.

"Here's a sandwich, to take to Sandwich," she said.

And so off I ran to Sandwich, my next stop after Margate, spending most of the run worrying that it wasn't hard enough, and that I wasn't doing it the "right" way, whatever that was. I was so busy worrying that I barely noticed my legs carrying me another 18 miles.

I took a selfie at the "Welcome to Sandwich" sign with my sandwich and went off to spend the night worrying some more.

Looking at the OS map now, I can see a footpath hugging the shore all the way from Sandwich to Deal, past the Sandwich Flats. According to the map, this trail forms part of Stour Valley Walk, the White Cliffs County Trail, the Saxon Shore Way and now the new England Coast Path. Given that the Saxon Shore Way alone has been open since 1980, I can only imagine that this footpath existed in 2015. Instead of running on it – this lovely, quiet, traffic-free trail that somebody had taken the time to maintain, exclusively for the leisure of pedestrians – I ran along the A258.

Why? Because I couldn't read a map. Because I didn't know that the footpath existed. Because, when cars were coming towards me at speed and there was no grass verge and I was attempting to flatten myself against a hedge, I had no idea how you'd go about finding an alternative route. I didn't understand about maps and footpaths and rights of way. I was just aimlessly piecing together a route from Google Maps, the odd signpost and some directions from strangers.

It seems utterly idiotic to me now, and I look back and despair at how much simpler I could have made things for myself. But I guess it just goes to show how little you actually need to know to have a go at something.

You don't even need much common sense, apparently.

———

I made it to Deal without getting run over, and on to Dover, where I stayed at a B&B that almost exclusively hosts channel swimmers and spent the evening listening to the owner tell me stories of their crossings, and then to Folkestone. I finally found some trails to run on, picking up the Saxon Shore Way that I'd managed to miss on the way into Deal. It was a stormy few days and I slid my way over the slick, grassy clifftop paths. As I teetered close to the edge, I was very aware of my own mortality again, but in a way that felt a lot more revitalising than when it's because a lorry might crush you at any second. This is what I had dreamt of – sea air whipping at my face, miles and miles of ocean stretching out before me, nobody else in sight. Every now and again the sun would shine out from behind the black clouds and I knew that this was exactly where I wanted to be.

It had always been my intention to "train on the job", so to speak, and build up my mileage as I went, upping the distances as I got stronger and the daylight increased. While I was doing the occasional longer run, like the 18 miles from Margate to Sandwich, mostly it was a lot less – under 10 miles, often. This is less than many runners do on a daily basis as fairly casual training, but it was still taking its toll. I just wasn't used to it. Every night, I fell into bed exhausted. I couldn't stop eating – more than I needed, probably, but it was the only thing that seemed to help the tiredness. I was getting niggles, like my sore shins, but moving off the pavement and onto trails did help those. The pack was the main issue – my back ached constantly.

I didn't feel capable of upping my mileage much at that stage, but the relatively short distances left me with a lot of time to spare. No matter how slowly you run 10 miles, it still doesn't take that long, not when you have a whole day to play with it. Trying to fill this time proved expensive. It often involved spending too much money on food and hot drinks just to have somewhere warm to sit.

It was early afternoon when I arrived in Folkestone. I found a cafe and tried to buy a jacket potato and cheese.

"Do you want to try that again, love?" asked the woman at the counter. I looked down at the slip that had just come out of the card reader. My card had been declined. I put my PIN in again. The same thing happened.

"That's weird, I'll just pay cash instead." I rooted around in my purse, found some pound coins, and sat down to try to enjoy my potato. But I suddenly didn't feel very hungry any more. My heart was beating harder, and I had a sinking feeling in my stomach.

I checked my online banking. My account wasn't empty, which was a relief given that this was supposedly where I was storing all the money that would last me for the next ten months. I had a habit of taking an ignorance-is-bliss approach to my finances, as if not knowing how little money was in my account would magically conjure up more. I relied on blind optimism until the moment I was at a cash point and the screen said insufficient funds, again, and the panic would set in.

I was relieved I wasn't at that point yet. It looked like my account had just been blocked for some reason. There was a branch of my bank just around the corner from the cafe, and I went to find out what had happened. The man at the front desk took my details and scowled at the computer for a while before leading me into a meeting room with a glass wall, a single table and a phone.

"You need to talk to the collections department," he told me, dialing a number and handing me the receiver. There was a voice on the other end of the line before I could think to ask why, and I relayed what had happened again to the woman on the phone.

"Oh yes, I can see that we've put a block on your current account due to an outstanding debt on your credit card. If you make a payment now we can get everything up and running again for you."

Credit card? I didn't have a credit card with this bank. Except... with horror, I remembered the card I'd maxed out while at university. A combination of a summer interrailing trip I couldn't afford, several pairs of Topshop heels I couldn't walk in and countless nights out that I couldn't remember.

I had taken out the credit card because I didn't have enough money, or felt like I didn't at least. Once I'd maxed it out and the minimum repayments started coming out of my account each month, I definitely didn't have enough. I embarked on a very questionable process that involved taking out another credit card and withdrawing cash on that to deposit into my bank account to pay off the original card.

I like to think I'm not a stupid person, but sometimes the evidence to the contrary really stacks up.

I continued this process for a while, taking out several cards. When that strategy stopped working, once they were all maxed out and the payments started bouncing, I cancelled the direct debits so I didn't keep getting charged by my bank. I started receiving lots of phone calls from various numbers I didn't recognise, but I just didn't pick up. Nor did I open the letters that were coming through the post on an almost daily basis. What you don't know can't hurt you, right?

Eventually the letters and the phone calls stopped. I was no longer being harassed and nobody was trying to take my money from me any more. Problem solved, I thought, and then immediately buried my head in the sand about it. Except here we were, five years later, and it wasn't problem solved. It was problem-turned-into-a-very-bloody-big-disaster.

"How much do I need to pay?" I asked quietly, remembering that I had owed £1,800 originally on that particular credit card.

"Well, the good news is that we're willing to offer a compromise to get this settled. If you pay £900 today, we can write off the debt and unblock your accounts."

On the one hand, I was essentially saving £900. On the other hand, I had completely screwed my credit score, would probably never be able to get a mortgage and – more pressingly – making the payment would eat up nearly a third of the money I was planning to survive on for the next ten months.

"I can't afford that, I don't have a job at the moment."

She asked how I'd lost my job and when I expected to be in work again. I tried to explain that I'd given it up voluntarily, that I wasn't really looking for a new job, that I was on an adventure. As you can imagine, this story didn't incite a huge amount of sympathy.

"You can submit an appeal, stating that you can't make payment, but we'll then perform an assessment of your incomings and outgoings and looking at yours," she paused, "I can tell you now you're unlikely to win an appeal."

Shame hit me like a ton of bricks as I thought about what she'd be seeing as she scrolled through my bank statements. All the meals out, unnecessary shopping trips on Oxford Street, rounds in the pub, a recent spending spree on outdoor gear... I suddenly felt very aware that I was crying, and that everybody in the bank could see me through the glass wall.

There was only one option, really. I agreed to pay the £900, my account was debited and my card was unblocked. I'd just have to figure out the rest later.

––––––––

In the beginning stages of thinking about my trip, I had started reading a lot about adventure therapy and the mental and physical health benefits of going outside. Somehow just taking ten months out to go on an adventure seemed a little frivolous, so I started telling people that I was doing it with the hopes of founding a non-profit or charity afterward, promoting what I was calling at the time "small-scale adventure therapy". I'm not sure where I got that from but it sounded good. It's what I told my boss when I handed in my notice, and what I wrote about in my application for the adventure grant I applied for. Somehow it made it all a little easier to explain, and put some weight behind what I was doing. And I wasn't lying – I believed that this is what I would do.

Spoiler: that didn't happen. There are hundreds of incredible projects and organisations offering the sort of experiences I was talking about, run by passionate, experienced and, most importantly, professionally trained people. I'm embarrassed now that I ever thought myself qualified to even be thinking about rivalling them. It's a sign of just how unqualified I was that I didn't realise how out of my depth I was.

But as part of that vague ambition, I had posted on my blog that I would love for people to come and run with me for a day, spend some time outdoors, connect. But when I started receiving emails from people saying they would like to do that, it suddenly it felt like a lot of pressure. What if they wanted to go faster than I could run? What if I got them lost? What if we had nothing to talk about? What if they went home and told people I wasn't a proper runner, that this was all a joke, that I had no idea what I was doing?

People kept saying nice things to me, telling me I was an inspiration, but they weren't seeing the full picture. They hadn't heard the phone call at the bank, they couldn't see how many times I stopped each day to sit on a bench and have a break, they didn't know quite how clueless I was. I was trying to be honest, but if they really knew, I was convinced nobody would be interested in following my adventure.

Some time in early November, I received one of those emails from a man called Travis, and instinctively started to have all of those worries. We arranged to meet in Folkestone and run 13 miles together, and just hoped I wouldn't disappoint him too much.

I woke up on the Saturday morning we were due to meet, the day after the credit card debacle, to torrential rain slamming at the windows. I was very grateful to have been put up by another B&B the night before and not in my as-yet-unpitched tent. The downpour didn't bode well for giving Travis the Best Day of Running Ever, aka the experience I, for some reason, felt the need to provide for everybody who ran with me. I met him at the station and we set out into the deluge.

It turned out that Travis was easy company, and the miles passed quickly. Having somebody there spurred me on a bit and we actually ran, rather than the stop-start shuffle I'd mostly been doing until that point. By early afternoon we had arrived in New Romney, soaked through and keen to get inside somewhere. We asked a passing man where the nearest pub was.

"Oh, it's a mile up there," he pointed, "you won't want to walk that, too far."

Travis and I exchanged a look and thanked him. It was easier not to mention that we'd already run from Folkestone that morning. Or the whole 5,000-mile run thing. Ten minutes later we were sitting in the pub, soggy kit hanging from the radiators, drinking a post-adventure beer.

"Cheers," Travis said, clinking his glass to mine. I cheersed back. A whole morning and some of an afternoon had passed, and I had barely worried about anything at all. I'd just done some running and chatted to someone friendly and now here I was in the most old-fashioned pub I'd ever set foot in, about to eat a pie, in a place I never would have visited otherwise. After lunch, Travis headed off and I made my way across the village to where I was staying with another family for the night. They let me have a hot shower and change into some dry clothes and then we sat on the sofa and watched a Pixar film together.

Maybe it was okay not to be in a jungle, sleeping under canvas, eating ration packs, I thought. Maybe just doing something different was enough, something that felt uncomfortable.

A few weeks later I got another email from Travis. He was going on holiday to Cornwall in a few weeks time. If I was nearby, maybe we could run together again. I guess I mustn't have been too much of a disappointment.

CHAPTER 5

I had last seen Greg in early October. He'd happened to be in London for meetings (or so he said) one day during my final week at work, and we met for lunch. I'd known him for more than a year at this point, and I can only recall one singular time we had seen each other without it being tacked onto other plans he already had. Whenever I suggested that maybe sometimes we could plan to do something for more than a couple of snatched hours it was always treated as a completely preposterous idea. Once, he told me he had a meeting at 3 p.m. and suggested we meet afterward. I said that sounded great, and that I'd finish work at 6 p.m. like I always did.

"I can't just wait around for hours for you, Elise," he had replied angrily.

I tried to squash the thought that I had been waiting around for months for him.

I can't remember exactly why we met for that final lunch, or under what guise. A month earlier I had actually managed to get him to spend a whole evening with me. We'd been for dinner in a French restaurant and he'd even let me eat the bread that came with my meal (not always the case – apparently carbs were evil and I didn't need them). Afterward, I'd sat on his lap on a bench on the South Bank and he'd held my face while we talked about what we'd do when I went running, how we'd make this work. I had thought we were making some progress then. Even just a week or so earlier he'd been sending me pictures of himself late at night and telling me all the things he wanted to do to me.

But sitting there in that brightly lit cafe, it felt like we were little more than acquaintances. We made small talk and ate overpriced salads and I think I knew then that we wouldn't be trying to make it work. We didn't discuss it, but then I felt like our whole relationship had been guesswork, smoke and mirrors, tip-toeing around on eggshells. We said goodbye, and I walked back to my office. I was relieved, in some ways, to feel that maybe this was the end. I had wanted this so badly, but perhaps if it was over I wouldn't have to spend quite so much time hiding in the toilets crying, which would be a nice change.

Later that afternoon, my phone beeped with a message from him.

"I had a cheque for £30,000 in my pocket for you today but I sensed that you're strong enough now, that you don't need it."

I believe that, in general, we expect people to be telling us the truth, especially people who we like and trust. You end up so far down the rabbit hole of lies before you start to realise that things don't quite add up. Over the months, there had been so many things that Greg had said to me that just made no sense whatsoever, from the mundane to the utterly outlandish. But I'd wanted to believe him, and so I had. I was embarrassed to tell my friends that he'd told me he was in New York hanging out with a supermodel who kept flirting with him, when I was certain he was actually at home, in his childhood bedroom. What kind of person did it make me, if I was stupid enough to believe a person like him?

But when I received that message, despite all the heartache, I could only laugh. Why would you still be sleeping in a single bed at your parents' house if you have a casual £30,000 lying around? Why was it that all these outlandish promises were only made after the event, so he never had to act on them? Why would you even consider giving so much money to somebody you couldn't make time to have dinner with more than once a month, who you clearly didn't really care about?

Why was I so afraid of cutting him out of my life when he contributed so little to it?

Why did he continue to tell me that he loved me, when he so clearly didn't?

And why did I continue to believe him?

––––––

After Folkestone and my day with Travis, I ran past Camber Sands to Rye, and then on to Hastings where Luke, a local runner, managed a hotel on the seafront. He offered me a room for the night and said he'd keep me company for some of the next day's run to Eastbourne. It was 21 miles, the furthest I'd attempted yet, and that night I'd be staying at the lighthouse B&B.

Luke planned to run the first half with me before turning back. I met him in the hotel reception that morning and he insisted on carrying my pack. He chatted away as we ran together, asking questions and telling me about his own running, and generally being great company. It should have been a good day. I should have been having a lovely time.

But, instead, all I could think about was the fact that I was supposed to be running this section with Greg.

Although it was patently obvious to anyone that I should have just made a clean break from him after that last lunch (or a long time before, let's be honest), for some reason we had carried on talking over the first few weeks I was running, playing the charade of being friends. While during more lucid moments I could recognise how unhealthy it had all been, in a way I think I romanticised how miserable I felt. If this just ended now, then what had it all been for? I needed it to have meant something, to have been worthwhile, and I kidded myself that if we could be friends then perhaps that was enough.

When Luke turned around after running 10 miles together, I felt both relief and guilt. I was so grateful to him for coming out with me but, really, I just wanted to be alone in my own head so that I could carry on torturing myself. I slowed to a walk as the trail ran alongside a railway line, the simple act of putting one foot in front of the other proving fairly monumental. I pulled my phone out to message Greg – if we were friends, surely I could tell him how I was feeling? I told him where I was and that I was finding it hard. His response came almost immediately.

"You just need to stop moaning, get on with it."

Why wasn't he finding this hard too? If he'd really felt all those things he'd claimed to, why was it only me falling apart? Every time I posted a video on my Facebook page people commented telling me how inspiring and brave I was. I was sure they wouldn't be saying that if they could see me crying by the train tracks about a boy. You couldn't run away from your problems, it turned out.

Somehow I kept moving forward. I'm really not sure how – I guess just because I had no other choice. I reached Eastbourne and then climbed up and out of town, onto the South Downs and towards Beachy Head. The light was fading, all the dragging my heels since leaving Luke had put me way behind schedule, and for some reason I didn't have a head torch. Storm Barney had just started to blow over the South Coast and it was a constant fight to stop the wind pushing me towards the cliff edge. I was exhausted in every possible way. Just as the last of the daylight leaked from the sky, I reached the lighthouse and knocked on the door. The B&B manager, Paul, showed me to my room.

"I'm cooking a curry, if you'd like some, to save you going back out?" he asked, "and how about a gin and tonic? There's a lovely bath in your room." I nodded a yes to all of his suggestions.

Later, once I'd eaten and warmed up and washed away the worst of the day, I recorded a video, attempting to make a joke about how I'd mastered the art of running, crying and breathing all at once. "I started crying, I'm not really sure why," I told the camera. Except, of course, I knew exactly why: I wasn't meant to be in that lighthouse alone.

I was on a 5,000-mile run, supposedly doing this huge, once-in-a-lifetime thing, and all that felt important to me was somebody who wasn't there.

———

Coasting

Storm Barney was raging even harder when I woke up the next morning.

"I don't want to let you go out there alone," said Paul as he heaped breakfast onto my plate. Apparently late November isn't prime time to be staying in a lighthouse hotel on the British coast, and I was the only guest. Hearing the wind buffeting the circular walls and the rain hammering against the windows, I wasn't sure that I wanted to go out there either. I only had a short day along to Seaford though, less than 10 miles, and I promised him that I'd be okay. I finished the last piece of toast, tightened the hood of my raincoat around my face, and set off.

Within seconds of stepping out of the door, a blast of wind had nearly knocked me off my feet. I could see the path ahead, trailing over the Seven Sisters, and I ran forward into the gusts. Anastasia's "Left Outside Alone" came on my playlist and I screamed along with the lyrics as I flew down from the grassy peak of the first cliff, rain lashing at my face.

I arrived in Seaford soaked to the skin but feeling a little better. I watched the news that evening and learned that Storm Barney had been causing devastation across the country, winds of up to 75 mph tearing through homes and ripping up trees. But for me, Barney had proved almost cathartic. It won't fix everything but there's something about running in a storm, screaming along to some angry lyrics, that makes the world make a little more sense again.

CHAPTER 6

The middle section of the south coast passed by in a bit of a blur. I ran across pebbly beaches and past brightly painted beach huts in West Sussex. I spent a rest day drinking hot chocolate in Bognor Regis. I got completely lost trying to navigate the waterways of the Pagham Harbour Nature Reserve, and filmed a very dramatic video clip about how I might die there before a dog walker rescued me. I came inland to skirt around Chichester Harbour and the squiggly Solent. I ran through the New Forest to Lymington, wild horses galloping beside me as the sun set.

It was a blur because almost every day as I inched my way along, somebody from the Yes Tribe came to join me. It had been going for less than six months at that point, but along with the people I had spent the summer camping with, there were thousands of people in the Facebook group. Lots of them were based around London and the South East, and they ran with me as if in relay for those few weeks.

Coasting

Astrid and Tom joined me from Seaford to Brighton, not minding too much when I got us hopelessly lost and we had to scramble up a cliff. Alice met me a couple of days later for the stretch from Lancing Beach to Worthing, which turned out to only be 5 km, and I worried for the hundredth time about what a fraud I was, proclaiming to be an adventurer and then only running a parkrun. Jenny drove all the way from Essex to West Sussex to run into Chichester with me, bringing with her a flask of tea and lots of biscuits. A band of merry women in the form of Becky, Terri, Fiona and Charlotte travelled by train, boat and car to meet me in Emsworth and run 16 extremely windy miles into Portsmouth, bringing with them multiple varieties of homemade flapjacks. Christina kept me company for an evening in Southampton where we drank mulled wine at the Christmas market to celebrate one month of adventuring.

I was still worried about letting people down, but with the Yes Tribe, I felt some comfort in knowing that they were just genuinely excited that I was having a go. It wasn't about being the best athlete out there, or setting any records. It was just about getting outside, trying something new, connecting with people, experiencing life beyond just what is expected of us.

And I was doing that, I kept trying to tell myself. Even on the days I was only running 5 km, even when I was staying with a lovely family instead of in a cold tent (something I still hadn't done), I was still at least having a go.

I started the South West Coast Path without really noticing. The 630-mile National Trail officially starts (or, more often, ends if you do it in the other direction) in Poole Harbour. I missed the commemorative marker because I was more preoccupied with running as fast as I could around to Sandbanks to catch the ferry over to Studland, avoiding a 20+ mile inland detour, having faffed around for too long eating breakfast.

I made it to the ferry with approximately 45 seconds to spare. The crossing only takes a few minutes and I'd soon disembarked, now in a hurry to beat the sunset and get to Swanage before dark. There was a short stretch along the road, before I dropped down to the coast path. I was running along the grass verge, and a car was parked on my right. I looked across and saw a man sitting in the passenger seat but nobody in the driver's seat, weirdly.

It all happened very quickly after that. My glance dropped and I saw that somebody was in fact in the driver's seat; they were just lying horizontally with their head in the passenger's lap. And the passenger wasn't wearing any trousers. And the driver's head was moving up and down.

Then, before I could look away, the passenger turned in my direction, caught my eye and winked.

I felt violated. This was meant to be a lovely, wholesome tour of the seaside. I'd imagined myself eating ice creams and scones and befriending fishermen and waxing lyrical about how beautiful our coastline is.

I hadn't imagined... this.

I broke out in a cold sweat and ran away as quickly as I could.

———

Coasting

Overnight a yellow weather warning was issued. Storm Desmond was on his way, bringing with him heavy rain and severe gales. I climbed up out of Swanage onto the coast path, which ran atop the cliffs, around Durlston Country Park. Up on the exposed tops, it was almost impossible to stay upright. I battled forward for a while, but it was useless.

I crouched down, lowering my centre of gravity in an attempt to stay on my feet, and tried to figure out what to do. That night I was being picked up by Peter, who owned an outdoor supplies company and lived nearby. He'd sent me a couple of parcels of snacks along the way and was letting me stay with his family tonight. It should have only been 14 miles or so along the coast path, a relatively easy day, but it was looking like it would be slow going at best, and that I might actually die at worst.

I saw a footpath sign off to the right, heading inland. I followed it hoping that the wind might not be so bad away from the cliff edge, having been buffered by trees and fences and lumpy bits of land before hitting me. The path lasted for a hundred metres or so, before depositing me out on a farm track. It was still windy, but there was less chance of me ending up in the sea, so that was a positive.

Over the howling I heard a dog barking and saw a very lively collie being held by the collar, desperately pulling to get free.

"He's okay, he just wants to say hello," the man holding the collar looked me up and down. "Where are you heading to? You've picked quite the day for it."

"I just need to get to somewhere near Kimmeridge. I was running along the coast path but it's too rough out there," I told him.

"You can't be out on the coast path by yourself today, no way. Keep going straight along this track instead. This is Priest's Way, named after the local priest who travelled along here between his parishes. You'll come out in Worth Matravers. Stop at the pub in the village, it's the best one around."

I thanked him and went to head off, relieved I could escape the coast path for at least a little while.

"Make sure you do stop at that pub, you really must," he shouted into the wind as he walked away.

It wasn't advice I normally needed giving twice, but as I reached Worth Matravers, I wasn't sure whether to stop. I had barely covered any distance yet and really needed to get a move on. But I was also soaked through and fed up with the day. The idea of being inside somewhere and having a break from being battered by the wind was definitely appealing.

When I saw the pub in the village square, my mind was made up. It did look very warm inside, and the old man had seemed *very* insistent. Who was I to let him down? I headed inside. There was straw on the floor and it was full of dogs and muddy boots and other people also sheltering from Storm Desmond. I ordered a pasty (the only thing on the menu) and a tankard of hot cider. Not necessarily traditional sports nutrition, I'll admit, but one of the main things I was learning was that actually you could eat almost anything mid-run, as long as you were going slowly enough.

The pub was exactly as you'd hope a pub that you stumble across in the middle of a storm would be like. I could have stayed for hours, drinking more tankards of cider and petting more dogs, but it was already mid-afternoon and the December days were only getting shorter. I needed to plough through a few more miles before calling Peter, or I'd be too behind schedule tomorrow.

Having been blown over more times than I could count and nearly losing my rain cover, gloves, phone... anything not attached to me, basically, I got to Kimmeridge, where Peter was picking me up. I wandered around the village for a while trying to find some phone signal and finally called him to be rescued. The inland route had ended up being a bit of a shortcut, and so it really hadn't been a very long day distance-wise, but I was so ready for it to be over.

After a night at Peter's talking about stoves (the latest project his company was working on) and being loaded up with snacks, he dropped me back to Kimmeridge where I was meeting up with local runners Kate and Sofia. Storm Desmond was hanging around but raging slightly less viciously today. It was still very, very windy, but I felt fairly sure that we could probably follow the coast path without being blown off a cliff.

After a few miles of running we reached the abandoned village of Tyneham. In 1943, during World War Two, Tyneham's residents were displaced just before Christmas so that the land could be used as a military firing range. When they left, the residents assumed they would return one day, but sadly they never could. Today Tyneham is a real life "ghost village" consisting only of some abandoned buildings and a restored church and school for visitors. A good spot for some map reading and to eat the chocolate cake that Sofia had baked. I looked at the map that Kate had brought along and pretended it meant something to me. Perhaps that would have been a good opportunity to get some lessons on actually reading one but I was too embarrassed to ask.

I only had about 10 miles to cover that day. It felt like a normal Sunday with friends: a reasonable-length run, some snacks, great views and a few laughs. I was still battling with myself whenever it felt too easy, but perhaps this was how it had to be. When you go out to do something for a few days or a week, maybe you can really hit the ground running and then end each day feeling broken and spent and like you've given your absolute all. But when you set out to do something over the course of nearly a whole year, you'd never make it through if you felt like that every day. It's the sum total of all the manageable parts that makes the big thing happen.

The fact I was worrying about this made me an enormous hypocrite. I kept talking about how much I hated the macho I-slayed-a-bear-for-breakfast narrative that often surrounds adventure. I kept telling people how lucky I was to be there, and that the whole point was to enjoy it. But then, every time I *did* enjoy it, I just felt guilty. It was very confusing. I just remember a constant, low-level headache throughout those first couple of months, where my thoughts were all a mess and I couldn't quite untangle them. I was so caught up in what I should and shouldn't be doing.

From Tyneham we carried on heading west. On the way down to Lulworth Cove, our finishing point, we took a wrong turn somewhere. The trail wound its way into some scrubby woodland and started to peter out, before vanishing altogether. We were on a sheer hillside, clambering through thickets of brambles.

Coasting

"I'm not sure we're on the coast path any more," Kate said, vocalising what we were all thinking.

"Erm no, maybe not," I agreed while being pulled back by a thorny branch that had attached itself to my leggings, scraping the skin underneath.

"I think if we just head that way," Kate said pointing directly upwards, "we'll rejoin the coast path."

Anything seemed better than the route we were currently pursuing. We retraced our steps for a while before scrambling up the hillside, eventually linking up with a much more promising-looking path that took us into Lulworth Cove.

During peak season, Lulworth Cove and nearby Durdle Door are heaving with beachgoers at the weekends. It was a lot quieter on a gloomy Sunday in December. Kate's partner picked her and Sofia up to take them home. Despite the fact I felt morally compromised for having enjoyed it, I had had such a nice day with them. I said goodbye, bought some fudge from the sweet shop before it closed, and then walked up to the youth hostel where I was staying that night.

The hostel was quiet, just as the cove had been, and I had a room to myself despite having paid for a dormitory, which was a nice surprise. I was lying on my bed, reading my book and thinking about how happy I was that I wouldn't have any strangers snoring in the bunk below me tonight when I noticed an unpleasant smell filling the room. I tried to ignore it for a while but it really was vile, a combination of stagnant bog and wet animal. I felt a bit weird about complaining – it was a hostel, you expect to rough it a bit. But perhaps there was a problem with the plumbing they needed to know about? Maybe there was a leak somewhere? This couldn't be normal.

I got up from my bottom bunk and put my shoes on to go to reception. I was halfway down the corridor when I noticed that the smell seemed worse suddenly and, actually, it was following me.

With horror I realised that the odour was, in fact, coming from my own trainers. All of the cow pats and puddle water that they had waded through over the past few weeks must have soaked into the fabric, and the heat from the radiator had warmed them up, now releasing the scent.

I sheepishly walked back down the corridor to my room, took my revolting shoes off and picked my book up again, feeling very grateful that a) I hadn't made it as far as reception to complain before realising, and b) I wasn't sharing a room tonight.

CHAPTER 7

The first stretch of the South West Coast Path is known as the Jurassic Coast. It starts in Swanage, reaches around the Dorset coast and into Devon, where it ends in Exmouth. It's England's only natural UNESCO World Heritage Site and sits within the Dorset Area of Outstanding Natural Beauty.

The Jurassic Coast felt like my introduction to "proper" coast paths. Narrow trails winding over exposed clifftops, brutally steep steps taking you into and out of the roller coaster of valleys, vertical scrambles down to secluded coves, rolling fields on one side and crashing waves on the other. When I think of running around the coast, this is the sort of terrain that first comes to mind. It was one of the earlier sections but even now, if you ask me for a recommendation, I'm likely to tell you to go to the Jurassic Coast.

My dad joined me for my last day on it, the first of what would turn out to be many, many visits. I saw him more regularly during those ten months than at any other time in my adult life. In turn, he saw more obscure places around the coast of the UK than I'm sure he ever imagined he would. I set out from Sidmouth while he drove his car to Exmouth, where the Jurassic Coast ends, and ran back to meet me. We met in the middle in Budleigh Salterton, one of my dad's favourite places for no other reason than there's a memorial bench dedicated to a man named Chuffer Hornby. If there's one thing my dad likes more than anything, it's a memorial bench.

During the summer months there's a ferry you can take from Exmouth across the Exe Estuary. It drops you in Starcross, where the South West Coast Path resumes. In the winter, when the ferry isn't running, the alternative is a 10-mile detour up to the first bridge over the river. I saw no reason whatsoever to be held hostage by the ferry timetables and happily let my dad do his best boat impression and drive me around the water instead. He headed home and I carried on to Dawlish Warren, where I was meeting Jazz.

I had met Jazz two months earlier, at Yestival. I'd been sitting next to her when Dave had called me onto the stage to announce my adventure to the entire audience. As I mentioned earlier, I spent most of that festival crying uncontrollably, so I potentially didn't make the best first impression. Despite this, Jazz very kindly invited me to stay with her family in Devon when I ran through.

We weren't far off the shortest day of the year and it was almost dark by the time I arrived in Dawlish Warren, just before four o'clock in the afternoon. It was pouring with rain and I wasn't meeting Jazz until five. The cafes were all shutting and I wandered around for a while before finding a strange kind of restaurant-cum-coffee shop that seemed to be open a little later. I was used to living in London where you could get anything you wanted 24/7. I was increasingly learning that this was not the case elsewhere.

I ordered a hot chocolate and sat shivering in my wet clothes. My minimal packing consisted of two sets of running kit: a dry set (which I put on in the evenings) and a wet set (which I actually ran in), and never the twain shall meet. I had started off referring to the dry set as the clean set, but by any normal laundry standards this was patently untrue, they just appeared clean in comparison to the other set which was normally covered in mud and sweat and sheep poo. I was desperate to take my sopping wet leggings off but I knew I'd regret it when I didn't have anything dry to put on later.

As I waited for Jazz, alone in that strange cafe wearing soggy leggings on a Saturday night, the world suddenly felt quite lonely again. It was always harder after somebody had visited. I'd had such a lovely couple of days with my dad – as well as running together, I'd taken a rest day to spend with him. He'd brought some "real" clothes for me to wear and we had been out for breakfast then to a carol concert at Exeter Cathedral. It was nice to just do something that felt normal and familiar with somebody I loved and who really knew me. Now he was gone and I was on my own, feeling homesick again.

Two hot chocolates later, Jazz picked me up and we drove to her village. I instantly felt better. It wasn't *home*, but it was *a* home. It was warm and dry and I got to take off my wet clothes and hang out with her dogs. Jazz's mum cooked a Saturday night roast dinner and I went to sleep feeling much safer and happier.

Up and down and up and down and up and down.

———

Jazz joined me to run the 20 miles from Dawlish Warren to Paignton. She had never run more than a half marathon before.

I always worried that I didn't look like a real runner, let alone an ultrarunner. I wasn't lean and strong-looking like the runners who won races. If anything, I had probably put on weight with the endless cakes I was being brought by people who ran with me, and all the home-cooked dinners made by the people I stayed with, and then the extra snacks in cafes just so I could sit somewhere dry. I had committed to fuelling with passion, despite the fact that on lots of days I covered less distance than I do now in my normal day-to-day life. I just happened to be joining those miles up in a long chain, which made it seem more impressive.

Maybe it was a good thing that I didn't look like an elite athlete though, that I wasn't running sub-8-minute miles all day every day. If I had been, I doubt as many people would have been inclined to say yes to coming with me and running further than they ever had before. Maybe the fact that I had no idea what I was doing made other people feel more comfortable to give it a go – like Jazz, on that Sunday in December.

Jazz has since become one of my closest friends. I admire her skills and competence in many, many areas. Hopefully, then, she can forgive me for saying that, at that time at least, trail running perhaps wasn't one of them.

Jazz's mum packed us up with lunch for our expedition – cheese rolls, crisps and cereal bars – and her stepdad dropped us back to Dawlish Warren. They were collecting Jazz from Paignton at the end of the day and had offered to take some of the contents of my backpack with them. Throughout the whole ten months, there was nothing that brightened a day more than the opportunity to lighten my load for a while. My back still hadn't got used to running with the heavy pack.

We settled into an easy pace, walking the uphills and jogging the flats and the downs. Heading towards Torquay, the coast path comes away from the cliff edge and takes you through some woods. The floor was claggy where it had been so wet in the days before. I lost my footing on a slick patch and slipped backward, landing in a puddle of orangey-red, clay-like mud which, in the process of standing up again, I managed to smear all over me.

"Don't worry, I've got some wipes in my bag," Jazz said. I stood very still and tried not to touch anything else while she looked for them.

"Oh no!" Jazz exclaimed. I looked over to where she was crouched over her backpack, looking slightly more shimmery than she had earlier. "My glitter has exploded!"

From her bag, along with the promised wipes, Jazz pulled an empty pot of pink glitter, the contents of which was now all over Jazz's hands, legs, shorts, hat, sandwiches... well, everything she owned really. The inside of her pack would probably never look the same again. We looked quite the pair running beside one another, me coated in mud and Jazz covered head to toe in glitter.

How to safely contain your pink glitter is an age-old concern for serious explorers all over the world. I'm sure that these are the same kind of hazards that Shackleton and Scott faced.

We stopped in Torquay for an ice cream to recover from the incident before running the final few miles to Paignton, Jazz sparkling in the sunlight.

———

Earlier that week, before my dad arrived, I had stayed with the Youngs. Rob Young was yet another person I had met through the Yes Tribe and he invited me to stay with him and his wife Veryan and their two children.

They arranged to meet me in Sidmouth on Wednesday afternoon, but I had a fairly traumatic afternoon on the way there. I got very lost in some fields and had to be escorted back to the coast path by a disgruntled farmer in his tractor. I wasn't in the best mood when I arrived, annoyed with myself for getting lost, and with the farmer for being *quite* so grumpy. Then I saw the whole Young family waiting on the esplanade holding signs with my name on and a flask of hot chocolate. The day really improved.

Over dinner that evening, Veryan said she might come and run with me the following week, if she could take a day off work. She sent me a message a couple of days later asking if Monday would be okay. I told her that I had 19 miles scheduled, from Paignton around to Dartmouth and that she was very welcome to come along.

Veryan had never run more than 10 km, or just over 6 miles, before.

Nowadays, if somebody proposed coming for a best-part-of-a-marathon run with me having never covered more than a third of the distance before, I might have some concerns. I'd be worried that they would do themselves some serious damage at worst, or at best just have a miserable time. Ignorance was still bliss back then though. I was so far out of my comfort zone that it didn't occur to me to be worried when somebody else was too. In fact, I almost found it reassuring not to be the only one. It was the days the "real" ultrarunners came to run with me that I felt most nervous.

I met Veryan on the seafront in Paignton at 9 o' clock on Monday morning. It was already raining hard and didn't look like it would be stopping any time soon. We set off into the low clouds and passed the miles chatting away. Veryan told me about the new job she was hoping to start soon, about the time her and Rob had spent travelling in New Zealand, and about the merino wool clothing company they had started there.

The South West Coast Path is a roller coaster from start to finish. Over its 630 miles, you climb the height of Everest four times. I can recall approximately two flat sections of more than a mile (one being along the River Taw estuary path into and out of Barnstaple in North Devon, the other a 5K stretch from Penzance around to Mousehole). It's slow going at the best of times; the elevation is absorbed by thousands of steps built into the steep valleys, making it hard to pick up any speed going down hills either.

The day I spent with Veryan was, I think we can safely say, not even close to being "the best of times" conditions-wise. All the rainfall of the past few months meant that the paths had been churned up and turned completely to mush. We reached the bottom of one particularly steep hill and started to make our way up it, but for every step we took forward we were sliding backward by about four times the distance.

I was wearing trail shoes with supposedly good traction but they were no match for the waterfall of muddy slop beneath my feet. I spied a fence to the right.

"We'll have to use that for support," I said to Veryan and we shuffled towards it. I was grateful to have something to cling onto, but there was something that wasn't ideal about our fence: it was barbed wire. I quite liked both my arms and my waterproof coat and I didn't particularly want to rip them to shreds. Although at that moment, given how wet it was, I was probably more attached to the coat than my limbs.

Through some trial and error, we developed a very sophisticated technique for hauling ourselves up the slope. We would crouch down slightly, hold tightly onto the non-barbed wire rungs of the fence with two hands and then lean to the left to avoid the sharp bits. Then it was a case of swapping hands and pulling your feet upwards. It sort of worked, but I was a long-distance runner (or trying to be, at least). I did not have the upper body strength for this. Every few metres we'd find a grassy tussock at the edge of the path, wedge our feet against it and stand up straight for a rest. It was a fairly exhausting process.

"Snack?" Veryan suggested when we reached the top, her breath short from the exertion of the climbing expedition we had just found ourselves on.

I literally never say no to a snack. As in, I genuinely can't recall a single time, in my entire life. My mum likes to tell a story about me, aged three, standing next to a builder who was doing some work for them saying "I like Kit Kats" on repeat, until he eventually started bringing two Kit Kats to work with him.

Coasting

I nodded a yes to Veryan, and we found a fence to lean against. These were not just any snacks, I soon discovered. Veryan had brought with her a bag of chocolate-coated gingerbread. Is there anything better when it's the 14th of December and your arms hurt and you're covered in mud and you're soaking wet and you still have ten more miles to run/walk/climb/slide/crawl? It's unlikely. Refuelled and with morale significantly boosted, we carried on.

"How much further do you think we have to go?" Veryan asked a few hours later. There had been a sign saying it was 4 miles to Kingswear (where Veryan would head home while I took the ferry over to Dartmouth) and then another claiming 3 miles, but a huge chunk of time had disappeared between the two. I normally calculated my day based on averaging about 4 miles an hour but it was taking much longer. It didn't *feel* like we were moving that slowly. I wasn't sure whether it was our legs or the signs that couldn't be trusted. It had been a dark day altogether with all the black rain clouds and night seemed to be coming in even earlier than normal.

One of the many good things about the South West Coast Path is that it's quite well marked on Google Maps as a footpath. Given that, as we know, this was my only real means of navigation, this was very useful. The less good thing is that my phone battery tended to die as soon as it got slightly cold. And on this day, it really was quite cold. I pulled it out to try to get some accurate information as to how far we had left to go, but just found a no-battery symbol flashing at me.

We would just have to keep going. It couldn't be too far now.

Slowly but surely, one muddy foot in front of the other, we continued creeping along the coast path until, at long last, we reached the top of the final cliff before the trail goes down into Kingswear. We saw the lights of the village below us and it was such a relief. When it felt never-ending I knew, rationally, that the ordeal would be over at some point, but it was hard to make my brain believe that. On the longest, wettest, hardest days there was always a part of me that wondered if perhaps I'd have to admit defeat and live atop the cliff forever. It was never until I could physically see the end destination that I really believed it was possible to get there.

We headed down into the village and I hugged Veryan goodbye. It felt fairly miraculous that she had managed to run three times further than she ever had before, in some of the worst conditions I'd experienced so far. I was glad she'd come for the day and hoped she was glad too. Although, right at that moment, I think she was probably more just excited for a hot shower and dry clothes and to be sitting down on the sofa.

But then isn't that why we do these things? For how incredible it makes something as simple as a hot shower and a warm pair of socks and a cup of tea feel? The pleasure and the pain, all wrapped up together.

———

I had been following George Mahood on Twitter for a while. He was famed (although, I'm sure, he'd disagree with that word) for attempting to cycle from Land's End to John o' Groats without any money, clothes, food, shoes… or a bike. He self-published a book about the trip and now lives in Devon with his wife Rachel and their three children, where he makes a living writing more books.

Coasting

When I got an email from him asking if I needed somewhere to stay for a night, I felt a little star-struck. It was like when I had met Anna – there's something sort of surreal about the people you follow on the internet turning into real people. Never meet your heroes, they say, but actually I was finding they were generally quite nice people. In the adventure world, at least. I can't vouch for any other industries.

George picked me up from Beesands and we drove back to his house. One of his daughters was with him and she told me about the school nativity play she had performed in that afternoon. That night, over a huge bowl of pasta and a lot of garlic bread, we talked over my plan for the next few days. I told George and Rachel that I was planning to run through to Bantham the next day, via the Salcombe ferry. They exchanged a look. It was about 23 miles, which I thought sounded doable, but I got the impression that they thought this might be a bit ambitious.

"And then what about when you get to Bantham?" George asked. "The ferry over the Avon to Bigbury isn't running at this time of year."

Of course, I hadn't looked at the route closely enough on any maps to know there was a piece of water that needed to be crossed, or a ferry in the first place, let alone that it wasn't running.

"How about you stay here tomorrow night too, then I can just drop you round to Bigbury to get going the next day?" George asked. This sounded like a great plan to me, obviously, but I couldn't quite believe that, once again, somebody would be willing to go so far out of their way to help me. George had already told me he couldn't join me for a run because he was almost ready to hit publish on his next book and was busy getting it finished. It was also the week before Christmas. Everybody had their own lives and families to get on with, yet here they were offering to ferry me around.

The next morning George made me scrambled eggs and toast with homemade bread for breakfast then dropped me back to Beesands. The best thing about staying for two nights was that I had got to leave most of the contents of my backpack behind, and I hopped out of the car feeling very light.

"Just give me a call when you're getting near to Bantham and I'll come and get you. Or if you want to be picked up sooner, that's fine too, no problem at all." I sensed there was still some doubt about my ability to do this section in one go.

These doubts were well founded, in fairness. It was 23 miles which, admittedly, would be the furthest I had run in one go so far, and the South West Coast Path website did describe this section as "particularly tough", along "a rugged, undeveloped section of coast". I had no choice but to make it though – if I didn't get to the estuary and George had to pick me up sooner, I'd still have the ferry issue the following day. I tightened my rucksack straps, crossed my fingers and got going.

Some time that afternoon, long before it got dark, I called George.

"I'm in Thurlestone," I told him, "so about 20 minutes away from Bantham."

Fuelled by the cheese sandwiches that Rachel had made for me using more of that homemade bread, and some Salcombe fudge that I had picked up after the mid-run ferry ride (a ferry that was actually still running in the winter, thank god), I had managed the full 23 miles. I hadn't needed to be rescued early.

Coasting

Although they didn't say anything, I think that George and Rachel were surprised. And so was I, to be honest.

I had been running for nearly two months – perhaps I finally knew what I was doing. I just kept putting one foot in front of the other, over and over and over again, day after day after day, and it had become a new kind of normal. I had a nice moment of thinking, for once, that maybe I wasn't totally useless.

It wasn't a feeling that lasted long.

CHAPTER 8

I went to university in Plymouth. As seemed to be the case with most things in my life, I didn't plan to. I was going to take a gap year after my A Levels but, on results day, the reality of having to stay at home to work and save up while everybody else went off to start their new lives dawned on me. I spent the weekend in bed crying, then, on the Monday morning, I logged onto the UCAS site and found a place at the University of Plymouth through clearing. Two weeks later, we packed up my mum's Suzuki Swift with all my most treasured belongings (and a lot of junk too) and drove 250 miles south.

I wouldn't say that I regret going to university. Looking back at it now, with the benefit of hindsight and being able to see how it all worked out for the greater good in the end, I'm glad I went. I met my best friends there. I got a degree, just about, for whatever that's worth. I probably wouldn't have got into running or adventure or the outdoors if it wasn't for the many societies I joined in my final year in a bid to pad out my CV a bit and make some new friends after lots of mine had already graduated.

But if we look at the specifics then sure, there's a lot I regret. We've talked about the credit cards and the debt already. Then there were the many, many black-out drunk nights. Waking up with an unexplainable injury, a lost phone and somebody in my bed whose name I didn't know. The debilitating hangovers. Flashbacks creeping in of all the mortifying things that had happened the night before. Friends filling in the blanks. Pictures uploaded to Facebook with people I didn't remember seeing. A cloud of shame hanging over me for days, weeks, months, forever. Sending drunken text messages on one night out to try to make amends for all the things I had done on another. Oversleeping, missing lectures, calling in sick to work, promising myself I'd be better tomorrow...

There was the person I was when I was drunk and then the person I was when I was sober. Or, more accurately, the person I wanted to be when I was sober but who I never quite got to be because I was too busy hiding from drunk me's mistakes. Bad decision after bad decision. Self-destructive behaviour that leaked into day-to-day life too. Endless procrastination. Nearly failing my degree. All those credit cards. My terrible taste in men and endlessly overlooking the red flags. Bury a problem, worry about it later, go on a night out instead, make everything ten times worse.

And it's all normalised because that's just what you do when you're a student, isn't it? You binge-drink until the point of hating yourself and nobody really questions that it might be a problem.

In the 18 months since finishing university, I hadn't necessarily curbed those habits, there were just fewer opportunities to display them. When I started working full time I no longer had the energy or the money or the same group of always-available friends to go out four or five nights a week with. But whenever I did drink, it was exactly the same. No matter how much progress I felt like I was making, I still didn't know my limits. Or if I did know them, I bulldozed right through them without a second thought.

Then suddenly I was on an adventure without any opportunities to go and be an idiot in a nightclub. I convinced myself that maybe I wouldn't be like that any more. Drunk Me seemed so far removed from Adventure Me and, even more so, from the exaggerated caricature of Adventure Me that I ended up portraying on the internet. My friends were constantly amused by what they called my wholesome alter ego. They threatened to set up an "Elise Downing Tells The Truth" account, exposing all the hangovers and bad decisions.

But what is the truth? If this was actually how I was spending my days now, just running and being outside and only being concerned about where my next slice of cake was coming from, then wasn't this just who I was now?

I was nervous running into Plymouth. I hadn't been back since graduating, and I didn't know how to reconcile this part I was playing now with the person I had been then.

I arrived on a Thursday evening just as it was getting dark. It had been a long day, well over 20 miles, and I was looking forward to taking the weekend off to catch up with some friends. I'd been averaging one rest day per week so far, but this would be the first time I took several days off at once.

Coasting

It was strange to be somewhere I knew so well. I ran through the Barbican and instinctively knew the quickest route into town, the shortcut through campus to the student union offices. I had got used to the constant feeling of unfamiliarity and I think that was part of the reason I was so exhausted all the time. You could never just switch off. It was comforting to be able to move around on autopilot again.

I was staying with my friend Alex that night. She worked at the student union heading up all the charity activity, and I had met her the year before during a frenzy of volunteering and extracurricular activities. I found her in her office and waited for her to finish work. We stopped at the Co-op for pizza and Prosecco and then headed back to Alex's flat.

———

I woke up 12 hours later to Alex shaking me awake.

"Elise, I need to go to work. You can let yourself out, just bring the keys to the office later." She left the room. I heard her picking up her bag and then the front door clicking behind her.

The last thing I remembered was being in the student union bar and sharing one, then two, then three bottles of their cheapest wine with Alex. We had met up with some other friends who were also still in Plymouth. We might have done a pub quiz, but that was hazy. I could vaguely recall taking a shot and maybe being picked up by somebody and then dropped again. I had a bruise on the back of my leg. Then… nothing. No more memories. My phone was on the table next to me, which was a relief. I clicked the home button and saw it light up with notifications from Facebook.

I vaguely remembered drunkenly posting something. My heart started to beat very fast. What on earth could I have written? I pulled open the app. There I was, being lifted in the air by Alex and our other friend James. At least that confirmed that I had in fact been picked up. The caption wasn't too horrendous, which was a relief given that more than 50 people had already liked it.

Looking at my phone caused a wave of nausea to wash over me. I ran for the bathroom and spent some time sitting on the tiled floor, not daring to move. When it felt safe, I ventured back to Alex's bedroom and checked the time.

It was 8.45.

Fuck.

I remembered with horror that I was due to be giving a talk at a local secondary school that morning. In 15 minutes, to be precise.

Fuck, fuck, fuck.

This should have been my second school talk. I'd hoped to do more but found it difficult making them work logistically, when I was never 100 per cent sure of my timings. Also, if I'm honest, I found them a little awkward. I didn't feel like I had any right to go and pretend to be "inspiring" when, behind the scenes, everything still felt like such a mess.

And didn't this just prove that? In a quarter of an hour I was meant to be telling these kids about following your dreams, about being brave, about having a go at something, about not just settling for what's accepted of you. Instead, I was in bed, half naked and hungover. I had no idea what I'd done last night but I knew, instinctively, that I'd embarrassed myself. I couldn't go and pretend to be motivational. I was a sham.

Coasting

I messaged my contact at the school and told him that I wasn't feeling well and wasn't going to be able to make it. It wasn't a lie, I suppose. I really wasn't feeling well. I ran for the bathroom again.

Eventually I mustered up the energy to have a hot shower, which made me feel better for approximately 30 seconds. I gathered my stuff from around Alex's flat and stepped out into the fresh air. Given the state of me, this was probably a bad idea. I doubt Alex would have minded me staying there for the day but, for some reason, I felt a bit weird about it. I felt like I needed to go and brave the world, but I wasn't sure where to go. I was staying with some other friends that night but had all day to kill before they finished work.

I remembered that a few years earlier, when there had been a mouse infestation in my student house and I'd been too afraid to sleep in case one got into bed with me, I had spent a whole night on a sofa in the university library. My still-a-bit-drunk brain told me that this was my best option. I was pretty sure I could sign in as a visitor and, best of all, I was almost certain that I wouldn't be the most hungover person in there.

And that's how I came to spend an entire 8 hours camped out on a sofa tucked behind a corner near the printers, only moving between the toilets to throw up again and the vending machine to buy another can of Diet Coke. In between, I tried to close my eyes and have a nap without anybody noticing. I don't think I'm being dramatic if I describe it as one of the worst days of my life. Even worse, perhaps, than that fateful marathon where I was the crying crayon. At least that had come with a medal.

I hoped that none of the students milling around the printers were the same people following my lovely, wholesome, brave adventure online. It really wasn't looking very lovely or wholesome or brave at all as I clapped my hand to my mouth and made yet another dash to the toilets.

I was eventually able to leave the library and I spent the rest of the weekend with Katie and Mary, two of my best friends, recovering from my hangover and laughing a lot. When I left to start running again, I nearly cried. As always, the loneliness always felt worse right after saying goodbye.

It was the Monday of Christmas week and I was meant to be running 22 miles to Millendreath, just before Looe, where a lady with a B&B was letting me stay for the night. The route from Plymouth to Looe passes a military firing range at Tregantle Fort, just before you get to Portwrinkle. You can check online which days shooting is taking place. I, of course, had not done this. I got to the edge of the range and saw lots of red flags flying, indicating that you shouldn't pass through. The alternative route follows the B3247 instead.

Even on the best of days, I imagine that the B3247 makes for a pretty hairy route on foot. It's a fast, winding, fairly narrow road, with lots of tall hedges and very few substantial verges. On that day, it also happened to be extremely foggy. I could barely see my hand when I stretched my arm out in front of me. I definitely couldn't see the traffic coming towards me. I would just hear the roar of an engine, then suddenly a car would be there, next to me, speeding past, a hair's breadth from brushing my arm. Even more worryingly, the opposite was obviously true too: the drivers couldn't see me either.

Coasting

I found a gap in the hedge and stepped off the road into the edge of a field. I messaged Mary.

"I'm not sure what to do, I'm stuck. The trail is closed and the road feels dangerous," I told her.

It did feel dangerous. I wasn't lying. But, still, at the back of my mind I wondered if I was just looking for an excuse to stop. If I was more adventurous, wouldn't I have just carried on, ignoring everything I knew about road safety? I couldn't tell.

"I can come and pick you up after work, if you need," Mary replied.

I peered out from the field again. Another car came rushing out of the mist. I decided that I did need rescuing. I didn't want to die today. I'd just have to come back the next day when the coast path was open again.

I carried on a little further, flattening myself against the hedge until I reached a village with a pub. I ordered a pot of tea and waited it out by the fire for the next few hours until Mary arrived.

What happened if you were on an adventure somewhere your friends couldn't come and rescue you? I wasn't sure, but I didn't want to find out.

———

I eventually made it to Looe, where I stayed with Jim and Shirley who owned a small B&B by the seafront. They made me breakfast in the morning and Jim walked around the harbour with me to take some action shots. We climbed the steps that join the harbourside to the sea road above, and looked down over the hotchpotch of coloured houses stacked up on the hills either side of the fishing port. I ran back and forth a few times so Jim could get some pictures.

"Are you okay?" Jim asked, a concerned look on his face. It took me a moment to realise he was referring to the limp I seemed to adopt at the beginning of every day, thanks to a pain in my right leg. I'd just got used to it but imagine it did look a bit alarming to an onlooker.

"Oh, yes, it goes off after a while." And it did, normally.

I thanked Jim again for letting me stay, and headed off. I followed the marine road for a while before it merged into the coastal trail. As I reached the end of the road section, I realised with some concern that my limp didn't seem to be "going off" today and, actually, it hurt quite a lot. The pain was enough to make me think that I should probably stop running, so I walked for a bit. It still hurt.

I sat down on a bench and thought about what to do. It was December 23rd, Christmas Eve Eve.

I was meant to be spending Christmas with Megan who I had met the summer before on a midnight run around Central London where we were, inexplicably, all dressed in tennis whites. Maybe Wimbledon had been on at the time, or perhaps the run was just led by a tennis enthusiast? I'm not sure. Either way, her family lived in the depths of Cornwall, and she had invited me to stay with them for Christmas.

Of course, I could have gone home for Christmas. It would have been easy to take a train back to Northampton, have a few days off and enjoy Christmas with my family. But that didn't feel very adventurous, so I had taken Megan up on her offer. It would be the first Christmas I'd ever spent away from my family. Somehow it felt like a rite of passage. The decision had not proven popular with everyone, though. Every time I had called my dad for the past month, he'd said "Elise, I had this awful dream last night that you aren't coming home for Christmas..." When Christmas Day did arrive, he wore black to signify his mourning.

The plan had been to run a bit further around the South Cornwall coast from Looe to Charlestown, near St Austell, from where Megan would pick me up and take me home for Christmas. My right leg seemed to be screaming a firm no to that idea though. I hobbled back into town, bought a pasty and looked up buses to St Austell, where I had already arranged somewhere to stay there that night. Maybe it made sense to take the bus, meet Megan and then retrace my steps back to Looe to start running again after Christmas. I imagined that a few days of rest and lots of Christmas food would miraculously fix my leg. Roast potatoes are well known for their healing properties, after all.

On the bus to St Austell, I looked up sports physios. I found one who hadn't packed up for Christmas yet and booked myself in for that afternoon. Just in case the roast potatoes didn't work.

I spent Christmas with Megan's family and it was lovely. I ate a lot of roast potatoes, but my leg still hurt. The physio I had seen in St Austell hadn't come back with anything concrete, just muttered something about overuse. A fair assessment, I suppose.

The day after Boxing Day my parents drove down. They had booked a cottage in Falmouth where we were going to stay for a few days and celebrate a second Christmas together.

Falmouth should only have been about another two or three days on from Looe, so I was anticipating being nearly there by the time my parents arrived.

Except, of course, by the time they arrived on the 27th I still hadn't run past Looe. They picked me up from near Megan's and we drove down to Falmouth. I took some more rest days, spending them in the cottage eating my way through the advent calendar that my mum had still bought me, despite me missing the whole of advent, watching Christmas television and trying not to be too grumpy. I think I might have failed a bit on that front.

The day before they left, we headed out for a test run together to see how my leg was doing. The answer came back loud and clear: not very well. It was a weird sort of pain. I couldn't quite pinpoint where it was coming from and it wasn't even pain, as such. There was just a general discomfort from the knee down and the feeling that something definitely wasn't right.

I was still planning to head back to Looe when they left and get going again. I could always just walk if I needed to. I was doing a lot of that anyway, thanks to the gradients of the South West Coast Path and the constant muddy slip-and-slide the recent storms had produced.

We packed up the cottage and I had a strop that was painfully reminiscent of the tantrum I'd thrown in Dartford station car park. I huffed and puffed about how I couldn't do this and I was clearly useless and I should probably just quit. None of this was my mum and dad's fault, obviously, but shouting at them helped to cover up how terrified I felt underneath. But still, alongside all the shouting and panicking, I kept insisting that I was going to start again that day.

Coasting

They say that life is what happens when you're busy making other plans, though. I guess that on that cold December day, life wanted to whisk me away down the M5 in my mum's Suzuki Swift. Maybe it was a gut feeling that it was too soon to press play again. Maybe I just needed a break. I don't know. All I do know is that by the evening I was safely ensconced under a blanket on the sofa, in the living room of the house I grew up in in the Midlands, eating Christmas chocolate and drinking a beer and feeling much, *much*, better for it.

And, weirdly, as soon as I got home, I felt something tugging me back. This whole adventure had been fuelled by a desire to fill my life with more of that sheer pinch-me-this-is-so-great joy that I only ever find outdoors. There had been a few glimpses of it so far but, mostly, those moments had been overshadowed by all the worrying and hangovers and self-destruction.

Sitting there happily under that blanket, I had taken the physical step of quitting already: I was home. I could have just posted a blog saying that the adventure was over, and left it there. I'd done enough. It already would have been a big enough achievement. But I knew that I wouldn't do that. I felt very clearly that I wanted to get back to the sea and start chipping away at those 5,000 miles again.

Those moments of joy were out there somewhere, I just needed to look a little harder for them.

CHAPTER 9

I ran up a hill – actually ran up it, lungs burning and legs screaming. Ahead of me, the sunset was breaking through the clouds. I was overwhelmed by the feeling that there was nowhere in the world I'd rather be than right there, on that hill by the sea, looking at the sky exploding into a hundred colours before my eyes.

My moment of contentment was quickly shattered when a herd of overly friendly cows appeared over the next hill. We had a face off. I swore a lot and then climbed over a fence to put some barbed wire between me and them. I scrambled through the bracken to rejoin the path, away from the cows, and ran down into Mevagissey as the sun dipped below the horizon.

It was the 8th of January. I was back on the coast and had been running again for three days. I was excited to be back and was trying out some new mind games. I told myself that each day was just a standalone run, a lovely day out in and of itself, rather than thinking about it as a tiny fraction of the coastal whole. It was a tactic I'd used semi-successfully at the beginning and I decided it was worth another shot. I wanted to be enjoying myself, that was the point of all of this after all.

I realised that I needed to start differentiating from the problems caused by running and being on an adventure, and all the pre-existing *stuff* in my brain that had always been there that I couldn't run away from. There had always been days when I was grumpy and tired and sad. Quitting my adventure to make them go away seemed like an easy fix but actually it would just mean getting rid of all the incredible parts too.

And I didn't want to let go of those bits. Taking that time off and going home had made me realise how much I wanted to carry on feeling excited by the cliffs and the coast and the Cornish air, by the fudge and the local ales and the crab sandwiches. I wanted to keep marvelling over how quickly the weather changes, turning from bright sunshine to blackened, hail-throwing clouds in a matter of seconds and how the storms stir up the sea into a rage. I wanted to be out there, day after day, running and scrambling and trying to embrace the fact my feet were probably going to be wet for the best part of the next year. I wanted to continue to feel overwhelmed with gratitude over the kindness I was receiving from perfect strangers, every single day.

Quitting might have got rid of some of the hard bits, but it would have wiped out all of those positives too.

———

Lawrence met me in Mevagissey the next morning. He was another person from the Yes Tribe and he was working nearby. Later that year he would join *another* Yes Triber, Laura, to run from "Rome to Home" along the old pilgrim route. I don't think he'd committed to that trip at this point though, he just told me that he had some interest in adventure running. Of course, I hoped to show him it at its best, give him an experience that anybody would want to repeat.

We didn't have too far to go that day, only about 8 miles to Boswinger where I was staying with a couple called Kay and Simon. They ran a vegan B&B from their home and were letting me sleep in their empty guest room for the night. From the moment Lawrence and I set off mid-morning, it rained. It was that really wet-feeling rain, buckets and buckets of it pouring from the sky. We were completely soaked through after just minutes but it was good fun, splashing our way along the coast path which had become a fast-flowing stream.

I knew that we needed to turn right off the coast path into Boswinger at some point, but it was raining too much to get my phone out and attempt any kind of navigation. It occurred to me that I hadn't actually checked what time Kay and Simon would be free and that, given the short distance and the lack of hanging around admiring the scenery, we were likely to arrive quite early. I hoped they didn't have plans that afternoon.

We made it to Boswinger just before lunchtime. I managed to dry my phone screen just enough to find their address and we headed to their cottage. They weren't home. Of course they weren't.

Boswinger is a small place. It's set in a beautiful location, but I think we can safely say that the village itself is not a tourist hotspot. It consists of some houses, a playground, a caravan park and a youth hostel that is closed in January. There isn't a pub or a cafe or anywhere else where you might be able to shelter indoors from a storm. Once again, I felt my chest tighten with the feeling of being stuck, of having nowhere to go.

At this point, Lawrence and I were both very, *very* wet. It wasn't really an option to just wait around outside for them. Lawrence, of course, could have just headed home and I wouldn't have blamed him for abandoning me in Boswinger to potentially drown in my own clothes. If the roles had been reversed, I'm sure I would have conjured up an elaborate excuse to leave. Thankfully, Lawrence is a nicer person than I am and stuck with me.

The last village we had run through was Gorran Haven, a few miles back, where we remembered passing a hotel that had looked open.

"Worth a try?" one of us suggested and we turned around to retrace our steps. At least we'd be moving – it was getting quite cold standing there in our wet kit.

We reached Gorran Haven and stood outside the hotel, peering in through the window. Then we looked at each other. Everybody inside looked very clean. They seemed to be having a nice, civilised time. They didn't have splashes of mud on their faces, for one. Meanwhile, you probably wouldn't have been surprised if Lawrence and I told you that we had actually been in the sea fully clothed, we were so wet, and had then rolled around in a field, we were so filthy.

"Maybe there's a cafe instead..." Lawrence said hopefully. We headed up the road and were relieved to see a sign for hot food. Weirdly, it was right outside the post office. We headed in.

"Erm, the sign outside said you might be doing food?" I asked the woman behind the counter, glancing around. It really did look a lot like a post office. So much so, somebody behind me was carrying a stack of parcels, and I could see they sold stamps.

"Oh yes, just take a seat over there," she pointed to the back of the shop.

There, the post office became less like a post office and more like a general store. And, surrounded by cleaning products and greetings cards and dusty bottles of wine, there was a lone table and two chairs. We sat down. Lawrence ordered a full English breakfast and I went for a pasty. We both asked for hot chocolate. Before long, our food was brought out from the kitchen adjoined to the post office.

It was all very surreal.

The woman from behind the post office counter, who was also the waitress and, I imagine, the shopkeeper too, asked where we'd been, where we were going, etc. I did my usual terrible job of explaining, feeling very awkward. She brought a plug-in heater and a chair over for us to hang our wettest layers on. My raincoat was making puddles on the floor.

I got a text message from Kay telling me that they would be in from 5 p.m., and to head over anytime after that. Once we had killed enough time by drinking several more hot chocolates, I said goodbye to Lawrence, put on every layer I had and set about heading back to Boswinger. It's a different kind of cold when you have wet layers stuck to you. I took my phone out to make a video.

"I'm going to make a bold claim here: this might be the coldest I've ever been," I told the camera, my face peering out from under three different hoods.

I made it back to Boswinger, where Kay and Simon showed me to a warm room. I had a hot shower and put my dry clothes on. They served up big bowls of vegetable chilli with homemade cornbread for dinner and, after a few hours of chatting and stroking their cat, I went to bed feeling very happy not to be shivering for the first time all day.

It had definitely been a memorable day. I hoped those moments of joy I'd returned to Cornwall in pursuit of would start to make themselves known in a more obvious format soon.

———

From Boswinger, I ran to Falmouth where I was planning to have a rest day. Having got to the stage before Christmas where I was ticking off consecutive 20-mile days without really thinking about it, it felt a little odd to be having a day off so soon after having started again. But the pre-Christmas strategy had left me miserable and injured. As my dad likes to say, "If you do as you've always done, you'll get as you've always gotten." I'm pretty sure that's a hash of a Henry Ford quote but the logic still stands. (And, as far as my dad's famous tips for life go, it's one of the better ones. His favourite is "always weed your patio". Useful in its own right, I suppose.)

It had stopped raining but it was still very muddy underfoot. Wet feet were my principal complaint at the time. I'd heard that waterproof trail-running shoes were pretty useless as water inevitably splashed in over the top and then didn't have anywhere to go. What you wanted was a pair with good drainage, and this was the strategy I'd gone for, buying a pair of waterproof socks to go with them. These socks might have been useful if you were heading out for a run in a few showers, but were, unsurprisingly, failing to withstand the daily total saturation I was putting them through. There were also now holes in them, having been worn for more than 500 miles at this stage. A fairly pivotal malfunction in a pair of waterproof socks. I did have another pair of socks, but these hadn't been waterproof to start with and also now had holes in them.

I still hadn't pitched my tent and my current not-camping strategy made it a lot easier to manage wet kit, but my shoes never really dried out overnight. Every morning, I dreaded the moment I had to prize my feet back into them, stiff with mud and bits of cow pat and endless puddle water. Perhaps it sounds silly, but it really was the worst part of every day.

When I first decided that I was going to set off on this trip, as far as I knew, nobody else had ever run the coast of Britain before in the way I was hoping to: carrying my own kit, no support vehicle, and sticking to trails rather than roads. It wasn't a huge part of the appeal for me – it would never be an official record or world first due to too many variables and a complete lack of any kind of data recording from my side – but it was a nice bonus.

Then, a few months before I was due to start, I heard about Wayne Russell. Wayne was also planning to run a lap of the UK coast and his trip looked almost identical to mine, even down to him planning to start in exactly the same place. I didn't really mind – I could still claim first woman, and youngest person. For two months I watched along as Wayne got his head start on me, trying to glean any useful hints and tips from the videos he was posting.

When I got going myself, I quickly found that any mild disgruntlement I might have felt at Wayne taking some of the shine off my own achievements was vastly overshadowed by the comfort of having somebody else knowing exactly what I was going through. My friends and family were great and when I called my mum four times a day to moan about various things she tried to be nice, but she didn't really know how it felt to have had wet feet for three months on end. From the very beginning, Wayne and I had exchanged messages and it was so good to talk to somebody who just *got it*, who knew exactly how this felt.

But even with Wayne's conciliatory messages, by the time I reached Falmouth, I'd just about had it with the wet feet. It was ridiculous: I'd managed to carry myself from London to Cornwall using just my legs and yet this was the thing that looked most likely to thwart the whole expedition. I made it my mission that evening to try and solve this problem.

First, I went to a shop and bought some new socks. As well as the issue of the holes, both of my pairs were stiff with mud and needed more than the feeble hand wash in a sink I could offer them.

Second, I took my shoes in the shower with me and tried to blast away the worst of the caked on mud. This, as anybody sensible would have been able to tell you, caused a horrible mess. I spent the next 45 minutes trying to scoop mud out of the plug. I had generously been offered a room in a lovely B&B by the seafront for the night and this is how I was treating it. I was the worst guest ever.

I had not timed my shoes' shower well either. I only had one pair with me and I needed to put something on my feet to go and get some dinner. Although they looked slightly cleaner now, they were also much, *much* wetter. I stood with my dripping trainers in my hand and wondered whether it would perhaps be better to just go hungry that night.

My stomach grumbled loudly in answer to that suggestion. Maybe not.

I stuffed the shoes with a combination of toilet paper and some leaflets I found in a drawer and then spent the best part of an hour attempting to blast them dry with a hair dryer. If you've ever tried to use a hotel room hairdryer, you can probably imagine how utterly useless this was. I'd have been better off trying to dry them by breathing heavily on them. They were just as wet as when I started, just slightly warmer now. The increase in temperature had also released their smell even more. The shower may have done some superficial cleaning, but they were clearly still harbouring a lot of… stuff.

I was hungry now, but couldn't bear the thought of putting my new socks into these damp, smelly foot containers. I rummaged through my rucksack for something useful and produced one carrier bag and a sandwich bag. I shook the crumbs out and stuffed my feet in, then put my shoes on. There was a definite rusting sound as I walked and I will say that having two lumps of sopping wet fabric attached to your feet isn't exactly a pleasant experience, even if they were separated from your socks by a plastic barrier, but it was better than nothing.

I looked forward to my next chat with Wayne so that I could tell him about my invention.

"Do you have wi-fi?" I asked in a cafe for not the first time that day.

"We do, but we're closing now," was the response. It was quarter to four in the afternoon. I was taking a rest day in Falmouth and was due to be giving a virtual talk to a class of ten-year-olds in America in 15 minutes. Unhelpfully, the whole town seemed to be shutting for the day.

"The library is open until five, maybe you could try there?" the cafe owner told me, which was the most useful suggestion I had received so far. I ran up the road and just about managed to log on in time for the talk and then answer all their questions before I got chucked out again.

Outside the library, I met Lorraine. She lived in Penryn, a couple of miles away from Falmouth at the head of the Penryn estuary, and had offered me somewhere to stay to bookend my rest day. We took the bus to her house and Lorraine told me about all the adventures she wanted to do with Millie and Jack, her two children, while they ran up and down the top deck of the bus, clearly thinking that was an adventure in itself. She was planning to spend the summer holidays walking a stretch of the South West Coast Path with them, wild camping along the way. I was struggling to look after myself on the trail and I still hadn't even pitched my tent. I couldn't imagine looking after two small humans as well.

Lorraine put Millie and Jack to bed and we ate roast chicken, rice and salad for dinner before sitting down to watch TV together. I absent-mindedly picked up Jack's Rubik's Cube. Two hours later, we were both hooked. Lorraine was furiously

Googling solutions and different combinations, shouting them out as I tried to make them work. We'd get so far, then I'd make a mistake, and we'd have to go back to the beginning. By 1 a.m. we still hadn't cracked it. I reluctantly put the cube down and went to bed.

As I was leaving the next morning, Lorraine handed me the Rubik's Cube.

"You got so far, you can't leave it now."

"But I can't take Jack's toy," I protested, the cube between us. I did *really* want to finish it…

"He won't even notice; he's never played with it. I'll get him a new one if he does, they're only a fiver."

The next night, I stayed up late again and finished it. It felt like a bigger achievement than any of the running had so far. I had visions of spending every spare minute of the next few months practising, and crossing the finish line able to do it in under 30 seconds. Of course, in reality I never picked it up again. But that's how I ended up running approximately 80 per cent of the coast of the UK with a Rubik's Cube in my bag.

CHAPTER 10

It was mid-January and I had committed so wholly to not pitching my tent that I had gone as far as sending my camping kit home with my dad on his last visit. It seemed stupid to carry the weight when I knew, if I was honest with myself, there's no way I would be camping until the summer.

I have friends who have spent lots of time wild camping alone, whether for weeks on end during big trips or just for odd nights here and there. They all tell me the same: it gets easier, you stop being so scared. I'm sure they're right and that the same would have happened for me if I'd just given it a go. And I could see the appeal if you were running through wild, remote places and it wasn't the middle of winter. I pictured myself running around the Highlands of Scotland in the summer when it was light until 10 p.m., pitching up in front of a loch with mountains in the background, miles from anybody, swimming naked and drinking water from streams.

But the reality of camping in the middle of a very stormy Cornish winter felt a little different. At the end of every day I was covered in dirt and soaked through after miles and miles of running through sloppy trails. It was dark at 4 p.m. My back was already being shredded by the weight of the gear I was carrying, the thought of putting extra warm layers in felt impossible. The idea of wild camping night after night, constantly being cold and filthy, my kit never drying... No thank you.

Luckily, the domino effect of hospitality kept going. When I managed to get out of my own head enough to stop worrying for a second, I could see what a privilege it was to be let into so many people's homes, like Lorraine's, and allowed a glimpse into their lives.

Something I get asked about a lot is what it was like adventuring alone as a woman. Wasn't I scared out there in the wild, all by myself?

Firstly, I think that it's important to differentiate between real vs perceived risk. Although it can feel a bit unsettling being completely alone somewhere remote, the chances of there being an attacker lurking in the bushes on a deserted stretch of coast path are distinctly less than the chances of me running into one walking home from the tube late at night in central London. And, as a paramedic I later stayed with near Edinburgh told me, you are much more likely to come to harm from somebody you already know. Male relatives are particularly high on the risk list. By spending the best part of the year almost exclusively with complete strangers, I was actually putting myself in a safer position, statistically speaking.

But still, there is the ever-present threat that, at any time, I could potentially run into somebody who wants to do something horrible to me. This is something I live with constantly, as a person in general maybe, but as a woman more so. I don't think I'm alone in that feeling. I strongly believe we should be concentrating on teaching our sons not to attack people rather than teaching our daughters how to not get attacked. But still, there were things I did to mitigate the risks.

I didn't have live tracking, because the idea of that made me feel uncomfortable. I never posted a schedule up in advance, despite being asked to. I avoided being too specific about my whereabouts until after I had already moved on from a place. I told my parents where I was staying each night and we had a set check-in time by which I'd tell them I'd arrived safely. I avoided staying with anybody who didn't have a connection to either somebody I already knew, or some kind of reputable organisation like a running club, or at the least were a family rather than an individual. I Facebook stalked everybody who offered me a place to stay and if I felt even the slightest bit uncomfortable about accepting, I would politely decline.

On the whole, I mostly felt safe. There were a few moments where I didn't but, actually, there were an awful lot fewer than in my non-adventuring life where I hold my keys in my hand on every single walk home after dark (so any time after 4 p.m. in the winter) *just in case*.

And I think that you also have to acknowledge that, on the flip side of any potential risk, there are advantages to being a woman too (even if they in no way balance out the added danger). I was a woman in her early 20s. I had blonde hair that I wore in braids. I was pretty unthreatening physically. Would so many people have welcomed me into their homes and let me sleep in their spare rooms, read bedtime stories to their children and play with their Rubik's Cubes if I had been a man?

I'm not sure they would have.

CHAPTER 11

"What is the most southerly point in England?" is a common pub quiz question. And the nearly as commonly given answer is that it's Land's End. This is incorrect. Land's End is actually the most south *westerly* point, an important distinction. Lizard Point, sitting at the tip of the Lizard Peninsula, is the most southerly.

A few weeks earlier Paul Beevers had got in touch. He'd walked the South West Coast Path in 2014 and wanted to pass on some of the kindness he had experienced. Paul lived with his wife and their two daughters near Helston, which is inland towards the top of the Lizard Peninsula. The plan was for Paul to run with me for a day and for me to stay at their house the nights either side. As always, staying anywhere for more than one night was the biggest treat as it meant I got to ditch most of the contents of my pack for the day. I was able to to leave my spare clothes, the Rubik's Cube, iPad and novel behind and just carry water and some snacks.

Paul picked me up from Helford Passage, where my run from Falmouth with Lorraine ended, and we compared notes about various sections of the path for the whole journey back to his. We arrived home and Paul introduced me to Clare, his wife, and Cecelia and Merryn, their daughters. They showed me the spare room and insisted I had a bath. I drew pictures with the girls and then read them a bedtime story. Instantly, I felt at home.

———

I'd often felt, for as long as I could really remember, this sense of lingering sadness and guilt. Guilt if ever I felt happy, because there are so many problems in the world and surely by feeling joy I wasn't taking them seriously. But then guilt when I was sad too because I was so lucky, what right did I have to feel down? I felt like I was in a fog a lot of the time. I'd have moments of clarity where I'd envisage how I might want my life to be, but I had no idea of how to get there, or I'd get the feeling that I didn't deserve it anyway, so I shouldn't even try. Cycles of self-destructive behaviour, feelings of pointlessness and hopelessness, wondering if anything was ever going to change.

I kept telling people that I was doing this adventure in the pursuit of happiness. In some ways, that was true. One of the charities I was raising money for was a children's mental health charity and I had a page on my website saying something about how "The world needs more happy people". I suppose I did like the *idea* of that. It sounded nice to not be weighed down by everything wrong in the world, all of the time.

But, also, a part of me almost judged anybody who claimed to actually be happy. With so many awful things happening in the world that people could be worrying about, how could they possibly waste that time feeling content? I felt, at times, as though happiness was almost a symptom of stupidity (as sad as it makes me to admit that now). Sometimes, when I was feeling particularly bad, I'd call my parents to quiz them about it. "How are you not miserable?" I'd ask them over and over and over. I just really didn't understand it. Didn't everybody feel like I did, secretly? But apparently they didn't – my dad's probably the most content person I know.

I guess, essentially, I did want to feel happy, because I knew in theory that it felt good. But I didn't want to tar myself with the same brush I'd tarred all of those happy people with. It was a real catch-22. I'm aware that this all sounds very melodramatic, but I guess that's kind of the point when you're just really bloody sad. It often is without rhyme or reason.

Another reason I didn't spend too much time attempting to achieve happiness was that I wasn't convinced it existed. I didn't really believe the happy people, maybe because it made me feel better to tell myself that they must secretly be miserable too. They might pretend, but surely they were also crying themselves to sleep?

But the more people I stayed with as I ran around the coast, the more I started to wonder if I'd got it wrong. I was meeting so many different people; families that all looked completely different from each other, people doing different jobs with different incomes, living in different sorts of houses, prioritising different things. Yet, fundamentally, despite their many differences, everybody seemed fairly content with their lives. Sure, I was only getting a snapshot and I'm certain that everybody had their own skeletons in their closets that I just wasn't getting to see, but I did find it hard to believe that they were all sobbing behind closed doors every night, when the world had gone away. And I didn't think that any of these people were stupid or ignorant. The opposite, in fact. Every day I was having conversations that made me feel wholly unintelligent. It was a bit of a revelation, honestly.

I started to wonder if perhaps I too could be happy one day? Perhaps I could stop wearing my misery as a badge of superiority? There was a lot of unravelling to do, but over the next few months it was something I would think about a lot.

———

I sat in bed in the Beevers' spare room, at the top of their house, flicking through my phone. A picture popped up on my Facebook news feed.

It was Greg, on New Year's Eve. He had his arm around a girl.

We hadn't spoken much over the past few weeks, but he still weighed on my mind a lot. It's hard to explain – things didn't make much sense at the time and even all these years on, they still don't fully. Although I knew that whatever had happened between us romantically was over (and was glad about that, mostly), I was still very much under the assumption that he would be in my life in some capacity. This feeling was only perpetuated by the sense of ownership he seemed to feel over my adventure. It was as though, by being the person to make me believe my idea of running around the coast was possible, he now had some kind of claim to it. And because I still hadn't managed to make sense of all the preceding months of negativity, part of me believed that this was true.

It was the same part of me that also believed that what had gone on between us had been mutually destructive. He'd done and said some strange things, I knew that, but it takes two, I thought. I felt utterly broken by the whole experience and couldn't even comprehend dating anybody else (even if I hadn't been living out of a backpack with no clean pants) and I assumed he'd be feeling the same.

Apparently not.

Just for my own peace of mind, I needed to know for certain if he'd moved on.

"The girl in that picture," I asked him, "is something going on with her? I'd just like to know."

"Yes," he replied. I thought the confirmation would hurt more than it did, but actually I felt okay about it. I guess this was just a drop in the ocean compared to all the times Greg had made me feel like my heart was literally ripping in two, or like I was going utterly mad.

He asked how I was. When I told him everything was going well – that I was doing it, at least – he managed to spin his response into a backhanded compliment as always.

I'm not sure where the surge of clarity came from, but for a moment I felt as though the fog lifted a little. I would never be able to untangle all the stories Greg had told me, work out which were true and which weren't, but I could make the decision to not listen to any more of them. And I suddenly felt, very clearly, that if I had any chance of reaching this mystical place of contentment I'd recently learnt existed (or, at least, of not feeling miserable all the time), then I *needed* to stop listening to them. I needed Greg to not be in my life. He could think what he wanted about me, it was irrelevant.

"I think that we probably shouldn't talk again," I told him.

I couldn't cut him out, he replied. He said that I never would have even gone on this adventure if it weren't for him, for his input, for his help. He told me that I wasn't strong enough, that there's no way I could do it on my own. How dare I not let him be a part of it?

For a moment, I wobbled, and worried that maybe he was right – perhaps I couldn't do it without him, perhaps nobody else would want me.

But he wasn't a part of it, not really. None of his offers of help had ever actually materialised. He kept offering to put me in touch with his supposed famous friends and powerful business connections, but I was becoming more and more certain that they didn't actually exist. Or, the people existed, but I was increasingly sure that Greg didn't know them.

Maybe he had been the extra nudge I needed at the start. Sure, let's credit him with that. But since then? He hadn't been a part of anything. This was my adventure. It was my legs that were doing the running and me who was doing all of the organising and admin and promoting. There were lots of other people involved too, of course. People cheering me on from the sidelines, donating to my charities, putting me up for the night, running with me for miles on end on dismal winter days. But Greg wasn't one of them.

I would be fine without him in my life because, I finally realised, he wasn't really in it anyway.

We argued back and forth for a while. It's easy to sit and write this in a very detached way, and make it sound as though I was cool and calm and resolute throughout this whole exchange. I wasn't. I knew that cutting him out was the right thing to do, but it was still hard to take those comments. As much as I tried to tell myself his opinion didn't matter, I did still care. But, this time, there was something stronger overriding the doubt.

The conversation finally ended when either I blocked his number or he blocked mine. I'm not sure which way around it was now but, for the next few months, there was no Greg. Every day, the fog lifted a little more.

———

Paul dropped me in Lizard village after my last night staying with them, and I headed down to the furthest tip of the peninsula. I made a video announcing to the world that I was officially the southernmost person on mainland UK but you could barely hear me above the winds. Behind me, seagulls circled over the crashing waves.

The day before, running with Paul, we had passed through Porthallow, the halfway point of the South West Coast Path. It was arbitrary really, but it felt significant in some way. I was two and a half months in and I had run over 700 miles in total, 315 of which had been on this one trail. People asked a lot about the running, but that was the easy bit. It was the rest of it that felt hard. I might have still been on home turf, technically, but there was a funny feeling of displacement, of not quite belonging.

Seven-hundred miles down, more than four-thousand still to go, if my estimations were right. I was as far south as I could go now. For the next five or six months I would be running north, pulling upwards, watching the seasons changing, seeing my leg muscles grow, spending more endless solitary hours with just myself for company, forced to come to terms with all the parts of me I usually avoided.

Maybe that's what I was finding so difficult, why I felt so unsettled all the time. We spend so much of our lives distracted, avoiding looking ourselves head on in the mirror. I was happy to accept my friends and family members with all their faults and imperfections, but I never gave myself that same luxury. I never just sat down with myself and said, "Well this is who we are, what are we going to do about it?"

But a long run gives you a lot of time for self-reflection. Too much, probably. You stop being able to hide from yourself. I didn't really know who I was, I realised. I was clouded by other people's opinions, their conflicting views and thoughts. And no wonder I was confused – each of those people would have drawn a completely different picture of me, yet here I was trying to be all of them at once. I needed to find out for myself who I really was.

I turned away from the seabirds and started following the path north, ready for whatever came next.

CHAPTER 12

Judy heaped another spoon of beef stew onto my plate and gestured to me to help myself to more potatoes. I had just been telling her that my dad was coming to visit in a couple of days, his first trip of the year.

"And you're meeting him in St Ives?" she asked.

"Yes."

"On Tuesday?"

"Yes, on Tuesday."

"As in, two days from now?" It was Sunday when we were eating the stew.

"Yes, Tuesday, two days from now."

"That's a long way to go in two days, isn't it, Mick?" Mick nodded.

Judy and Mick were keen walkers and had just been telling me about some of the trips they had been on. Judy had shown me photos of them hiking all over the world, tackling strenuous multi-day routes. They clearly knew a lot about the outdoors and it concerned me a little that they thought I was being too ambitious.

They lived in St Loy, a wooded valley that was one of the most remote on the south coast of Cornwall. Their garden extended right down onto the South West Coast Path. There really can't be many places more idyllic to live. I was planning to run around to St Just the next day, via Land's End, and then on to St Ives the following day. It was only 35 miles in total. It hadn't occurred to me that I would have any issues at all covering that. On paper, it looked fine.

It's true that the South West Coast Path website described this section as "one of the toughest sections of the entire Path", calling it "a strenuous journey of roller coaster climbs". But hadn't the rest of it been tough and strenuous and a roller coaster? I respected Judy and Mick's opinion and did feel concerned by their concern. I'd been doing this for nearly three months by this point though, and how many times had I heard similar comments? I hoped that I was strong enough.

Judy made me breakfast the following morning and then she and Mick waved me off. It was an early start because they were heading out themselves that morning, into Truro where Mick had a hospital appointment. It was Blue Monday, supposedly the most depressing day of the year. But as I edged my way further around the coast path, breathing in that clean Cornish air and feeling my legs propelling me forward, the only thing that seemed particularly blue was the sea, and the slither of blue sky peeking out from behind the clouds. After about 8 miles of trotting along, having quite a nice time and listening to Atomic Kitten, I reached Land's End.

Coasting

It was a bit strange, really. Normally Land's End was where people started or finished their big trips, but here I was just passing through. It's a fairly bleak place, especially in the winter, with its closed-up outlets and arcades. I decided I should mark my visit in some way and stopped at the Land's End Hotel for a cream tea. I did it the Devon way – cream first, jam second – and hoped this wouldn't offend anybody too much. Could they throw you out of Cornwall for doing your scones the wrong way?

I reached St Just just before dark. I was staying with Laura and her 25-year-old cat. Laura asked me where I was staying the next night. St Ives, I told her.

"You can't run all the way there tomorrow. It's a very long way, you know."

But I felt unusually optimistic. Perhaps I was starting to have a little faith in my own abilities. I set an early alarm; we weren't exactly swimming in daylight at that time of year and I needed to get going first thing if I was going to make it.

It wasn't ideal, then, when I overslept the following morning.

I find that when you've got too much to do and not enough time to do it in, a rigid plan is the only solution. Without a plan, I would end up haemorrhaging time looking at views and strolling up hills and taking pictures. I split the day into four chunks of five miles, with the promise of a sit down and a snack break between each. After five miles I ate a Cadbury caramel egg and some Haribo. At 10 miles it was a cheese roll and an apple. I tried to make my legs move as fast as possible in between snacks.

It was slow going. I was starting to see where the website had got the words "strenuous" and "roller coaster" from.

It was impossible to gain any momentum – as well as the hills, underfoot was a sea of sinking mud, with slippery rocks scattered about that you could attempt to hop between – and 19-miles was starting to feel more like 40.

Late afternoon came and I was just starting to worry that the light was dimming when I slipped in the mud for probably the tenth time that day. Perhaps they'd all been right. Even if I did make it, why was I bothering? I was cold and wet and, frankly, not having much fun at all. I had mud in my eyebrows, in my plaits and even, I would discover later, in my bra.

Swearing under my breath and cursing having even started this whole stupid thing, I crested a hill and ahead of me, the lights of St Ives were twinkling. I stopped swearing. It was four o' clock. I still had nearly an hour of daylight to play with, and not too much further to go. I'd done it – the hardest part of the whole South West Coast Path, apparently, and I'd ticked it off in one day.

I thought, not for the first time, about how I couldn't believe I was really doing this. I still didn't feel like a real runner. I was slow and I'd never won any races and I still didn't have the lean physique of the people I thought *were* real runners. But maybe it wasn't about that. Maybe it wasn't about being the best.

Maybe it was just about putting one foot in front of the other and not giving up. We all know the story of the tortoise and the hare, after all.

―――――

My dad found me in St Ives and I took a couple of rest days to spend with him. We stayed in a cottage by the sea and one morning, as I sat on the sofa drinking coffee and watching trashy daytime TV, he went out for a run.

"I'm only doing four miles, I'll be back in about half an hour," he told me and sprinted out of the door. Since the marathon I'd made him run dressed as a fairy a couple of years earlier, he'd got the bug, and was now desperately trying to train for a sub-3-hour one. He'd only really started running with any regularity in his 50s and apparently there was no time to lose when it came to fulfilling his athletic potential.

Over an hour later, he reappeared, plastered in mud and breathing heavily.

"It's quite hilly out there, isn't it?"

Yes, dad. This is what I had been trying to explain for months. People pictured the coast and imagined long, flat proms. As I had discovered, it wasn't really like that.

I woke up in the holiday cottage after two days and felt, with every fibre of my being, that I couldn't be bothered to go for a run. I always expected to feel refreshed after a rest, but more often it was the opposite. It was as though my body remembered how nice it was just to do normal things for a while, to not run miles and miles each day and always have wet feet, and then staged a protest. I lay in bed for 45 minutes thinking of every possible excuse under the sun to not go for a run. None quite held up though and I reluctantly got up, put my kit on and set off.

The plan was for me to start out from St Ives alone while my dad drove around to Portreath, the end point for the day. He'd then start running back along the coast from there and meet me en route somewhere. It would be about 18 miles for me, in total.

Perhaps strange for somebody who had chosen to spend a year of their life running around the coast, but there was one thing I was learning that I hated above everything else, and that was sand. I liked nice, firm trails that ran alongside the sand. I liked looking out from clifftops over the sandy beaches below. I liked sitting on a rock at the edge of the sand to eat my sandwiches at lunchtime. I did not like actually coming into contact with the sand. I especially didn't like having to run on sand. It was hard work and it got in your shoes and it always put me in a terrible mood.

It was unfortunate, then, that from Hayle through to Godrevy Point the coast path winds through the sand dunes. These dunes are supposedly rich with wildlife and a real treat to explore. Sadly, I was too busy being grumpy about losing the waymarkers and scrambling up and down sandy mounds to pay any attention.

Eventually, I emerged from the dunes near Godrevy. In front of me, like a beacon of hope and joy, was a cafe. I headed inside. I needed cake.

A little while later, feeling restored, I headed back out. I was about to start running again when I heard somebody calling my name. There, in the car park, was Judy from St Loy.

"I've been out walking with my daughter," she told me, "I saw you running through the dunes and thought I might catch up with you at the cake shop."

My habits were proving to be embarrassingly predictable.

"I'm sorry if we were a little quiet the other day," she went on to say. "We really wanted to help you out but, you see, Mick's not very well at the moment. The appointment at the hospital was about some potential treatment. It was playing on his mind, he's normally very chatty."

I felt quite overwhelmed that they'd invited me to stay even with so much else going on and I couldn't help but feel a little sad as I ran off to find my dad. I may have only met them briefly, but they were such a lovely couple. I hoped that Mick would be okay.

————

The sun was shining and I didn't have my backpack on. I was running with Kerstin and her magnificent dog, George the Pointer. George made light work of the coast path, bounding along, leaping over rocks and sprinting up hills. I wasn't finding it quite so easy but I was still having an above average day. More than I had for quite a while, I felt like I liked running again. Breathing in the clean sea air, wind on my face, cheeks colouring with the sun… it's hard to say why these things make you feel so much better, but somehow they just do. I'm not religious and I don't believe in a god, but when you're outside on a beautiful day and your body works how you want it to, it's hard to believe there isn't something more at play. I generally struggled with finding the meaning in things, but somehow, in moments like those, I didn't worry about it so much.

Kerstin was telling me about how she had grown up in Germany but moved to England when she was 18. Now she lived in Cornwall with her husband, Martin, in the house where they were letting me stay for a couple of nights. Martin was a music teacher and I was sleeping in the spare-cum-music-room, right next to his piano. Kerstin told me about the ultras she ran, about her children, about how energetic George was.

It was a beautiful, bright day but the trails were still wet from all the rain that had come before. In places, the path had turned into a stream. For the first few minutes of each day I attempted to dodge the water, skipping from side to side in a bid to cling onto my slightly drier feet. It was completely fruitless and within a mile they were sodden again. I still hated having wet feet but the winter sunshine at least made me feel like summer might come at some point.

Kerstin was just ahead of me as we headed down a gentle slope. She leaped forward, straight through what we both assumed was just another puddle. I watched as she sank down about two feet until she was thigh-deep in sludge.

We were wrong. It wasn't just a puddle.

The run-off from the farm above had created a kind of sinkhole in the path. It smelled awful and, now, so did Kerstin. She pulled herself out of the sewagey pit and back onto firmer land and we burst out laughing, doubled over, tears streaming down our faces. It was approximately 50 per cent awful and 50 per cent hilarious. The "awful" portion was mostly just to do with the stink – it really wasn't pleasant.

There was nothing to do but carry on. A few minutes later we came across a stream dissecting the path. Kerstin braced herself as she plunged into the clear, cold water and attempted to wash herself. She looked a lot better afterward but she still smelled fairly terrible. I was silently relieved that it hadn't been me – at least Kerstin had a whole wardrobe of clean clothes at home, whereas I only had one set of kit. I would have been carrying that smell around for months.

Coasting

During my one night in St Just with Laura, I'd taken a brief break from stroking the cat that was older than me to go and record an interview for the Marathon Talk podcast in her spare room. It came out a week later, while I was staying with a friend of a friend, Faye. I had a vague memory of being fairly open during the interview and felt like I needed to listen to it, as I couldn't quite remember what I'd said. I asked Faye if she minded if I played it over breakfast.

Thinking about it now, I can't quite believe that this was something I suggested. I literally cannot think of anything more horrendous than listening back to a recording of myself, let alone in front of somebody else. I guess I just really needed to know that I hadn't revealed anything too terrible. So, we sat there over porridge and listened to me waffle on about running, as if I had any idea what I was talking about.

Martin, Marathon Talk's host, asked me about the mental side of doing a big adventure. I told him that I tended to have a propensity towards the negative, towards doom and gloom and thinking the world is about to end. The biggest challenge for me had been to try and get over this, to be a bit more glass half full and find the positives in all the wet feet and rainy days. It had been a big learning curve, to say the least.

"That surprised me," Faye said when it had finished, "I don't think of you like that at all, you always seem really upbeat."

I started to wonder: how much of who we are is just a story we tell ourselves? I always thought that I'd somehow managed to trick people into thinking I wasn't as glum and miserable as I actually was. But if I wasn't always feeling that, and I wasn't portraying that or acting like that, then had I just got myself wrong?

I had spent so many months listening to Greg tell me that I was too negative to ever really be happy. I'd absorbed it as the complete and immovable truth about myself. But I didn't agree with him on so many other things. The man didn't believe in eating bread, for god's sake. If for no other reason than this, he clearly couldn't be trusted. And, as hopefully has been made clear by now, there were plenty of other reasons too.

Yet, despite all the evidence mounting up against him, I chose to believe him on the one thing that was more important than anything else: who I was. Let him reject carbs. Let him fantasise about the life he was living. Let him conjure up whatever other stories made him happy.

But why on earth was I still giving more weight to Greg's opinions about me than I was to any actual evidence, or to the opinions of all the people I loved and trusted and agreed with on other things? It's not easy to change the stories we tell ourselves, but I knew I needed to start trying.

I spent the rest of the day with Faye laughing, watching rubbish TV, eating pasties and hanging out with her dog Molly. That day, the truth was that I did feel pretty cheerful.

CHAPTER 13

After staying with Faye, I ran to Tintagel, home to the famous Tintagel Castle and all the legends surrounding King Arthur. From there, my next stop was Bude, 19 miles away. This stretch included Scrade, one of the deepest and steepest valleys on the Cornish coast.

After a few calmer days, Storm Gertrude had hit and the winds were picking up again. It had been a headwind for most of the morning, which meant that I was okay while I climbed up the hills, with the lump of land in front shielding me. But when I reached the top, I'd immediately be buffed in the face and suddenly struggling to stand upright. The force of it literally knocked me to the ground a couple of times and both times I landed in a thorn bush. I made a video in which I was on the verge of tears, rambling about the splinters in my hands and how hard it all felt.

The conditions were terrible and I felt bone-tired. Even though I'd scrambled my way into and out of lots of steep, deep valleys so far and I knew this one couldn't be that much worse, the thought of tackling Scrade was looming. I didn't think I could make it the whole way. I knew that if I made it to Crackington Haven, around 11 miles in, there was then a bus I could take into Bude where I was staying with local runners Annie and Graham for the night. I just had to get that far, I kept telling myself. A few more miles and I could stop.

By the time I got to Crackington Haven, I was exhausted, mentally and physically. The sheer effort of battling the wind and the mud, the fear of being blown off a cliff at any time... you couldn't just switch off and let your legs go. It was relentless. I bought a can of Coke and a slice of cake in the tiny village cafe. I needed sugar. I was shaking.

I wanted to get on that bus so badly. I wanted to be somewhere safe and warm and dry. I didn't want to be out on the exposed cliffs any more.

But more than that, I didn't want to quit. On other days I'd bailed early, but it had been fine to retrace my steps and make up the lost ground the next day. It wouldn't be that easy on this section. I was about to cross the border onto a remote section of the North Devon coast. I still wasn't camping (and thank god, I thought, not fancying the chances of my tiny tent against those gusts), and it had been hard to find places to stay that were en route. Losing a day would throw my whole schedule off. And it would be a false economy anyway – I'd still have to do it tomorrow, when the weather wasn't looking any better.

The realisation came with a certain amount of horror: not quitting meant carrying on.

I sat in the cafe watching the clock. I saw it approach the time the bus was due, then the minute hand ticked over. I didn't move. I pictured the bus pulling away out of the village, without me on it. There were no more buses coming that day. I'd just have to get on with it. I drained the last of my Coke, sucking up any remaining droplets of energy, and reluctantly headed outside.

I put my headphones in and pressed play on my motivational noughties pop playlist, but I couldn't hear a thing over the screaming winds.

These were the days that made us stronger, I tried to tell myself.

Several hours and some very slow miles later, I reached Widemouth Bay, home to a cluster of holiday homes, a pub and a cafe that sits about 3 miles south of Bude itself. The worst was over: I had survived Scrade and I knew that it was easy from there, just a grass path over the clifftops. But it was getting dark and I didn't have any nerve left. I didn't have it in me to set out in the dark along the cliff edge by myself.

Maybe I could just catch a bus from here, I thought. It was only a few extra miles to add onto the next day, no big deal. The setting sun was really just a conveniently valid reason to cry "safety" and stop. The truth of it is that I just didn't have anything else left in me. I'd been empty 15 miles earlier. I was really bloody empty now. But my phone had done its thing where it died in the cold again though and I couldn't see any bus stops to check a timetable.

Ahead of me, I saw some lights just down the road glowing in the darkness. A beacon of hope – or at least that's how I see it now, in retrospect. As I got nearer, I saw that it was the Wet Fish Shop. I'd never been to a wet fish shop before. I'd never even heard of one. The smell that hit me when I opened the door made it clear that this was a shop that sold fresh ("wet") fish, as opposed to the cooked variety. There was a man working behind the counter.

"Hello, are there any buses going to Bude?" I asked him.

"Yes," he said, "but you've just missed it and the next one isn't for two hours."

The thought of standing outside in the rain for 2 hours was almost worse than the idea of running there. Almost, but not quite.

"Is there a footpath along the main road?" I asked. Maybe I could just about force myself to walk a couple of miles on a road, I thought. *Maybe*.

"Not the whole way," he said.

I'd had enough hairy experiences on tight, fast roads already that I knew I wouldn't be risking this one in the dark. That about-to-cry feeling surfaced in my throat. I needed to get to Bude but all the options to do so seemed terrible. I was frozen, my teeth wouldn't stop chattering and a dark cloud had descended in my brain. The world suddenly felt like a very lonely place. I wandered across the shop and pretended to browse some non-wet-fish-filled shelves while I figured out what to do. Then –

"If you wait ten minutes," the man said, "I can drive you down."

It kept happening, but I was still so surprised every time anybody offered to help me like this. A few months earlier, I would have said no. Whether out of pride or politeness, I'm not sure. I would have said no and carried on standing there panicking about what I was going to do instead. But I kept trying to remind myself of my earlier realisation that people didn't generally offer to do something unless they really didn't mind doing it, so instead I said "Yes please" and stood by the wet fish waiting for him to finish. It was a bit smelly inside but it also wasn't raining, so that seemed like a fair trade-off.

We got into his van and he asked me about what I was doing. It was a fair question, I suppose. January isn't exactly prime time for tourists and I'd turned up in his shop just as it was getting dark, covered in mud and sweat, on the verge of tears. I told him that I'd run from Tintagel that morning, that it'd been a long day and that I was tired. I left out the hundreds of miles before that. I couldn't summon the energy to pretend to be excited about adventuring. Right now, I was just happy with small talk.

I expected him to just drop me in the centre of Bude, but he insisted on taking me right to Annie and Graham's front door. I said thank you and goodbye and that I hoped he had a nice evening, and that was that. The Wet Fish Man, my saviour, was gone.

Graham answered the door. He told me that Annie had been worried and headed out along the cliff to make sure I was okay in the dark.

"I'll just give her a call and tell her you're here, she'll be back soon."

I was a total stranger, I couldn't believe they cared enough to have worried like that.

Graham looked me up and down. I'd been submerged knee-deep in mud for most of the day, with Storm Gertrude whipping the ground up from underneath my feet and plastering the rest of me with it too.

"Erm, there's a hose around the back, would you mind…" he asked, and directed me through the side gate into the garden. When I saw how clean and light Annie and Graham's home was, I was grateful to have had the opportunity to get the worst of the mud off before going inside. It's generally not great house guest etiquette to turn all pale surfaces a shade of brown.

When Annie arrived home she said maybe the best words I have ever heard spoken aloud: "We have a hot tub, if you fancy a soak."

I very much fancied a soak. I took a quick shower so as to not completely contaminate the water and then, less than an hour after my panic in the Wet Fish Shop, I was in a hot tub with a gin and tonic in my hand. How quickly things turn around. Later, Annie cooked dinner and we talked about running and how great Cornwall is and other trips we'd been on. The dark cloud lifted a little, the tension in my shoulders that I hadn't even realised was there started to release. The world felt a lot less lonely.

———

Scrade might have been the deepest valley on that stretch of coast but it certainly wasn't the only one, as I discovered over the next few days. From Polzeath to Westward Ho! is 85 miles and I was tackling it over four days. I sound like a broken record by this point, I know, so I'm going to avoid beating around the bush and just sum it up in three words for you: mud, storm, hills.

These days, I'm a morning person through and through – give me a 5 a.m. alarm over a midnight bedtime any day – but this definitely hasn't always been the case. I was really struggling to get myself going in the mornings. As a result, there ended up being an awful lot of panics towards the end of each day, when the sun was setting and I wasn't at my destination yet and I couldn't make my legs move any faster.

It was beautiful, though. Maybe that's something I'm not emphasising enough. It was hard and horrible at times, and the wind knocked me over regularly and I hated having wet feet and I doubted myself constantly. That's all true. But the backdrop to all that was happening was truly stunning.

It was all worth it for the moments when the sun came out and, looking out over the turquoise seas and soft white sand and rugged cliffs, you could be anywhere in the world – it looked like a holiday brochure. Even on the stormy days I felt in awe of the landscape. This was South West England at its wildest, its most rugged and its most brilliant. Being out there day in, day out, rain or shine, you didn't miss anything. Seabirds swooping through the stormy clouds. Seals bobbing around in the rough water and basking on rocky outcrops. Sodden sheep huddling together, eyes shining through the low cloud of a misty afternoon.

The endless slippery ascents and hundreds of steps were tiring, sure, but then you'd get a rare gentle descent where you could stretch your legs out and it felt like flying. The cold, fresh air against your skin. Rain in your hair. Sprays of seawater on your face. It wasn't even February yet but I already had a strong runner's tan emerging, cheeks glowing permanently and a strip of dark skin around my ankles where my leggings didn't quite meet my socks.

It was beautiful and wonderful and hard and terrible – all at once, often. I swung wildly between loving it and hating it, with mere seconds of transition between the two. Sometimes I felt so utterly certain that I wanted to quit altogether, then a majestic landscape would unfold in front of me, or somebody would make me a hot cup of tea at the end of a cold day, and there was suddenly nowhere else I'd rather be.

I was tired after the 85-mile roller-coaster stint across the North Devon/Cornwall border and up to Westward Ho! I had a short day pencilled in next, just a couple of miles across to Appledore. I was finding that it was always on those easier days when I crashed though – no adrenaline to keep you buoyed up, a lot of time to kill, loneliness creeping in.

I was getting better at dealing with the wobbles though. I called Dave from the Yes Tribe who gave me a pep talk. I had a cry, I had a bath and, after a good night's sleep and four chocolate brownies from the village deli (John's of Appledore if you're ever passing – the best brownies ever), I felt a lot better.

My next stop was Barnstaple. The South West Coast Path follows the Tarka Trail (inspired by the route followed by Tarka the Otter) for this section, tracking the River Taw. The route is mostly along old railway tracks and, as a result, is flat for an entire 13 miles. It had been months since I had run that far without a gradient. It also wasn't raining. I couldn't believe how quickly the miles ticked by when I was actually running, rather than hauling myself up hills via barbed wire fences and brambles. It felt like a miracle.

There's a retail park just before you reach Barnstaple town centre. To celebrate those flat miles, I went to the Pizza Hut buffet and ate approximately 16 slices of pizza, one portion of pasta and two bowls of mixed salad covered in those crunchy bacon bits (fun fact: these bacon bits are, surprisingly, vegan). My friend Katie, who had come down to spend the weekend with me in Plymouth, lived near Barnstaple and I was staying with her that night. I whiled away the afternoon at the buffet, waiting for her to finish work.

Katie picked me up and we headed back to hers. I don't think Katie would mind me telling you that she is absolutely not a sporty person, not remotely interested in the idea of running or spending long, cold days outdoors. That night, we went out for a curry and talked about everything under the sun except running or adventure. We talked about boys and work and Katie's flatmate. I was still wearing my running kit and my muddy trail shoes, but as long as I didn't look in any mirrors, it just felt like a normal evening out with a friend.

The next morning, I found that Katie had bought me an avocado to have for breakfast. I was very excited. It goes without saying that I massively appreciated everybody who put me up and fed me, but I think they thought "runner" and immediately just thought I needed to be endlessly carb-loading. And I can't complain; I was doing that to myself too. Exhibit A: The four chocolate brownies in Appledore. Exhibit B: The Pizza Hut buffet I'd willingly taken myself to the day before.

But still, I did think I'd probably feel better if I ate some more vegetables, and that avocado tasted like heaven. I'd lived with Katie at university, so sitting on her sofa, eating avocado on toast as I had done so many times, felt like a kind of home away from home. I almost forgot that I had to head back and start running again soon.

Not for the first time, I found that I enjoyed the adventure most when it didn't really feel like I was on it.

————

It was 11 o' clock in the morning and I was soaked. As in, really soaked, down-to-my-pants soaked. I'm no weather expert, but I was fairly certain it was the wettest day of the whole year so far. I didn't understand how the sky could possibly have held as much liquid as it was currently throwing down. I was running from Ilfracombe to Lynton and I wasn't having a very nice time.

The coast path took me through a village and I saw a pub on the high street. It looked a bit dubious but it had a roof and, I imagined, some heating, which would be a big improvement on the current conditions outdoors. It wasn't even midday yet, but when I opened the door, I was greeted by what looked to be the entire village drinking bottles of Smirnoff Ice. An odd choice at the best of times if you're not a 15-year-old at a house party and definitely not the drink I'd go for at 11 o' clock in the morning on a cold, wet Saturday in February.

I ordered a hot chocolate and the barmaid gave me a funny look. I wasn't sure whether that was to do with the hot chocolate specifically or just the fact I'd ordered anything except a Smirnoff Ice. I didn't care – they could stare however much they wanted, it was dry inside and that was all that mattered. I found a quiet corner to make puddles in and drink my hot chocolate. This was a challenge given how much my teeth were chattering.

I only had two more days left on the South West Coast Path after this and I was sad that I wasn't enjoying it. I wanted to finish the trail with a streak of life-affirming days, bounding along breathing in big lungfuls of fresh sea air, not shivering in this strange pub full of alcopop drinkers (I never did find out the reason behind this). I hoped that tomorrow would be better.

I looked at the map on my phone (thank god for Google – I still hadn't learned to read a proper map). There was a quiet-looking, or so I hoped, country road running roughly parallel to the coast path for most of the rest of the way. Taking it would shave a couple of miles off and hopefully it would be a bit less muddy than the trails. I drained the dregs of my hot chocolate and headed back out, looking wistfully over my shoulder at all the Smirnoff Ice drinkers as I left the pub. I was probably wrong to judge – they were about to have a much more pleasant afternoon than I was.

I had been right: the road route was shorter and less muddy. However, without any drainage on either side of the road, the torrential rain was collecting and filling it up like a bathtub. With hedges on both sides, the only way out was through. A Land Rover came past as I waded through one particularly flooded section, up to my knees in murky water.

"We saw you in the village," the driver wound down her window to tell me. "Where are you headed to? Would you like a lift?"

I really wanted to say yes. I had another 8 or 9 miles to go to until Lynton, where I had a room at a B&B for the night. If I got in this woman's car (which looked as though it would almost definitely have heated seats), I could be there within 15 minutes. Within half an hour, I could have stripped off my sodden kit, had a scalding hot shower and be sitting in a fluffy white towel drinking a cup of tea.

I would have chosen a hot shower and that cup of tea over a million pounds in that moment.

And all of that was just one word away. I just had to say "yes", get in the car, and I'd be there. But instead...

"No, thank you, I'm fine. Only a few miles to go! It's fun really!" I plastered the biggest smile I could muster onto my face, probably coming across as quite manic. The woman drove away looking confused. I could understand that: I was questioning my own choice too.

———

The next day was just as wet, and so was the one after that. It looked like my dreams of finishing the South West Coast Path in a blaze of sunshine and glory weren't going to come true.

My final day on the path dawned. I was in Porlock and only had 9 miles to cover to Minehead, where the South West Coast Path ended. I awoke to the sound of wind thrashing against the single glazing, rain hammering down. I headed down to breakfast. Steve, who had been my host for the night, was cooking sausages and eggs.

"I'm not sure you should go out there, you know," he said, putting bread into the toaster. "It sounds bad enough down here, it'll be ever so blowy on the tops."

Looking out the window, I'll admit that the idea of heading out for another day's soaking didn't seem enormously appealing. I had in my head that this was it though – the last day. I didn't want to delay it. I went back upstairs to pack my stuff and looked at the South West Coast Path website's description of this section, to see just how stupid I was being.

Coasting

There were two route options for this section, it turned out. There was the rugged coast path that tracked the cliff edges more closely, then an alternative route that took you further inland, over the moors. It would still be gusty up there, but I was less likely to actually get blown into the sea, I imagined. It didn't seem like too much of a bad idea.

As soon as I started running that morning, something just clicked. I could barely feel my backpack and my legs were fine, and instead of begrudging the weather, I was embracing it. It was wild and unpredictable and it chewed you up and spat you out. It felt like a fitting end to the nearly two months I'd spent following little yellow acorns (the symbols that you find on the waymarkers signing every National Trail route).

The path climbed upwards and then I was on the moors. I rounded a corner and one particularly strong gust blew me several metres across the wide path. I felt very glad then that I wasn't on the coast path. I skidded to a halt and saw a herd of cows sheltering behind a tree.

Normally I was terrified of cows. A significant chunk of the trip so far had been spent avoiding them – climbing over barbed wire and electric fences and taking utterly ludicrous detours. But on that wild, windy Monday morning, I almost felt something like a connection to them. We were all out there, bracing ourselves against Mother Nature, doing what we needed to do to survive.

I'm not sure the cows were quite on board with my whimsy. They looked at me, bemused. *Who is this fool in a purple coat sliding around out there? Why isn't she under a tree, like us? Go home*, I could see them thinking.

Those 9 miles flew by. Before I knew it, my legs were carrying me off the moor and down into Minehead itself. I reached the seafront and saw the statue that marked the end of the South West Coast Path (or, for those doing it in the other direction, the start). I was actually out of breath. I hadn't moved fast enough to be out of breath for weeks.

I hung around by the sign for a while, hoping that somebody might come along who could take my picture. I was keen to mark this moment after missing the start of the path altogether, not realising what a huge part of my life this one route would become. Nobody came though. Apparently a wet and windy Monday morning in February wasn't prime time to be hanging around by the sea. I took a selfie instead and went off to find a sandwich.

The bigger moments in life often end up being underwhelming, I think. You think about them so much, build them up, pray for them... then they're just there. Most of the time, I'm not sure it's possible for those moments to live up to what you imagine. Can reality ever feel as big as a dream?

More often, is reality a selfie and a sandwich by yourself?

Finishing the South West Coast Path was bittersweet, too. I was proud of myself and it felt momentous, in some way. With the 630 miles of the Path and the 300 odd miles preceding it, I had run nearly 1,000 miles in total. That's a hell of a journey on its own. If, a year earlier when I first dreamed up this whole thing, I had told people I was just running the South West Coast Path, that would have sounded like an unfathomably huge adventure in itself and I'd have finished there in Minehead probably feeling as satisfied as I was ever going to. But instead I'd felt it necessary to chuck an extra 4,000 miles on and I was nowhere near finished, and I felt like I was going to be running literally forever more.

Coasting

It's hard to explain. Physically, I was holding up well. My thighs were doing a commendable job of turning cake into muscle and, nearly three months in, I was yet to have a single blister. There were days when – please excuse the cliché – I felt like I'd been born to run. Days like this one: flying across moors, up and down hills, battling the elements, feeling invincible.

But while my legs felt strong, so often my head felt like spaghetti. It's a feeling I had been trying – and often struggling – to convey. How do you explain brain spaghetti? It was confusing to feel and live through. It's even more confusing to attempt to recall and describe. Irrational, illogical, a tangle of self-doubt and unease, peppered with moments of joy and wonder and pride.

I had fallen in love with the South West Coast Path, unequivocally. Alongside all the brain spaghetti (or, perhaps, an integral part of it) was a dizzying, all-consuming, heart-soaring obsession. Before I had even finished it, I was already thinking of ways to go back and do it again. Despite this though, the whole experience was clouded by the shadow of wondering, "Will this ever end?" It was strange because I don't think I actually wanted it to end, I maybe just wanted the end to be an option.

And there was an option. At any time I could get on a train that would take me home and it could all be over. Any time I wanted, easy as that.

Except, of course, I knew I wasn't going to do that.

I simultaneously had absolutely no idea *how* I was going to run another 4,000 miles or keep myself going for another seven months, yet felt very sure that I would.

No matter what logic, reason, my own doubtful mind and, sometimes, the words others had spoken aloud said... no matter what they said, I was going to do this.

CHAPTER 14

"I don't like that, not on my television, not in my house."
Jeffrey stood up from his armchair and left the room.

I sat very still, feeling very uncomfortable.

"Oh, don't mind him," his wife Sarah said, gesturing towards
the slamming door with one hand. "He gets like this sometimes."

Except, actually, I did mind. I minded quite a lot. We had
just eaten fish and chips for dinner and we were in the living
room watching the TV. Some sort of mid-week drama was on
and two men had just kissed. Clearly, Jeffrey didn't think this
was acceptable.

In almost any other circumstance, I would have questioned
him, or at least been vocal about the extent to which I disagreed.
But I was in his home. He and Sarah had invited me to stay for
the night as I ran along the Somerset coast. They had insisted
on buying me dinner. They had laid the bed with fresh sheets
and let me do a load of laundry so that I had clean, dry kit to
put on in the morning.

Coasting

Should somebody be entitled to have their own opinions in their own home? Or, by inviting a relative stranger in, are you opening yourself to being questioned? Was it my duty to be an ally, to try to broaden his mind, to question his outdated, prejudiced, sometimes dangerous opinions? Or, as well as accepting the good things from strangers – their kindness, their generosity, their warm beds and their washing machines – did I also have to accept the ways in which we differed too?

Jeffrey came back into the room. I sat there quietly and I didn't say anything. I made my excuses and I went to bed.

I don't believe that this was the right thing to do. I regret it a lot.

Nothing changes by people staying quiet and going to bed.

CHAPTER 15

It was Sunday morning in Bristol and I was traipsing around the city centre with Georgia, one of my best friends from university. We were using the Find My Phone app on my phone to try to locate hers, which we hoped would be in her handbag.

The app told us that we would find it right in the middle of a pedestrianised street. We made a beeline for the spot it specified, like pirates looking for some really shit treasure. There was a lot of rubbish and debris scattered across the cobbles but nothing that remotely resembled a phone or a handbag. We were, however, standing outside the bar that was the last place either of us could remember being the night before.

"Maybe the GPS is a bit off and it's actually in Lost Property inside?" I suggested.

"Maybe," Georgia half-heartedly replied. We went to Starbucks to kill some time before the bar opened again. We both ordered lattes the size of our heads and collapsed into a sofa in the corner to feel sorry for ourselves. I took one sip and felt my stomach churn. Perhaps a big, milky drink hadn't been the best idea.

I had detoured away from the coast slightly to come into Bristol and spend the weekend with Georgia, before crossing the Severn Bridge over to Wales. So far, my rule of thumb had been to always cross an estuary or river (or any other kind of water that got in my way) at the first possible opportunity. Sometimes this was via a ferry or bridge, at other times I could finish a day on one side and start the next day from the other. Occasionally, none of these options were possible and I had to run around. I was generally very grateful to anybody who had decided to build a bridge or put on a ferry, especially when the body of water in question was as big as the Bristol Channel.

I arrived at Georgia's on Friday evening. On Saturday, there was a big rugby match that we had been invited to Georgia's friend's house to watch. I was quite keen to not wear my increasingly tatty running kit. Unfortunately, Georgia is about half a foot and two dress sizes smaller than me, so finding anything in her wardrobe that I could borrow was tricky. She managed to dig out some very stretchy jeans and a baggy-on-her-but-not-on-me jumper. I paired them with my revolting trail shoes, which were more hole than shoe at this stage, and my down jacket. It was a winning look. We stopped by the supermarket on the way to her friend's and picked up a bottle of Prosecco and some beers. Once again, I got carried away with feeling normal for once and forgot that I had barely drunk for months and that I definitely couldn't keep up any more.

I had woken up the next morning in Georgia's bed with a throbbing headache, a chipped front tooth, a receipt in my purse for a pizza I didn't remember eating and a hazy half-memory of having been very close to a man's face. Georgia had woken up next to me without any of her possessions.

I'd done it again.

I was meant to leave Bristol that day and run to Chepstow. A group of women had got in touch a few days earlier asking if I fancied company for the day, and I had happily accepted. However, from the moment my eyes opened and I took a sip of water that made me retch, I knew that I wouldn't be running anywhere. I sent them some kind of excuse, said that I wasn't feeling well (again, not actually a lie). I went back to sleep until Georgia shook me awake a little while later and said we needed to go and find her stuff.

I felt awful, especially about having let down the women who were going to run with me. More and more people were following my Facebook page and watching the video clips I was posting (mostly thanks to my brother's admirable campaign to spam every running page going with my name and face). I tried to be honest about how hard I found it at times, and every time I opened up online I'd be flooded with comments from people telling me to keep going and that I was inspiring them. Yet here I was, schlepping around with a hangover, having to cancel runs and letting people down all over the shop.

If I sit here now and try to put things in perspective, I can admit that maybe I was being a bit harsh on myself. I had been running for nearly 100 days at this point and this was only the second time I'd let anybody down. It wasn't exactly like this was happening all the time. And if I read that one of the people I followed had drunk too much at a rugby game and had to cancel a run? I would have laughed. In fact, I would have loved to read that. I would have found that so much more relatable and been relieved that they weren't as wholesome and pure and perfect as they perhaps sometimes appeared.

But, of course, when it's yourself you're talking about, it's not that easy. Yes, I wanted other people to be flawed and imperfect and relatable, but when it came to me and the stories I told about myself I wanted to be perfect. I couldn't slip up, at all, ever. No mistakes. No being a normal 23-year-old on a night out with her mates. Nope, what a failure that would be.

———

I stayed at Georgia's an extra night then, on Monday morning, carried the lingering hangover blues with me over the Severn Bridge to Chepstow. I was spending my first night on Welsh soil in a hotel where some of the reviews warned about bed bugs. I didn't think you still got those in the UK in 2020. I really just felt like I needed somebody to give me a hug, pat me on the head and tell me that everything was going to be okay.

My general feeling of misery was only compounded when I walked for 10 minutes from the hotel to get fish and chips for dinner, then walked all the way back and realised they'd forgotten to put the salt and vinegar on my chips. Is it even fish and chips without salt and vinegar? So dry, so potato-ey. I struggled through a few before putting them in the bin and got into bed fully clothed. It was hard to sleep through the smell of grease and the constant itching. Was it bed bugs or was it just in my mind? It almost didn't matter, the net result was about the same.

For obvious reasons, I wasn't that keen on eating breakfast at the hotel. The following morning, I walked up the high street and found a cafe that looked clean and which was proudly displaying its 5* food hygiene certificate. I was tired from the terrible night's sleep and the after-effects of Saturday night and just couldn't bring myself to get going. I spent far too long in that cafe, eating croissants and drinking coffee, looking at my phone and pretending to do "admin". I just wanted my mum and my own bed (which was most definitely bed-bug-free) and to be home.

But the sun was shining and I still had a long way to run, so I prized myself out of the cracked leather cafe armchair and out into the fresh air. The first thing I needed to do was find the official start of the Wales Coast Path, which I knew was by the old bridge over the River Wye, somewhere near the castle. I headed towards the river and found that you couldn't really miss the trail start. It was signified by two different marker stones (one made of local Pennant sandstone and the other of Halkyn marble from Flintshire) and one beautiful ceramic map laid into the pavement.

It was a beautiful morning. The sun was shining and I felt a lot better for being outside. I'm not sure why this was a lesson I didn't seem to be able to absorb. I *always* felt better when I just got on with it and stopped faffing around wasting money on overpriced drinks and snacks just for an excuse to be inside. I touched the marker stones, made a quick video and set off towards Newport. The Wales Coast Path was a go.

I was running across the mudflats of the Caldicot Levels when a barefooted man with a beard ran towards me. I recognised him as Aleks Kashefi, better known as Barefoot Aleks.

Coasting

Aleks had completed a barefoot Land's End to John o' Groats run the year before and was planning to run the length of Europe next, starting at the continent's most northern point in Nordkapp in Norway and finishing at the southernmost tip in Tarifa, Spain. All without any shoes on.

Aleks had messaged me a couple of days earlier saying he might come and run with me during February half-term, and here he was. He introduced himself and then immediately offered me a lolly from his pocket.

"The best running snack," he assured me. "You just suck on it as you run and get a constant sugar hit."

One of the main life lessons I'd learned as a child was to never run with a lollipop in your mouth, but I was only about 7 miles into a 24-mile day and I was already starting to flag a bit. I figured it was worth a try.

I've come to spend a fair amount of time with Aleks over the past few years, including once running from London to Birmingham with him in the middle of January. He's one of the best long-run companions you'll find – always upbeat, super easy to chat to, hilarious, often plays motivational Beyoncé songs when you hit a dark spot. He brought all of those characteristics with him when he came to run with me that day in Wales. In return, I brought absolutely nothing to the table. My brief spell of optimism in the sunshine in Chepstow had quickly evaporated and every single step felt like a chore. Probably not helped by the fact I hadn't packed anywhere near enough snacks to get me through the best part of a marathon. Thank god for that lolly.

Aleks ran with me for 10 miles or so and I was terrible company throughout. If I'd just admitted I was in a bit of a grump that day, it would have been fine. I could have had a moan, we'd have laughed about it, Aleks would have played some Beyoncé and I'm sure I would have felt a lot better. Of all people, I think Aleks would understand the spaghetti-head thing. He'd done a lot of adventuring himself – he knew you had good days and bad days. But for some reason I insisted on pretending everything was absolutely fine while quietly panicking in my head about it. Between the running and the worrying, that didn't leave a huge amount of energy left for witty or insightful, or even just pleasant, conversation. Aleks had come all this way to run with me (he lived in the Peak District, where he was a teacher during term time) and I was being an utter bore.

We reached the turn-off to the lane where Aleks had parked his car and we said goodbye. Even though I hadn't been adding any value whatsoever to the conversation, having Aleks there chatting away beside me had really helped me get through the day so far. I felt a drop in energy almost instantly when he left. It was late afternoon, there wasn't too much daylight left and my phone battery was dying. I had run 18 miles and had at least six still to go. It felt like a mammoth task.

I passed Goldcliff, the last village before the coast path takes you up the River Usk and into Newport. I was standing there wondering what to do, feeling very sorry for myself, when in the window of what looked like a regular residential bungalow I saw a sign saying "open". I hopped over the low wall and found there was a tearoom. They were closing soon, but I managed to buy a can of Coke and a Mars Bar and was able to sit inside to plug my phone in for a few minutes.

As my phone warmed up and came back to life, it started to light up with notifications, including some messages from

Coasting

Georgia who had clearly been reunited with her lost handbag. She had had lunch with some of her work friends and they'd been chatting about Saturday night.

"Do you remember going off with my friend Will?" she had written, then "hahahaha". Well, I guess that confirmed my vague memory of a man's face being close to mine.

He was the first person I'd kissed since Greg. This wasn't quite how I'd envisaged moving on would look, I had to admit.

I had daydreamed about wild romances I might have as I ran around the coast. In these fantasies I conveniently forgot about the fact that I only had two pairs of pants and hadn't shaved my legs for weeks and generally smelt like a damp dog most of the time. I'd imagined all the handsome fishermen I would end up chatting to in tiny village pubs, or the rugged hikers I would meet on remote coast paths and then have to camp with for a week when a storm came in. I'm sure you get the picture.

What I didn't imagine was leaving a bar with Georgia's friend from work on a night out that I don't remember in the middle of Bristol. I felt my chest tighten at the thought of it. Sometimes, it's just better not to know.

I left the cafe and decided to follow the road into Newport, rather than the coast path. I knew that I wouldn't get there before dark and had a feeling of unease crawling all over me, more uncomfortable than the bed bugs in Chepstow. I played a game with myself where I just had to run to a lamp post, walk to one, run to one, walk to one. Occasionally I managed to run to two or three without taking the walk.

It took a while but eventually I reached Newport. I'd covered nearly 26 miles that day in the end. I found an Italian restaurant and spent too much money that I didn't have eating enough pasta to feed the entire population of Wales for a week and then fell into an 11-hour sleep.

Although I'd somehow managed to trick my legs into running all these miles, and I was slowly getting to grips with the logistics of organising an adventure, the financial side was still a constant concern. There were now thousands of people following my journey online, and they kept using this word "inspiration". But I wasn't an inspiration: I was the same person I always had been, with all the same flaws I'd had before.

I wondered what they'd say if they knew I'd already run out of money. I still hadn't pitched my tent, I wasn't even carrying it with me at this stage, and although I was mostly staying with all the incredibly kind people who kept putting me up, occasionally I'd have to pay for a hotel which would completely blow my budget. Then there was all the food and coffees I bought just so I could be inside somewhere warm and feel a little happier for a few minutes. I'd started doing some, frankly, pretty dodgy online copywriting to fund the trip. I'd heard about "copy mills" where basically you churn out articles containing keywords on a variety of questionable topics, and get paid abysmally for the privilege. It suited me though, as long as I put my morals aside.

If I had an evening alone, or found myself sitting in a cafe drinking one of those coffees that was slowly bankrupting me, I'd log into the site, assign myself a few articles, and get writing. The most worrying one I wrote was "Five Tips for Recovering From a Vasectomy Reversal Operation". Of course, I'm not a medical professional and I have no idea how one goes about recovering from such an operation. I kept them vague: stock your freezer with food beforehand, make sure you have some new films to watch, invite your friends over to keep you company.

I imagine that the people following me thought I spent my down time doing all manner of rugged, adventurous things: lancing blisters, foraging for berries, brushing up on my celestial navigation. They probably didn't picture me writing articles about how to care for your testicles, but there we were.

Sometimes you just do what you have to do.

CHAPTER 16

Sometimes things have to get worse before they get better.

After 11 hours of sleep and armed with an emergency Boost chocolate bar (the secret weapon of every long-distance runner, according to Barefoot Aleks), I left Newport. Over the next couple of days I ran through Cardiff and Barry and Rhoose. The rain set in again and, once more, everything I owned was damp and I was plastered in mud at all times.

A few weeks earlier I'd received an email from a man I didn't know who lived inland a little from this section of the coast, asking if I needed somewhere to stay when I passed. I largely avoided accepting accommodation offers from lone men, preferring to stick with families or women. I know that the majority of single men who live by themselves no doubt have entirely altruistic intentions and would never cause any harm to anybody, but better safe than sorry, I thought. As much as I'd only met very trustworthy people so far, there was still a part of my brain that always imagined the worst.

Coasting

But Facebook stalking Jeremy told me that he was an ex-colleague of somebody I'd been to university with (a fail-safe vetting process...) and I figured he was fairly unlikely to murder me. I replied to his email saying "yes please" and we arranged for him to meet me near the beach. We drove to his house in a village a few miles away from the coast. He made me a cup of tea and a sandwich, which I was very grateful for after another cold wet day.

"What do you fancy for dinner this evening?" Jeremy asked as I finished my tea. "I can cook, or we can get a takeaway, or head out to my local."

"I really don't mind, whatever's easiest," I told him. It was the truth. In my normal life, that I have full control over, I do perhaps have the tendency to be a little uptight. Maybe not uptight, just "inflexible". I like things to be how I like them to be. Don't we all? But one good thing to come out of staying with so many different people was having to overcome that entirely. You also certainly couldn't be a fussy eater. Whatever weird and wonderful concoction was put in front of me, I smiled and said thank you and ate it all and told them it was delicious. Usually I was hungry enough for this to mostly be the truth.

Sometimes hunger wasn't enough to mask the strange concoction I was served. Like the time I was given caramelised peaches and new potatoes for dessert. Or the vegetable peelings pie served with an entire head of broccoli on the side, boiled whole. But I was still very grateful.

"Let's go to my local then, no washing-up," Jeremy decided.

I showered and changed into my dry clothes. Jeremy had said I was welcome to do a load of laundry so, before we headed out for dinner, I took my muddy kit downstairs to put into the washing machine.

"Do you want to stick your shoes in too?" Jeremy asked, looking over to where they were festering in the corner. They were looking pretty grim. I'm sure I could see some sheep droppings hanging from the laces.

"Ah no, it's okay. I don't have any spares so I need to wear these if we're going out. Don't worry, I'm used to the wet feet by now."

"Do you want to borrow a pair of shoes? What size are you?"

"Erm, I'm a size six or seven, but really don't worry. I'm fine with these!" I tried to protest. This fell on deaf ears: before I knew it, Jeremy had gone to his shoe rack and found a pair of size 10 men's leather brogues for me to try on.

"I think they might be a bit big... I'll be fine with my own shoes, honestly."

"We're only going around the corner, better to have your shoes nice and clean for tomorrow, I think." We went back and forth like this for a while and I tried to protest, but it didn't seem to work. They were my feet, attached to my body – I'm not sure why I didn't insist a bit more firmly. I just found arguing with someone in their own home very awkward, even when what they were suggesting made me feel uncomfortable, as I'd found with Jeffrey in Somerset. My grandma's constant emphasis on politeness as a child had clearly been drilled into me a little too well. Perhaps sometimes we need to be a little bit impolite.

I really did not want to wear this man's shoes, but that's what I ended up doing. It goes without saying that I looked utterly ludicrous, heading out in patterned running tights, a merino wool long-sleeved top, a down jacket... and smart leather shoes that were four sizes too big. *Oh well*, I thought, *it's just the local pub, I'm sure it'll be very casual and it won't matter what I look like.* I don't think it was particularly presumptuous of me to think this. I was a little surprised, therefore, when Jeremy said "We're here," and opened the door to what was clearly a very fancy seafood restaurant.

"Hi Jeremy," the head waiter called as we walked in. At least this clearly was actually his local; that much was true.

We were escorted over to a booth where the only seating arrangement was side by side. Had I been on a date I would have thought what a lovely, romantic setting this was. However, as it was, I was out for dinner with a complete stranger who was 30 years my senior, *wearing his shoes lest we forget,* and I felt deeply uncomfortable. When I saw the prices on the menu, my mood plummeted even further. Even the cheapest main course would eat up several days of my adventure budget, and I was already having wine poured into my glass and being offered bread from a basket. I'd have to write about 5 hours' worth of vasectomy-reversal recovery tips to cover my share of the bill, I calculated.

After what felt like the longest evening of my life, we finished eating and it was time to leave. Jeremy insisted on paying, which I was grateful for but didn't feel entirely comfortable about. As soon as we got in, I made my excuses and headed up to the spare room. I brushed my teeth and went to get into bed, but when I pulled back the covers I found the sheets were covered in dubious looking yellow stains and strewn with dark hairs. I shuddered. The rest of Jeremy's house seemed clean enough, I couldn't understand what on earth had happened to the spare bed. I lay a clean towel on top of the duvet, then rolled out my sleeping bag and got into it fully clothed. I passed the night not sleeping at all and just trying to not touch anything.

The next morning, I left as early as I politely could and, safely back on the coast path, just tried to tell myself that at least this would make a good story one day. That day I ran another 21 miles, to where I was staying with Nicola, who'd been following my Facebook page. She met me just as it was getting dark, took me back to her house and introduced me to her lovely family.

I loved staying with Nicola: the bed sheets were clean and nobody made me wear their shoes.

———

From Nicola's, I ran around to Porthcawl, where I stayed in a strange hostel-type place. There were lots of bunk beds in every room but I seemed to be the only person there. It was right behind a fairly bleak-looking amusement arcade containing a Wimpy with a 1* hygiene rating proudly stuck up in the window. Could you actually be awarded zero? I wondered.

I wandered back into the town centre and couldn't seem to find anywhere open that would sell me anything resembling dinner. I ended up in Subway, yet another exotic destination to tick off my adventure to-do list, then went to the Spar and bought some porridge pots to have for breakfast the next morning. After the warmth of Nicola's home, Porthcawl felt pretty bleak.

While I was eating my Subway sandwich, my cousin Kelly was driving to Wales. She had offered to join me for tomorrow's run, which I'll admit I was a little surprised by – she's not necessarily the most outdoorsy person you'll ever meet. I imagine she was questioning her decision too when she arrived at the address I sent her and I let her into the hostel via the back door, which opened onto an alley of wheelie bins. Not quite the luxury hotels she typically prefers.

The next morning we poured hot water into the porridge pots and cooked up an unappetising grey sludge. We tried to liven it up with a few blueberries and washed it down with an equally dismal instant coffee. As always seemed to be the case whenever anybody came to run with me, it was absolutely bloody hammering it down. At least Kelly was well equipped for the weather: she was wearing her six-year-old son's Spiderman backpack and a waterproof coat that turned out to not be remotely waterproof. She locked her overnight bag into her car, which she was planning to get a taxi back to later, and we set off into the storm.

It was 10 miles to Port Talbot. Kelly had been doing a bit of running, but not much distance. We decided to just take it steady, run as far as we could, and then walk if we needed to. This section of the coast path was almost dead flat, taking us behind the dunes of Kenfig Sands Beach, but the weather was just getting worse and worse. We ended up only running about 3 miles, leaving us with a solid couple of hours of walking in the rain.

Kelly has a propensity to feel the cold at the best of times, and the not-at-all-waterproof coat wasn't helping. I could tell that she was struggling but I wasn't really sure what to do – we were over halfway to Port Talbot in the middle of a nature reserve. We may as well have carried on as turned back.

I attempted to keep her distracted from the fact she was steadily turning blue with a range of thrilling sophisticated games like "I went to the shops", but it didn't really work. I tried to look at a map and see if there were any shortcuts we could take but, once again, my phone had got cold and switched itself off. I didn't want to ask Kelly to look at hers in case we were further away from Port Talbot than I thought – ignorance was bliss to keep her moving forward. We'd just have to keep following the signs and hope for the best.

Eventually the signs took us out of the dunes and into some kind of civilisation, where the footpath ran parallel to the M4 for a while. It was a very scenic place to die of hypothermia. We walked through the outskirts of Port Talbot with dense sheets of rain falling in front of our eyes. Visibility was low but suddenly, just ahead of us on the residential street we were walking down, we saw the unmistakable bright lights of hope: a chip shop.

"Can we go in there?" Kelly asked, teeth chattering at a rate of knots. We headed inside and I ordered some chips for us to share. I was alarmed when Kelly said she didn't like vinegar. As you know, I like mine to be drowning in it but, given the worrying shade of blue she'd gone and my hunch that she really needed something warm inside, I left that debate for another time.

Kelly looked marginally less like she might literally be about to die after a few hot chips and we decided to take a cab back to Porthcawl to get her car together, and then decide what to do from there. The original plan had been to have lunch together in Port Talbot and then she'd head home to leave me to it, but it was clear that Kelly needed to put some dry clothes on as a matter of urgency.

Coasting

The taxi arrived and I made small talk with the driver while Kelly concentrated on Olympic-grade shivering. Back in Porthcawl, not a place I was thrilled to return to, Kelly changed into some warm clothes in the back seat of her car and put the heaters on full blast, and we started driving back to Port Talbot.

We had made it approximately half a mile down the road when she pulled over, dramatically flung the door open and threw up down the side of her car.

"I don't feel great," she confided, sitting back up and wiping her mouth.

"No, you're not looking amazing either, I have to say."

"I think I need some sugar." She rooted around in the back seat and produced some lemon drizzle cake bites. After a couple of those and a few minutes of sitting still, Kelly declared she was okay to drive again. She dropped me straight to the B&B in Port Talbot where I was staying that night.

"Going to have to skip lunch, sorry cus'."

I waved her off, feeling a bit concerned that she was now about to attempt to drive nearly 200 miles home. It had been another miserable day, another failed attempt at sourcing appropriately condimented fish and chips, and now I'd nearly killed my cousin too.

Perfect.

Running around Wales was going really well so far.

CHAPTER 17

My friends Alex and Rosie lived in Swansea, which was my next stop after Port Talbot.

I had met them when we all signed up for the Everest Base Camp trek while at university. Until now, that had been my biggest adventure. The whole trip was a comedy of errors. I was loosely assigned as "Adventure Leader" and my co-leader pulled out a few weeks before the trip, citing a dying pet lizard as his reason. Our tour company went into liquidation while we were halfway up the mountain, leaving us unsure whether we had any return flights booked. The local newspaper in Plymouth published a wildly inaccurate front page headline announcing that "Charity Will Pay to Get Them Home", the reader comments on which were fairly abusive. I managed to fall over on the second day and land on my knee, causing it to triple in size. I had to complete the rest of the trek using some borrowed walking poles essentially as crutches and our Sherpa insisted on giving me some rather dubious "sports" massages involving attempting to dig his fingers under my tendons while asking if I had a husband. Oh, and let's not forget that when we got back to Kathmandu, we went out to celebrate our achievements, all got horrendously drunk in an Irish bar and one of the boys missed the toilet, defecated on the bathroom floor and I ended up cleaning it up.

Yeah, it was a weird trip.

But despite that, I apparently still had a pretty fantastic time. I came home and wrote a Facebook status about how I was "increasingly realising that the only way I'm ever going to be happy is to be this tanned and exhausted and proud on a frequent basis", posted alongside a picture of us in a tea house at the end of the trek. I would question the use of "proud" but as I ran around the British coast, I was certainly frequently tanned and exhausted.

I ran into Swansea on a Sunday afternoon. It wasn't too far, only about 9 miles from Port Talbot. It was wet and windy and the Wales Coast Path mostly ran alongside a dual carriageway but, for some reason, this felt great fun. There was no rhyme or reason to what made a good day or a bad day.

Alex and Rosie lived with Alex's family and I stayed with them for a few days. Some familiarity felt like just what I needed. I took a rest day, unpacked my bag, borrowed some non-lycra clothes, went out for ice cream with Alex and Rosie's friends, laughed a lot, ate dinner with Alex's family... Nobody made me borrow their four-sizes-too-big shoes and I also managed not to nearly kill anybody with hypothermia, so it was a resounding success really.

After my day off, Alex joined me for a day to cover the 18 miles from Swansea around to Oxwich Bay on the

Gower Peninsula. The Gower was the first place in Britain to be named an Area of Outstanding Natural Beauty, and for good reason. The coast path winds over grassy cliffs, across beautiful bays and through wooded areas. It's tough going with lots of loose sand to plough through and steep steps to haul yourself up. But it's immediately worth the effort when you stumble across a hidden cove, or climb out of a valley to see miles and miles of blue water and craggy coastline stretching out towards the horizon.

It was a bright, sunny day. It felt like spring was coming – I even ended up taking my shoes and socks off and paddling. In February! I had spent the whole winter saying that I'd cry with joy the day that it stayed light until 6 p.m. and we were getting there.

People often asked why on earth I set off at the beginning of November, heading straight into winter. Mainly it was just because Greg suggested it and I didn't really think about it much beyond that. He knew about adventures. If he thought that was the best time to go, then that was the best time to go. And, actually, on this he was right. It might seem like a strange choice but, looking back, I feel certain it was the best way to do it. The plan was to be away for ten months, which meant I was going to be running during most months regardless. I could have started a couple of months later, say in early February, and then finished up the following November, therefore skipping December and January which were the worst months in terms of both daylight and weather. But it would have meant going from summer back into autumn and winter. Going from long, hot days full of ice creams and breaks on the beach back into dark nights and cold feet. Mentally, I think that would have been so much more demoralising, even if it would have saved me a few storms.

The way I did it, it was really bloody hard at the start and then it just got better and better. The weather got warmer, the days got longer and the running got easier as the paths hardened again. Mentally, that was a huge pick-me-up. That day walking around the Gower with Alex really felt like a turning point. Maybe this whole thing was going to start being a bit more how I'd imagined.

————

A few days later, I turned 24. My dad came to visit and booked an Airbnb for us to stay in for a few days. As always, just having a base was so nice. I thought about running 24 miles to mark my 24th birthday but instead opted for a more leisurely 12. My dad ran with me and the Wales Coast Path took us around Rhossili Bay, its 3 miles of perfect sand making it one of my favourite beaches in the world. We ran over dunes and through little pockets of woodland, finishing at the pub for a birthday lunch. Later on, back at the apartment, I insisted on decorating my own birthday cake and wasn't too offended when my dad called me a control freak because of it.

I had been at work on my birthday the year before. All day, Greg had made hints that some kind of surprise was on its way to my office and would be arriving any second. I kept glancing at the clock as the hands ticked closer and closer to 6 p.m. I faffed around at the end of the day, thinking that maybe if I just stayed a little longer, a delivery would arrive – or maybe even Greg himself. By 6.30 p.m., nothing had turned up.

"What are you still doing here?" Ellie, my manager, asked, "It's your birthday. Go and have fun!"

Apparently, that day, "fun" looked like pacing up and down Oxford Street crying. Then crying in the shoe department of Topshop. Then crying on the bus home. Then on my flatmate's shoulder when I got there. Then crying a bit more over the birthday burger he insisted we go out for. Then finishing things off by crying myself to sleep.

I was upset that Greg had let me down again, obviously, but it was more than that. We had been seeing each other for nearly six months and were just at the point where everything had stopped making sense. He would say things that appeared to totally contradict something else he'd said just a few days earlier, then outright deny it if I questioned it. I would lie in bed at night reading his messages over and over again. I was certain that the words I was reading said one thing – that he was on his way to my office with a present, for instance – but I didn't trust myself enough to be right any more. Maybe I really had misunderstood? I knew that if I said anything, he'd just tell me I'd got it wrong, that he'd never said anything of the kind. Of course he hadn't sent a present, what a ridiculous thing to expect, how much time did I think he had to waste on things like that?

All in all, it hadn't been a great day for me. Turning 24 was a big improvement – I spent it hanging out with my dad, somewhere beautiful, eating birthday cake, and nobody made me cry.

On the day he was due to leave, my dad suggested I take a day off and we visit the Big Pit National Coal Museum together. Part of the reason I had wanted to do this adventure in the first place had been to explore my home country and, given that I had no knowledge about South Wales mining history, this sounded like a valid way to spend a day. So that's where we went – we ate leftover birthday cake in the car, we learned about mining and, afterwards, dad declared that he might have just had the best day of his life.

Then, before I knew what was happening, we were on the M50 driving towards Northampton, instead of heading back west to pick up the coast again.

I was going home.

And I was really happy about it.

I'm not sure why I was so obsessed with not going home but, the same as at Christmas, I just felt like I shouldn't. It felt like cheating. If I had chosen a more far-flung adventure, I wouldn't have been able to just pop home and see my mum. I felt like I was giving myself an unfair advantage by making the most of being so near to home. Which was ridiculous, obviously, but I guess that's easy to say in hindsight.

I needed a few days off to do some planning, swap my socks (which were on their last legs again), sleep, not be polite to anybody, quieten my brain... that sort of thing. Plus my grandma had written a book of family history and her book launch was that weekend. How could I miss my own grandma's book launch?

———

A week later, I took the train back to Swansea. After a few days of looking at maps and poring over the Wales Coast Path distance charts, I felt a lot better equipped to tackle the rest of Wales, especially some of the more remote parts. I sent

Anna McNuff a picture of the provisional schedule I'd put together, which would take me all the way to Edinburgh.

"You're a planner like me, I knew it!" she replied.

And I think she was right. I had spent my whole life being the most disorganised person I knew and it was hard to shed that badge of honour (as dubious an honour as it was). The chaos didn't make me happy though, perhaps it never had. The chaos was just part of the cycle of self-sabotage and self-loathing, debt and stress – all the things that made me hate myself. What did make me happy, it turned out, was a spreadsheet and a to-do list.

From Swansea I planned to catch another train and then a bus back to the last spot I had run to on the Gower Peninsula. From here, I would start running again. There was just one problem: I couldn't stop crying. I sat curled up in a ball on the train, head against the window, sobbing. When the train pulled into Swansea, I moved my crying to a cafe, where I ordered a coffee and a slice of cheesecake, which I made soggy with tears. People kept asking me if I was okay. Understandable, as the way I was carrying on they probably assumed something serious had happened.

"I've got to go for a run," I just about managed to get out in halted breaths. Nobody seemed particularly sympathetic.

Unable to get it together enough to catch my second train, I paid too much money for a hotel room 50 metres up the road from that coffee shop in Swansea and went to bed at 4 p.m. instead. I slept like a dead person for a solid 16 hours, only waking up for another brief crying interlude at around 1 a.m.

When I woke up the next morning, I couldn't fathom how I had ever run anywhere before. My legs felt so heavy, as did my head. Just walking across the room felt like dragging ten tons of both physical and metaphorical lead behind me. I had been planning to run to Kidwelly that night, where Sally had offered me a bed. Clearly, I wasn't running anywhere, so I took the bus there instead. I called my dad to cry some more and he said he'd drive down the next morning to help me sort this mess out.

I knocked on Sally's door and she greeted me with a plate of freshly baked Welsh cakes. I felt like an idiot – she was being so nice to me but I hadn't run for over a week at that point. I went to bed early again and waited for my dad to rescue me. I couldn't get myself moving, that much was clear.

He arrived bright and early the next morning. Sally ran a small B&B and had another spare room, so my dad arranged to stay that night too. Sally then offered us a lift back to Llanelli, so we could run through to Kidwelly together. It was all getting so complicated, so much back and forth, and it just made me feel worse. I'd come on this trip for the A to B simplicity of it all, but it turned out I wasn't good enough to do it like that.

Llanelli to Kidwelly is about 13 miles. I would love to be able to sit here and tell you that once I started running again I remembered how much I loved it. I would love to describe a glorious, life-affirming day running along breathing in the sea air with my dad.

Unfortunately, that's not what happened. There's a long stretch along the beach and it was a windy day. The sand was whipping me in the face, getting in my eyes. I pulled my buff up and my hood down until I could barely see. Even if I was feeling on top form, it wouldn't have been a great day. As it was, I felt utterly miserable. I sat down in the sand and cried (again). My dad had to physically pull me up and coax me on to Kidwelly. We got there, eventually, but it wasn't enjoyable for anybody.

Sorry Dad.

––––––––

The next day we ran from Kidwelly to Carmarthen. I only cried once, which apparently meant I was safe to be left alone, so my dad left me to it (probably relieved to be rid of me for a bit, I imagine).

I wasn't alone for too long though. That weekend, my friend Adam drove to Laugharne – my next stop after Camarthen – after his night shift to come and run with me for a few days. Welsh poet Dylan Thomas lived in Laugharne with his family and I was thrilled to be staying at his favourite pub, Brown's Hotel: he had famously given the bar's phone number as his own.

When Adam arrived I hadn't washed my hair for nine days and, the night before, I'd eaten a packet of biscuits and some fizzy sweets and called it dinner, so I'll admit that I wasn't acting like somebody who had got their shit together. I was starting to see the light at the end of the tunnel though. I wasn't exactly enjoying it again yet, but I had stopped crying, which was a big step forward.

I had first met Adam the year before at a Yes Tribe camp out. When we started chatting, we realised we'd done the same local marathon a few months earlier and, after some digging, it turned out we were actually in the same photo. Adam was easily recognisable because he was wearing a sombrero. From then on, sombreros became a bit of a theme of our friendship. It was only fitting that he arrived in the depths of South West Wales wearing one.

We ran 21 miles together on the first day of his visit. From Laugharne we crossed the border into Pembrokeshire and then ran through to Tenby. It was a lot harder to feel sad running beside a man wearing a sombrero as I was mostly too busy laughing instead. That night, we stayed with professional cake baker Sandra and her husband Will.

I was so hungry when I arrived that I ate a packet of biscuits in the shower. As Sandra showed us her cake-decorating equipment after dinner I realised, with surprise, that I was actually having fun again. It was a constant cycle of wanting to quit, then having a moment of belief that perhaps I could do it after all. On the best days, I felt that not only was I able to finish it, but that more importantly perhaps I actually *wanted* to.

CHAPTER 18

I ran around Pembrokeshire via a web of connected people.

In Pembroke I stayed with Neil and Cathy, who told me stories about all the cycling touring trips they'd taken. They cooked up a feast, but one that was full of vegetables and made me feel like I actually had some energy to run on the next day. They understood what you needed to keep yourself moving day after day. Cathy sent me off the next day with a packed lunch of sandwiches, boiled eggs and fruit, and the phone number of her friend Debbie in my pocket.

"She lives on the Marloes Peninsula. Run about 20 miles and then call her, she'll pick you up for the night," Cathy told me.

I did exactly as she said. That evening, after a dinner of pasta, sausages, taramasalata and carrots (an odd combination, I'll admit, but not necessarily a bad one), Debbie took out her old photo albums. In the 90s Debbie had been cycle touring around Asia and managed to get into Tibet just as the borders reopened. She showed me pictures of a very different adventure to the one I was having – one where she had called home once a month via a pay phone. Meanwhile, I was calling my mum about five times a day and finding it fairly unreasonable if she was ever busy and didn't want to chat.

Debbie ran with me around the Marloes Peninsula and pointed out her office, which sat right at the tip of the land. She told me how she ran along the coast path to work. I don't imagine there are many more scenic commutes out there. By lunchtime we had reached Little Haven, another 20 miles ticked off. The miles had flown by, spurred on by the good weather and the company and the incredible views. That night, I stayed with Carrie and her husband. They told me all about how they had eloped, and showed me pictures from their idyllic-looking wedding.

And so it went. Every night, somebody would tell me that they had a friend, a friend of a friend, who lived a little further around, and they'd put me in touch. Or I would arrange to stay with somebody independently, from an email or a Facebook message they had sent, only to find out that by pure coincidence I had stayed with their colleague, or their brother-in-law, or their old cat-sitter, the night before. I felt buoyed on by all the people I was meeting with their incredible stories of so many adventures completely different to my own, and to those that happened within the echo chamber around me.

I still felt tired from the long days of running, but tired in the good way. I felt physically tired now, from all the miles and the hills and the hours spent outside, rather than the mental exhaustion I kept getting tangled up in. I knew how to deal with the physical fatigue: eat, sleep, rest, listen to motivational power ballads. That was something I could manage.

And with the weather finally improving, the days getting longer and spring creeping in, I felt like I could finally appreciate all the beautiful places I was running through. The Pembrokeshire Coast Path is 186 miles in length, starting in Amroth in the south, where I'd begun it a few days earlier, and taking you around to St Dogmaels in the north. I'd heard that it was super varied in terms of the landscape, and I was already finding that to be true. In a single day you could find yourself running past a mixture of pristine beaches, red standstone bays, volcanic headlands, winding estuaries and glacial valleys...

Every day, I looked around and wondered why we ever bothered travelling abroad when all this was right here, on our little island.

———

In Fishguard, I was due to be staying with Jackie, who was one of the connecting links at the centre of everybody else I had met. She worked at the college in Haverfordwest and seemed to know everybody.

As I headed towards Fishguard, I was listening to a true crime podcast about a US soldier who was held captive by the Taliban. Running around Strumble Head, I convinced myself that a soldier was going to pop out from behind every rock and hold me hostage. It wasn't a very relaxing experience. I'd just about got over this trauma when I rounded a corner and saw an entire herd of cows scattered across the coast path. There was literally no way I was going to be able to force myself to run through them. Aware that this fear was getting out of hand, but powerless to do anything about it in that moment, I trespassed across a few fields (sorry, farmers) and took the road instead.

A few miles later, a car slowed down beside me. My immediate thought was, of course, *here they are, they've come to kidnap me.* Luckily the passenger wound their window down and I realised that it was just Jackie and her daughter Abbie, who was home from university for the weekend. They'd decided to come out for a drive and see if they could find me but, unsurprisingly, weren't expecting to find me right here, nowhere near the coast path.

"Fancy finishing up for the day?" Jackie asked. "I've got a Sunday roast cooking at home."

It was already late afternoon and I was only a couple of miles out from Fishguard – I could make those up no problem.

"Yes," I told Jackie, "I'd like that a lot," and climbed into the back seat, trying not to smear too much mud around.

Jackie had asked in advance if I wanted to stay for two nights and have a rest day and, as soon as I arrived at her house, I was glad I'd said yes. It felt like home – not my home, but definitely *a* home, which was enough. I spent my rest day hanging out with Alfie, Jackie's Miniature Schnauzer, watching trashy TV with Abbie and eating lots. It was great.

I didn't really want to leave. I was finding that being on the move constantly really accelerates your ability to settle in somewhere. And once again, it was those moments of normality that I enjoyed the most. I never wanted to take for granted the privilege of being invited into people's homes.

———

I was sad to leave Fishguard and Jackie and her family, but was helped by the fact that my own mum was on her way to visit me. That day, I ran as far as Newport, where my mum picked me up and we drove ahead to Cardigan, 19 miles further on, where we were staying for a few days. We planned to get the bus back the next day and then run that section into Cardigan.

The following morning we waited at the bus stop for well over 30 minutes, but the bus didn't turn up. This being the middle of West Wales, I didn't feel hugely concerned by the no-show and, to avoid wasting any more time, suggested we just run this section in reverse and then get the bus back to Cardigan at the end. It was the last section of the Pembrokeshire Coast Path and it did feel a bit strange to finish it backward, but it seemed like our best option.

The sun was out and we were stocked up with simnel cake and hot cross buns from the bakery. We ran along the cliff paths, climbing up and down over grassy humps of land. Wild flowers were blooming and we could hear the waves crashing against the rocks far below us. It was Good Friday and it was proving to be a very good Friday.

When we got near to Newport, I decided it would be nice to take a shortcut across the beach. From where we stood on the other side of the harbour, the sandy beach stretched out before us and it looked like an easy walk across, with just a slightly damper patch of sand in the middle.

Unfortunately, when we got a bit closer I realised that it wasn't just a damp patch of sand – it was an estuary, a fully-fledged flowing stream of water.

I looked at my watch. The buses on the coast of West Wales aren't exactly plentiful and I knew that we would miss the last one if we went back and followed the coast path route inland.

"We're going to have to wade across, Mum. I think you'd better take your shoes off."

She didn't look particularly pleased by this idea. Something you should know about my mum is that, just like my cousin Kelly, she has a tendency to feel the cold. We really didn't have another option though, so we stripped off from the knees down and set off. My tactic was to splash through as quickly as possible. My mum's tactic was to try and pick between the shallower spots. Within seconds she'd fallen quite far behind. Her tactic wasn't proving enormously successful.

"Elise, I've got brain freeze from my feet. I don't like this."

I reminded her of the imminent arrival of the bus and that spurred her on a bit. We made it to the other side, pulled our shoes and socks back on, and rushed into the village to wait at the bus stop outside the pub.

We needn't have hurried. Half an hour later, we were still standing at the bus stop. Again, being the middle of Wales, I assumed that it was just running a bit late. When 45 minutes had passed and there was still no sign, my mum decided to go inside the pub and ask if the timetable had changed. A couple of minutes later, she reappeared.

"The buses don't run on bank holidays," she relayed.

Ah. That would explain why the one this morning hadn't turned up either.

We went back into the pub as it was getting a bit chilly outside and the barmaid called what would prove to be quite an expensive taxi for us. My mum paid, which I felt bad about given it was my mistake, but not bad enough to offer to contribute given my dwindling funds.

Maybe not such a good Friday after all.

———

The next day we were running in the right direction and, although my mum did have a bus to catch later, it wasn't a bank holiday, so things were looking more promising all round. On the downside, it was pouring down with absolutely torrential rain and there was a yellow weather warning out for the gale force winds.

My mum is a petite person – you know, in the way that some people just have small skeletons. I had horrible visions of a sharp gust of wind blowing her off the cliff and – more terrifyingly – of me having to call my brother and sister and explain that I'd lost Mum. We decided to take the inland route instead of the coast path. This had the advantage of saving us a few miles as well as potentially saving my mum's life.

Within minutes of setting off, we were soaked. We tried to chat but could barely hear one another above the wind. We wondered, not for the first nor the last time, why we didn't spend quality time together by going to a spa or going out for lunch like other people did with their mums. Why did we always choose an activity that involves spending hours outside in unpleasant weather conditions?

By the time we got to Aberporth, where my mum was planning to catch a bus back to Cardigan to pick up her car and head home, she had started to go blue and her teeth were chattering furiously. *Not again,* I thought. I saw a cafe and ushered her inside.

Coasting

I'm going to make a bold claim, but one that I feel 100 per cent confident in saying: I have never received a warmer welcome than the one we got in that cafe. Within minutes of us walking in, shivering and dripping everywhere, we had been surrounded by electric heaters, handed giant mugs of hot chocolate with cream and marshmallows and had orders taken for steaming bowls of Welsh cawl (a traditional lamb stew). I saw the colour come back into my mum's cheeks and felt very relieved that I'd got away without giving another family member hypothermia.

It's hard to make conversation when all you can think about is the fact that you can't feel your fingers and how hungry you are, but once we'd eaten and warmed up a bit, we got chatting to Ellen, who owned the cafe. She asked why exactly we were out on such a horrendous day (a valid question) and I told her what I was doing. This resulted in a minor argument when she didn't want to let us pay for lunch and my mum being offered a lift back to Cardigan by another man who had overheard our conversation, instead of having to wait for the bus.

"I'm going that way anyway," the man told her. We weren't convinced that this was the case but she very gratefully accepted.

I ran on for a few more miles to Llangrannog where I was staying in a farmhouse for the night. The room I was sleeping in was freezing so I put my down jacket on and got under the covers in an attempt to warm up. I ate a slice of squashed simnel cake and half a bar of chocolate I'd found in the bottom of my bag for dinner. Both were a bit damp but I was just happy to be inside.

As I lay in bed that evening my mum phoned me, sounding quite embarrassed, to tell me that she'd left a puddle in the man's van seat where her clothes had been so wet. Her visit hadn't been without its hiccups, but I was glad she'd been able to experience first-hand some of the kindness I'd been telling her about for months.

————

When I was miserable in Kidwelly, after the Swansea meltdown, I had made a deal with myself: two more weeks. Just run for two more weeks, I told myself, and if you still want to go home after that, you can. This was meant to be fun, after all. I had a very keen awareness that I had chosen to be there and I knew how fortunate I was to have been able to make that choice.

Adventures like this – the meandering, wandering, self-indulgent kind, as opposed to the breaking new ground, exploring type – were to be enjoyed and not just endured. They are about grasping life with both hands and living out all of your most wild and wonderful dreams. Running 5,000 miles really serves no useful purpose beyond that and so I think I was right to worry when it started to feel miserable. If you're not enjoying it, on some level, then what's the point?

It ebbs and flows, of course, and there are always going to be bits that are hard and times you feel scared, but I felt strongly that it shouldn't be one long miserable experience, and if it was I was either doing it wrong or maybe it just wasn't for me. So when I felt really low, I always told myself I just had to stick it out for two more weeks, and if I had a great day in that time, then the clock reset itself.

Coasting

And guess what? There was always a good day before two weeks were up – often, there were lots of them. Laughing until my stomach hurt because my friend was running through a field of cows wearing a sombrero. That moment when I ran down to Freshwater West Beach in the early evening light and it looked as beautiful as anywhere else in the world and my legs didn't hurt and I felt overwhelming gratitude that this was how I got to spend my Mondays now. Curling up on Jackie's sofa with Alfie the Schnauzer and wondering what on earth we ever did to deserve dogs, and if Jackie would notice if I took him with me. Sitting atop a cliff eating the best hot cross bun I've ever had with my mum and thinking we spotted a seal on the beach below.

It had taken me just over two weeks to run from Kidwelly to Llangrannog and, in that time, there had been so many moments that were worth resetting the clock for. It was never easy – I don't know why I ever expected it to be – but I was glad I hadn't quit. Really, really glad.

CHAPTER 19

On Easter Monday, I declared it shorts season and ran/slid/ marched my way through nearly 27 miles of the Ceredigion Coast Path. It was the first time I had ever run more than marathon distance and it felt like a truly life-affirming day. It was a beautiful, remote stretch of coastline and the sun was shining. I had been forecast to have a date with Storm Katie but she didn't show and I've never been so glad to be stood up. I was joined for a few miles by Andrew, a theatre professor at Aberystwyth University, who came to chat about a running and a performance project his students were doing.

After hills upon hills upon hills, I made it to Ynyslas, just north of Aberystwyth. I was staying the night with Rachel, whose holiday home I'd stayed in back in St David's. Every time something like that happened, every time one place linked to another in some obscure way via the people I met, it made the whole country feel a little smaller and the whole adventure feel a little less daunting. It was a nice feeling. Rachel and her family were going on holiday the next morning and, as they rushed around me packing, I got the impression that it probably wasn't enormously convenient to have me stay that night. I felt even more grateful that they'd invited me.

Storm Katie caught up with me the next day. I woke up to the sound of rain lashing at the windows – but I'd already declared it shorts season and there was no going back on that. When I went downstairs to leave and say goodbye, Rachel's husband Ben nodded at my legs approvingly.

"I cycle a lot," he told me, "and we always cover ourselves in baby oil. Skin's waterproof, of course, but the oil just helps you repel the water. Want to try some?"

"Erm, okay." It was an unusual suggestion, but not the worst I'd heard. At least nobody was trying to make me wear their shoes.

Ben went off upstairs and came back with a bottle of baby oil that looked older than me. He handed it to me and I smeared the oil over my legs, trying to not get it onto my clothes too much. *Either this will work,* I thought, *or it'll make for a good story.* I can confirm that I've never again covered myself in baby oil before a run, so I'm sure you can guess which of those it ended up being.

From Yynslas, the coast path follows the Dyfi Estuary inland. As I ran through the wooded valley, rain sheeted down. I didn't notice that I felt much warmer, particularly, just rather greasy.

———

"How are you girls STILL chatting?" asked a man as Anna and I overtook him near the top of a hill. "I'm struggling to walk up here and you've run it without pausing for breath once."

He might have had a point. I could probably count on one hand the amount of times we'd paused for breath in the entire last 24 hours since Anna had arrived in Wales, and most of those were while we were asleep.

This was Anna McNuff of "The Email" fame, who I've mentioned several times already. She had come to run with me for a few days and we had arranged to meet in Machynlleth. Here, the coast path does a U-turn to take you down the other side of the Dyfi Estuary and deliver you back to the sea. I still wasn't camping and Anna wasn't sure where her tent was anyway, so I'd found us somewhere to stay on Couchsurfing. com. Although I'd done a lot of unofficial couch surfing on this trip, it was my first experience via the official (and somewhat notorious) site. I'd heard a few horror stories, but Sam, whose ad I had responded to, sounded friendly enough. He said he'd be in all afternoon and to just show up.

I arrived in Machynlleth before Anna and went to find where we were staying. Let's not forget that at this point I was soaked through from a very wet day's running and also still covered in baby oil. Sam answered the door and showed me around the house, which was part of a housing cooperative. It was a big place and there were quite a few of them living there. One housemate was away and Anna and I were sleeping in their room, so I guess we were actually bed surfing rather than couch surfing. Sam showed me where the shower was and left me to get changed. I was just in the bedroom sorting my stuff out when I noticed something on the duvet cover. I leant over to pick it off, thinking it must be a bit of fluff or something.

Coasting

It was a slug.

On further inspection, I noticed the rest of its slug pals gathering near the window. This one must have been feeling particularly intrepid when it ventured across the room. I'm quite good at getting rid of spiders and other creepy crawlies, but I had no idea what you're meant to do with a slug. In the end I went for the method of picking it up and throwing it out the window. I instantly felt very, very guilty. That poor slug. I was glad that Anna was the adventurous type – I wasn't sure how many friends would forgive me for arranging a bed full of slugs for them to sleep in.

After de-slugging the bed and de-baby-oiling myself, I went back downstairs and chatted to Sam some more while I waited for Anna. I learned with some surprise that, as well as Sam and the mysterious housemate with slugs in their bed, the then-leader of the Wales Green Party also lived there.

After a fairly damp night's sleep, Anna and I met her friend Emily for toast and coffee in a cafe.

Emily has done a huge amount of long-distance cycling and she arrived at breakfast on her bike, mid-training ride. Later that summer, she won the 2016 Transcontinental Race, a 4,000K self-supported ride across Europe, so I guess the training paid off. Emily was one of the people I followed on Twitter who seemed like Proper Adventurers. I guess the only thing that qualified these people for that title was the fact their Twitter bios told me they'd done some adventures, but in my head it was a birth-given gift and one I could never attain. I was merely somebody posing as a Proper Adventurer. It felt strange to be sitting eating toast and sharing a milk jug with these two, who were the real deal. It was even stranger to realise that they were just normal, nice people like me or you (if you are, indeed, a normal, nice person too).

After consuming most of a loaf of bread each, Anna and I set off. I was a little nervous to run with Anna, but it ended up taking the top spot for one of my favourite days so far. Given how many miserable days I've described to you, I'll admit that doesn't sound like much of an accolade, but honestly: West Wales really put on a show for us that day. It was really out-of-this-world wonderful. The sun shone in bucketfuls, Anna had brought an excellent buffet of snacks and the views were epic.

We ran up and up through the woods, where the walker commented on our non-stop chatting, then suddenly we were at the top of the hill. Where we had been sheltered before, now the views opened up before us. The landscape was a patchwork of fields made up of a hundred different shades of green, dotted with the occasional cluster of stone buildings. In the distance, we could just about see the sea sparkling – Anna's first glimpse of it, as we'd been running along the estuary the whole time so far. Even we were silenced for a few moments and Anna pulled out a bag of Haribo to toast the moment with.

The atmosphere was ruined when a flock of inquisitive sheep came over to see what was happening and I had to admit to Anna – bona fide Proper Adventurer, lest we forget – that actually I was a bit scared of sheep, too, and could we move on quickly.

"I could feel your fear," she told me later.

We ran down to Aberdovey and carried on for a few more miles. The coast path takes you straight across the wide sandy beach to Tywyn. As we know, running on sand isn't my favourite, but this sand was compacted enough to not be too traumatic, and how paradise-y it felt made up for it anyway. Anna took some very Baywatch-esque pictures of me gliding over the sand (if Pamela Anderson had also plaited her hair, wore thermals and sported a tapestry of chafing scars on her back...). We stayed in a youth hostel that night (no slugs, thank god) and the next day we ran another wonderful 18 miles together, before it was time for Anna to head home.

The whole still-not-camping thing did rule out spontaneity to some extent, but I was grateful to still be receiving so many offers of places to stay, from a huge variety of people – friends, friends of friends, B&B owners, the people watching my videos and following along online. It was this latter group who humbled me the most. Would I open up my home to a stranger on the internet? Maybe I would now, having received that kindness myself, but I'd be wary, for sure. I couldn't believe that people trusted me so much.

Organising the logistics of this was a task in itself though and, whenever I had a rest day, this was what I spent the majority of my time doing. I guess this is why people have teams behind them sorting out the admin. I liked being a one-man-band though. It still felt like a bit of a cop-out that I hadn't camped yet – the least I could do was sort my own logistics. It was nice to have something to think about aside from running too. Sometimes I thought I was much more skilled at the behind-the-scenes stuff than I was at the physical bit – but then, I suppose doing the bits that feel hard is what makes a challenge a challenge.

It was a constant juggling act of trying to keep track of offers I received (often somebody from Scotland would email while I was still in Cornwall, for instance) and then marrying them up with my provisional schedule which, despite my best intentions, ended up changing a lot depending on how tired or grumpy or distracted I got.

Understandably, when somebody offers you a bed for the night, they tend to like to know when you're going to turn up, which meant I was generally working on a lead time of a few days at least, and often a week or more. This had positives – it gave me a deadline, something to work towards. If I'd been able to just fling my tent up whenever I wanted, I'm not convinced I would have had the willpower to make it through the longer, harder days. It was generally the incentive of not wanting to let somebody down, and knowing I had a hot shower and some home cooking waiting for me at the end, that kept me plodding on.

This did all mean that it was very rare for me to start a day not knowing where I was going to end it, but that second day with Anna was one of those. I guess I must have just got swept up in all the excitement of having a nice time.

I hugged Anna goodbye in Barmouth and watched her get into her car and drive away. Then I sat down on a bench outside the Co-op and had a cry. I'd had such a great few days and now I was alone again. It always felt like this and it made me almost not want people to visit. A group of my friends had wanted to visit over Easter weekend and I had faffed around and made some excuses and generally made it very difficult for them to plan anything, until in the end they gave up trying to organise it. It just felt easier to separate my life out – there was all the stuff going on at home without me, then there was my adventure life that was happening around the coast. They both worked fine independently, but every time the two met I found myself having a wobble.

Coasting

I was just about to see if there was a hostel or anywhere nearby with a bed I could book for the night when I remembered a message from a Tom in Tywyn, the place with the Baywatch beach we'd run through the day before. He and his housemate Helen were outdoor instructors for Outward Bound and he had messaged me on Facebook to ask if I needed a place to stay when I ran through. At the time, I'd replied to Tom saying thank you but that it didn't quite fit with my schedule.

It was only a few stops back on the train though. Maybe the offer would still be open – it would save me some cash and it would be nice to meet some more people. I messaged Tom saying I'd messed up my plan and any chance he still fancied a house guest for the night?

"Sure, I'll pick you up from the station," he replied almost instantly.

I got on the train – which you had to flag down at some of the smaller stations, making me feel like I was in the Railway Children – and headed to Tywyn. I knew I liked Tom from the moment I got into his van.

"We're having a barbecue on the beach tonight," he said and we headed to the supermarket to pick up food.

Less than 2 hours after I'd been crying in Barmouth, I was on the beach in Tywyn, sitting around a campfire with a beer in one hand and a burger in the other. I had felt a bit weird messaging Tom so last minute, thinking perhaps it was too cheeky but, as kept happening, when I let them, things seemed to just fall into place.

CHAPTER 20

I spent a lot of my childhood holidays in Porthmadog and Criccieth, and I have some great memories of them...

There was the time our ancient car broke down on the beach and my aunt had to try to tow it with a 1-metre length of rope. The holiday cottage with a fire alarm that was set off by some bacon and then rang for 15 hours straight. The leaking tent that flooded with rainwater and had to be bailed out with a saucepan. When I tripped over a step, whacked my head and an enormous cartoon-style lump popped out, that my aunt tried to soothe it with some frozen turkey legs which she then fed us for dinner. All the times my dad tried to convince us to climb the wall into Portmeirion, the tourist village where *The Prisoner* was filmed, to avoid paying. The fateful walk to Criccieth where we got caught out by a surprise Welsh heatwave, had no water or sun cream with us and everybody got heatstroke. The tantrum I famously threw after that walk when I wanted lemonade but all that was on offer was water, coined "The Lemonade Moment".

Just your standard idyllic family holiday kinda fare.

In particular, I have vivid memories of spending hours upon hours of my school holidays on Black Rock Sands beach, rain or shine. There are pictures of my aunt cooking sausages wearing her swimming costume with two fleeces, a hat and a scarf. *No such thing as bad weather, just not enough items of fleece clothing,* as they famously say.

I ran across Black Rock Sands on the first Sunday in April and it was nice to be somewhere familiar. The start of April had marked the halfway point time-wise, if my ten-month estimation stayed true, although I was nowhere near completing half of the distance. I tried not to think about that too much. I felt like I'd been doing this forever, but I still had such a long way to go. I had been in Wales alone for over six weeks, and covered nearly 700 miles of its coast, but still had 200 miles left before I was back in England. Then there was Scotland, another whole country, to get around.

It felt never-ending. I needed something to get excited about, something to achieve in the short term.

Enter "Project Peninsula".

———

The Llyn Peninsula is a finger of land that sticks out of the north-west corner of Wales. It is sometimes called the "Land's End of Wales" and has 110 miles of coastline running around it, if you call Porthmadog the start and Bangor the finish. The peninsula has protected status and as such is one of the least developed parts of the whole Wales Coast Path. It's full of history and wildlife and Welsh culture, with endless, remote stretches of sea views. The Wales Coast Path website suggests that you walk it over nine days. I thought I'd liven things up a little by attempting to get around it in four back-to-back marathons.

The first mistake I made was that I didn't call Porthmadog the start. From the Wales Coast Path website you can download distance charts covering the entire route, all 870 miles of it. They are very useful. I would highly recommend taking a look at them if you're ever planning a trip. However, being over three-quarters of the way around the country at this stage, I had spent far, far too much time staring at those charts. I don't have the best eyesight and all the tiny boxes had begun to blur into one. I misread the charts in my planning stages and thought that my four-marathons-in-four-days needed to start in Pwllheli, not Porthmadog.

This meant that when I set off from just past Pwllheli on what I thought was the first morning of my fun, exciting challenge, I was actually 18 miles too far along the route. This unintentional head start kind of ruined Project Peninsula, turning my four marathons into a less impressive sounding 3.5. To make things worse, for the first 5 miles of that day I was running along with a hot, greasy sausage in my pocket, wrapped in a serviette, which I had felt too rude to leave at breakfast that morning. I wasn't sure how much throwing a sausage into the hedge would help the local ecosystem and it was a while before I found a bin.

Project Peninsula wasn't off to a great start. It didn't get much better.

There was a coast path diversion in place, which meant several miles of navigating a labyrinth of sheep fields, knee-deep in mud for the most part while the sheep baa-ed at me aggressively, clearly as unhappy as I was about me being in their fields. I also seemed to be having some kind of allergic reaction to my backpack – I could feel the pin-pricking sensation of chafing, which was starting to burn.

I ran to Aberdaron, where my first full day on the peninsula was due to end. I hadn't been able to find anywhere to stay there so had booked a bed in a bunkhouse that was inland a little, not too far away but in the middle of nowhere. The internet assured me that there was a bus that would take me there. I dashed into the chip shop, picked up some fish and chips for tea, and rushed to the bus stop.

"Can you drop me here, please…" I asked the bus driver, showing him the name of the bus stop on my phone.

"Oh, we don't go there," he said.

"But you're the bus to Abersoch, aren't you? It says you go down this road."

"Yes, that's us, but I don't know where that stop is." I showed him the route map on my phone. "No, no idea at all. Sorry love."

"But you do drive down that road, don't you?"

"Oh yes, we do go that way."

"So maybe if I keep an eye out on my phone, could I just tell you when we're near, and then you can drop me at the closest stop."

"If you want love, but how do I know how much to charge you if I don't know where I'm taking you?"

"I can just pay the full fare to Abersoch, if you like, then it won't matter where I get off?" My chips were getting cold, I had layer upon layer of mud and cow muck and sand drying in solid lumps all the way up my legs, and I just really wanted to get on the bus. The driver agreed to this plan, although a little reluctantly, and off we went.

I watched the blue dot on Google Maps (my trusted companion) move along as we swerved around the narrow country lanes. When it looked like we were getting close to the elusive bus stop, I pressed the bell. Not a minute later, the driver pulled up to a bus stop sign sticking out of the hedge, exactly where my map told me it should be.

"Oh, you should have told me you meant here, love!" he said as I disembarked.

I wasn't sure how exactly I could have made it much clearer, but was relieved to have made it.

The bunkhouse was adjoined to a farmyard. I walked around, knocking on a few doors and disturbing some chickens, but couldn't find anybody. I turned a corner and saw a building that looked like it could be the bunkhouse. Inside, I found a group of walkers, who I'd be sharing with for the night, and an envelope with my name on, containing a key.

"Mountain biking?" one of the walkers asked, looking me up and down. I followed her gaze. I was quite muddy.

"Erm, no, running. Flooded sheep fields." She laughed and called some of the rest of the group over to take a look at me. They were in their late fifties, I guessed, and were here for a few days to do some walking around the peninsula.

"We're heading into Abersoch to find a pub for dinner, if you want to join," somebody offered. On the one hand, the idea of a beer was very appealing. On the other, I'd already eaten and just really wanted to have a shower and sit quietly and not talk to anyone. The prospect of the latter won.

"I'm okay actually. Thanks though, have a good evening."

Coasting

We chatted a bit longer and then the walkers left for dinner, leaving me with the place to myself. I headed through the bunkhouse to find the shower room, stripped my disgusting kit off and inspected my back in the mirror. It was not a pretty sight. It was bright red and covered in angry raised sores where my pack had rubbed. There were gooey patches where the clasp of my sports bra had embedded itself into the skin and then been prized away. I can't think of many sensations more unpleasant than water on friction burns, and I knew that showering was going to be a grim experience. If I didn't have about five fields worth of mud attached to my body, I probably would have skipped washing and just gone dirty for the night. That didn't really seem like an option, sadly.

I turned the hot water on and edged myself under it, inch-by-inch, limb-by-limb. I went in front-first but soon the water started dribbling down my back too. It felt like I was being assaulted by thousands of tiny, hot pokers. I screamed aloud with the stinging shock of it. I lasted long enough to get the worst of the mud off, then turned the water off, slightly breathless with the pain of it all.

I wasn't carrying a towel with me, having not deemed it essential (unlike other things – the Rubik's Cube, for example, which I was still carting around). Normally this meant attempting to dry myself using the corner of a T-shirt or something, but it turned out that not having a towel wasn't too much of a problem that day. There's no way I could have rubbed myself with it anyway. Instead I stood in the cold shower room to drip dry, then dressed again, wincing.

It's difficult to convey quite how awful chafing is, if you've never experienced it badly. I remembered myself on Day One, complaining about the tiny strip of redness on my lower back. *She had no idea,* I thought.

––––––––

I caught a bus back to Aberdaron the following morning and, with the help of most of a tub of Vaseline, made it through my second peninsula marathon without losing too much more skin on my back. I stayed at a pub in Nefyn that night, where I ate a lot of chips and went to bed at 8 p.m.

From Nefyn, the Wales Coast Path stops following the coast so closely and instead you start climbing upwards. Of everywhere I had run so far, the history on this section felt almost tangible. First you reach St Beuno's Church, a twelfth-century place of worship, sitting on the old pilgrim route. From St Bueno's you cross National Trust land towards Nant Gwrtheyrn, the Welsh language centre located in a former quarrying village. The village, which sits in the shadow of the Yr Eifl mountain range, was abandoned when the quarries closed in the 1930s.

Nant is nestled into the hillside above a pebble beach. As I descended towards the water, I was joined briefly by wild goats that ran ahead of me on the narrow path, before realising I was there and darting away into the bracken. It was an overcast day and the rusted relics left behind by old industry appeared spookily out of the mist.

I reached the visitor centre and figured this was as good a time as any for a break. It was here, lingering over coffee and wi-fi that I realised my mistake in miscalculating the mileage for Project Peninsula. I was looking at the distance charts, feeling slightly melancholy about the fact it would soon be time to leave Wales, and realised that Nefyn and Clynnog Fawr, where I was due to finish up that day, were actually only 13 miles apart. This was both a pleasant surprise (I was kind of tired by this point) and a disappointment (I stubbornly didn't want to be defeated in my mini challenge). My options were either to carry on to Clynnog Fawr as planned and take the afternoon off, or push on further and get ahead of schedule.

I was mulling over which option to take as I left Nant Gwrtheyrn. I climbed an inexplicably steep hill and saw a cluster of signposts pointing in various directions. A quick spot of googling told me that these marked the trails that would take you either up and over or around the three peaks of Yr Eifl. In a desperate attempt to prolong my time in Wales and absorb a little more of the peninsula, I quickly let go of my afternoon off and went and climbed a mountain instead.

I reached Bangor the following evening having run 92 miles in four days, including one surprise mountain. I might not have quite managed four full marathons, but Project Peninsula had served its purpose: I felt like I'd crossed a finish line, like I'd achieved something. The past few days had felt like a real adventure, whatever that was. The creeping boredom had been blown away.

But perhaps the biggest thing I took away from those few days was discovering the surprising sanctuary a Wetherspoons can provide, after whiling away several hours in one in Caernarfon. It's cheap, you get unlimited free coffee refills, there are plug sockets and good wi-fi, there's no judgement from anybody when you stay for hours and you can almost certainly guarantee that you won't be the scruffiest person in there. A kind of safe haven for adventurers.

CHAPTER 21

It was my last Saturday in Wales and I was sitting on the floor in front of a building site in Llandudno with Harriet and Chris. Chris was somebody else I'd met through the Yes Tribe in London and his girlfriend Harriet's parents lived in North Wales, so they'd come to run with me for the weekend.

"We'll bring lunch," Chris had said – as if I needed any persuasion to have some company.

We had met at the train station in Conwy that morning. Unintentionally, we had all managed to wear entirely matching running kit (unintentional on my part anyway – given that I only had one set of clothes that had been visible in all my pictures and videos, it's entirely possible that Chris and Harriet had planned this). We made our way around the Creuddyn Peninsula looking like a fairly rubbish amateur sports team.

It rained heavily all morning, which is why when we reached Llandudno we chose to stop for lunch in the bus shelter behind the building site. It wasn't the most picturesque of spots but it was undercover. I had been running behind Chris for most of the morning, trying not to get dropped on the uphills. I hadn't been able to help but notice that his rucksack looked quite full, considering they'd come from Harriet's parents that morning and we were heading back there together that evening.

Sitting in the bus shelter, I learned that when Chris said, "We'll bring lunch," he had really meant it. Out came a feast including, but not limited to, some incredible roast chicken sandwiches and a whole red velvet cake. We were lacking in utensils, but I ceremoniously cut the cake with my slightly rusty penknife.

Earlier on in the day, Chris and Harriet had mentioned they were keen to go for a post-run swim. Here's where I have to make a confession: I had been running around the coast of Britain for nearly six months at this point and, with the exception of that one paddle on the Gower with Alex, I still hadn't got in the water. Admittedly it hadn't been the most swimming-friendly weather, but this didn't change much once summer arrived either. Given that I'm a fairly fanatical all-year round swimmer these days, I'm sure this will go down as one of my biggest regrets in life. So much wasted opportunity.

We finished up running for the day in Colwyn Bay, where Harriet's car was waiting, and decided to start heading back to her parents' and find somewhere to swim en route. I'd run past countless tempting-looking swim spots over the past months, even if I hadn't been getting in the water. So many secluded bays with golden sands and sparkling turquoise water. The stuff of holiday brochures. As we drove along, I imagined myself running into the water somewhere like that.

Instead, we pulled up beside the Menai Strait, the narrow strip of water separating the Isle of Anglesey from the mainland.

It's potentially the muddiest, sludgiest, least alluring stretch of the Welsh coast you could possibly choose for a dip in the sea.

We got changed in the car, rain lashing at the windows. None of us actually had any swimming kit on us – Chris had it easy with boxer shorts and I was wearing my running shorts and sports bra. Harriet decided to brave it with knickers and a sports bra. There was nobody else around (weirdly the Menai Strait in the rain isn't a tourist destination) so it didn't really matter what we looked like. We were just about to get out of the car when a mother and child appeared.

"Erm, Haz, maybe we should wait a minute," Chris warned when he saw them. Admittedly, a leopard print thong maybe wasn't top of the list of child-friendly swimming attire. We waited for them to walk a little further away and then made a run for it.

It was equal parts invigorating and gross.

Afterward, we drove back to where Harriet's parents' family lived and spent the rest of the afternoon drinking beers in their swimming pool, walking the dog and eating everything in the fridge. The next day, Harriet and Chris ran another 14 miles with me around to Prestatyn.

I was excited to run to Prestatyn. It was the scene of one of our most memorable family holidays when, one year, we had strayed from Porthmadog to go to Prestatyn Pontins instead. Legend has it, there was a sign on the front door of our apartment saying that, in case of fire, please make sure you take the cutlery with you. I would have only been about nine at the time, but when I ran past on that gloomy Sunday afternoon, the holiday camp looked even more like a correctional facility than I remembered.

I was a little sad – I'd missed a trick by not trying to book in there for my last night in Wales.

———

Monday morning dawned and it was my last day of running in Wales. It passed by fairly uneventfully, a blur of hot cross buns, satsumas, Elton John albums and thoughts about how nice it was that my feet were dry (as most of those last 25 miles were on the road, away from any mud). The official Wales Coast Path route finishes a bit further inland along the River Dee, but I swung a left at Queensferry and ran beside the A494 until Google said I'd crossed the England/Wales border, where I pronounced Wales finished. Nothing like a dual carriageway to mark the end of something special.

Although not the most breathtaking of days compared to some of the scenery I'd run through in other parts of the country, in a way I was happy that my last day had been so uneventful. Wales as a whole had been an emotional roller coaster. There had been times when I thought I might flood the south coast with all my tears, but also countless really, truly amazing days. All the incredible people who had opened their homes to me and made everything seem a little less scary, a bit less lonely.

And the actual running itself – finally, I felt like that I was something I was able to do. There was a lot of trial and error going on and maybe I still didn't look like you would imagine a serious ultrarunner to, but my legs were happily churning through mile after mile, day after day, without too much complaint. What more is a runner than just somebody who runs? All it takes to be the kind of person who does a thing is to actually do that thing – there is no more context needed than that.

I had one and a half countries left to run around. I still felt terrified by that prospect but I also felt that perhaps it was possible. I wasn't sure how I had got this far, but I had, and that had to count for something.

CHAPTER 22

I stayed with Jo in Chester for the first two nights I was back on English soil. She went out to work while I had a rest day and I got to hang out with her two lovely dogs. Perhaps more than the running or the people or the sense of achievement, it was the amount of time I got to spend befriending other people's pets that made this whole thing feel worthwhile.

From there, I ran around the Wirral, where I met my dad for his monthly visit. We took a ferry 'cross the Mersey and were thrilled when they played the song during the crossing. We ran through Liverpool together, past the Bootle Docks and out to Crosby where Antony Gormley's 100 cast-iron figures are scattered across the beach.

My dad had brought with him two things for me: a new pair of running shoes, and my camping gear. As the days were starting to get longer, the weather warmer and the terrain more remote, I figured it was probably time I started to think about pitching a tent. One problem: I wasn't sure how I was going to fit it all into my bag. Somehow, although I thought I'd packed lightly, my stuff seemed to have expanded to fill my whole pack each day. And perhaps I hadn't packed that lightly – I was still carrying that Rubik's Cube around, after all.

Before he could leave, we spent about an hour trying to wrestle my tent, mat and sleeping bag into my rucksack. We just about managed it, utilising every outside pocket and stretching the front mesh to its max capacity, and my dad triumphantly pulled the drawstring closed and fastened the straps. We still had the problem of how I was going to run with it though – my pack had felt heavy enough even without the camping kit in it.

I hugged my dad goodbye and left him leaning against his car, watching as I took my first few steps with the added weight. It felt like running through treacle, like I was hopping from foot to foot on the spot without making any forward progress. I could feel the straps of my pack pulling down against my shoulders.

I had nearly 3,000 miles left to run. If I was to keep to my original ten-month plan, I needed to run them in less than half the time I'd taken to cover the first 2,000. I was heading into the more remote sections, as I attempted to navigate my way around the Scottish Highlands, and now I had this monster strapped to my back.

I wasn't sure how exactly I was going to manage it.

———

Back at that first Yes Tribe campout, where I'd stood around the campfire and announced my plan to run around the coast of the UK, I had met Sean, who I mentioned had recently completed a Land's End to John o' Groats, length-of-Britain triathlon. Shortly after, he set off in his next adventure – a coast of Britain triathlon. Our paths crossed in Southport while he was on the cycling leg of this challenge, which would become the world's longest continuous unsupported triathlon (4,200 miles in total).

We met for lunch in Frankie and Benny's. In a bid to take on calories quickly mid-adventure, Sean has a reputation for eating fairly horrifying things like a roast dinner blended into a smoothie. I was pleased that we just ate some pasta together instead. We spent an hour or so exchanging adventure stories, before Sean had to shoot off to ride a few more miles before dark. His schedule was clearly a little tighter and less aimless than mine.

We were leaving the restaurant when a couple with a small child appeared in front of us.

"We're big fans," they told Sean, "we really wanted to say hello. We saw you go in but didn't want to interrupt your lunch. Could we have a picture?"

Sean took a picture with the family, clearly unphased. This must be what it was like to be a celebrity, I thought. It wasn't just fans following Sean around though – the world's longest triathlon attempt was being filmed for a documentary on the Discovery Channel, so he also had a film crew travelling with him. As I said goodbye to Sean and walked away, I could hear him chatting to the cameramen.

"We've found somewhere for some good shots – can you head there and cycle up and down the hill a few times?" they asked Sean. I decided then that pro adventurer life maybe wasn't for me. I had a hard enough time finding the energy to run up each hill once.

I was planning to camp that night, in my newly retrieved tent. I was happy to be able to tell Sean this, when he asked my plans for the evening. I still felt real imposter syndrome whenever I spoke to anybody I deemed to be properly adventurous (and to most other people too, actually), and saying "I'm going to stay with a lovely family and eat a home-cooked meal and let them do my laundry" just didn't help my case.

I still wasn't quite ready to brave wild camping, but there was a scout campsite by the seafront that looked like a good bet. The website showed that there was plenty of space but the online booking form wasn't working, so after saying goodbye to Sean I headed to the campsite to ask if they had room for me.

"Yes, we have plenty of space," the man on duty told me.

"Great – how much is it for one tent? Do I pay now?"

"Oh no, you can't stay tonight, sorry."

"Why...? Is it caravan only?" I asked, although looking around I could see plenty of tents.

"No, we just can't take bookings on a Saturday I'm afraid."

"But there are lots of other people pitched up..." I gestured to all the people around me. It was late afternoon, people were cooking sausages on their camp stoves and opening bottles of beer, kids running around playing. These people were very clearly staying there tonight.

"Yes, you can *camp* on a Saturday, but you need to book in advance. We can't take payment on a Saturday."

It was one of the most ridiculous things I had ever heard. There was an empty pitch, I had a tent, I was offering money to put my tent in that pitch. I was always seeing people fundraising for the Scouts yet here they were turning down my money. It seemed absurd. I carried on trying to persuade him for a while, asking if I could pay cash, or pay tomorrow instead, or do a bank transfer. I came up with plenty of sensible options but it was clearly no use. And I'd made myself so well known to this man now that I couldn't just quietly pitch up in the corner and make a donation later.

I walked away from the campsite feeling very disgruntled and, for a lack of other options, found an overpriced hotel with some availability to book into instead. Another dent in my budget that I very much didn't need. Although quite how much I didn't need it, I wasn't sure – I was still avoiding my bank balance like the plague.

————

Four nights later I finally got to pitch my tent, at a small campsite on a farm just north of Blackpool.

It had taken me nearly six months to put that tent up and, when I finally did, I made a terrible job of it. The outer sheet didn't line up with the inner, and I hadn't pulled the ropes taut enough. I woke up freezing cold with damp material flapping in my face, my lightweight sleeping bag maybe not warm enough for the still-quite-chilly April weather. Perhaps it was for the best that I hadn't attempted to camp during the winter.

But still, I felt accomplished waking up in that tent. I'm not sure why I cared so much, but the entire time before that I'd felt like I was cheating somehow – camping seemed like such an integral part of everybody else's adventures and I had copped out by avoiding it for so long. It felt like a real relief to not be carrying the burden of that worry any more. Just as a physical weight had been added, equally an emotional one had been lifted.

The next night I camped again, this time right by the sea in Bolton-le-Sands, just north of Lancaster. I did a better job with tent erection that night and woke up to the most incredible sunrise over Morecambe Bay as my reward, a kaleidoscope of reds and pinks and oranges.

I didn't feel like I was cheating any more.

———

From where Wales ends to where Scotland begins is a relatively short hop up the western coast of northern England. Or so I thought at the time, at least – evidence of how warped my sense of time and distance had become. From Morecambe Bay I had just over 150 miles left until I reached Scotland, which would take about a week, I hoped.

Except, I found I suddenly had no motivation. My legs weren't playing ball and while Cumbria itself is great, home to the Lake District and a paradise for anybody who likes walking, or running, or who has eyes, I probably wouldn't recommend travelling around its coast on foot. The Cumbrian Coastal Way once would have guided you around, but it's no longer endorsed or maintained by Cumbria County Council, nor is it marked on OS maps any more (of course, not an issue in itself for me given that I still couldn't read an OS map at this point). In its absence, I plotted myself a hodgepodge route made up of the occasional nice trail connected by various roads, which varied from a bit hairy to downright dangerous.

Some of the waymarkers for the Cumbrian Coastal Way were still up and occasionally I tried to follow them. This was generally a bad idea, as I found out running from Grizebeck to Haverigg on my way on from the Furness Peninsula and back towards the coast proper.

I was only about 3 miles into the day when the no-longer-maintained coast path signs vanished completely, leaving me stranded on the A595. If you're not familiar with the A595, it is one of Cumbria's primary routes, linking the south of the county with Carlisle and Scotland in the north. It's a notorious bottleneck, a fast and busy road, and the stretch of it that I was standing crying beside had no footpath, no verge of any significance, and was full of tight bends and tall hedges. Think of a road that's absolutely not suitable for running down, then amplify that, and you're probably not far off the A595.

I tried one footpath sign coming off the road, but it took me to a dead end. I came back to the road, cried for a while (a tactic that had proved entirely useless in every difficult situation so far, but one which I persisted in trying) and then saw another footpath off to the left just ahead. I vaguely knew of a path running alongside the estuary, roughly parallel to the road a mile or so away, and thought that perhaps this footpath might connect to it. I headed down it, feeling hopeful.

A few hundred metres down the track I came to what looked like a derelict farmhouse. There was nobody around and it looked a bit dodgy, but the footpath sign was definitely pointing me through so I unhooked the stiff gate and pushed it open.

Out of nowhere, I heard the snap of a chain being pulled tight, and then there was a huge, black dog baring its teeth at me and going for my ankle. Thank god it was on a chain or I think it would have had my foot off. I backed out of the gate in shock, and headed back up to the track as fast as I could, wanting to be as far away from the farmhouse as possible.

I really wasn't sure what to do next. A farmer on a small ride-on lawnmower appeared just as I was having a moment of particularly snotty crying.

"What's the matter, eh?" he asked. I explained about the dog and the Cumbrian Coastal Way signs and how lost I was.

"Just walk across this field and you'll find another footpath to take you down to the estuary. You'll be there in no time." He was right, but I still felt a jolt of panic every time I saw a dog for the next few weeks.

———

As well as the route-finding stress, the Cumbrian weather gods didn't seem to have got the message that a) it was spring, and b) I had embarked on my camping career at long last. As I made my way north, I was hit by day after day of hailstorms. I had sent my running leggings home with my dad thinking I'd be fine going shorts-only from here on in, which was proving to be a huge mistake. Hail on skin is an unpleasant sensation, to say the least.

A few days after dog-gate, I was running beside another A-road (luckily this one had a footpath, but still not exactly the sort of terrain you dream of as a trail runner), being attacked by the stones falling from the sky and really questioning my life choices. Then, up ahead, like a beacon of hope shining out through the dense grey sky, I saw a New Balance factory outlet store. I couldn't believe my luck and headed straight inside to buy some new running tights.

"Can I use the changing room to put these on?" I asked the cashier once I'd paid. She looked me up and down, saw my pack and my now red-raw legs, and clearly decided not to ask what I was doing running along such an uninspiring route in such horrible weather. I was glad she didn't ask – I would have struggled to give her any sort of plausible explanation.

I was wondering the same thing myself, to be honest.

CHAPTER 23

It was the end of April but there were weather warnings for snow across the country. I wasn't enough of a sadist to carry on camping in those conditions (further proof that my original plan to camp all winter would never have worked) and I booked into a bunkhouse for my last night in England before I crossed the border into Scotland. As it happens, I probably would have been just as warm in my tent. And not only was it freezing, the bunkhouse had the added disadvantages of also being filthy and full of snoring men. It wasn't the best night of my life and I woke up early the next morning eager to leave, having slept in my coat.

I was terrified about running around Scotland. It felt like a huge, looming unknown; I just knew that it was big and remote and I didn't like Irn-Bru. I think my fear of getting around the UK's northernmost country played a big part in a lot of my earlier wobbles, even if I didn't quite realise it at the time. It was the awareness of the fact that no matter how far I'd already run, there was still this hulking great country that I hadn't even started yet. Around the time of my Swansea wobble I had even considered turning this into a duathlon, and cycling the Scotland leg instead of running. It would be quicker on a bike and I would be able to get further in a day, useful if I needed to escape from anything. It felt less daunting that way.

Considering the amount of time I had spent thinking about, and dreading, my entry to Scotland, it was largely unremarkable. The route over the border took me along the Hadrian's Wall Path into Carlisle, then on footpaths alongside dual carriageways and then onto a B-road that runs parallel to the M6 and takes you into Scotland. It was perhaps the least scenic stretch of my whole run so far, but that was okay. I had half expected to be plunged into wilderness as soon I stepped over the border. However mundane this alternative was, it made it easier to imagine myself surviving Scotland.

After 13 miles, and having taken about 50 selfies by the "Welcome to Scotland" sign, I reached Gretna Green. I ducked into the Old Toll Bar Cafe to find a toilet, as my A-road/ motorway route had been lacking in facilities. At least, I thought that the Old Toll Bar was just a cafe. It turned out that it was actually Gretna Green's historic wedding venue and for the small price of £310 I could invite ten friends to witness my legally binding nuptials. Sadly I didn't have a spare £310, ten friends or anybody to marry in the near vicinity, so it wasn't a deal I could take advantage of.

I carried on up the road a little and came to the Gretna Gateway Outlet Village. Inside there was a Cadbury chocolate discount store so I went and bought some misshapen chocolate instead. This seemed like a better memento from Gretna Green than a husband.

I had been offered a B&B room for the night, which I was very happy about given the sudden return of winter. I was standing outside the shopping centre looking at my phone and trying to figure out where to go when a passer-by stopped and asked if I needed directions. I told her where I was going.

"Oh, but that's another mile away. You won't want to walk that far, will you love. The bus stop's just across the road."

As always, I thought it was probably easiest not to explain.

———

It rained solidly for the first five days of May and then, less than a week after the weather warnings in Cumbria, summer arrived in Scotland while I was somewhere between Kircudbright (pronounced Kir-koo-bree, apparently, not Kur-cud-bright) and Gatehouse of Fleet. It happened rather abruptly – so abruptly, in fact, that I finished the day with a very fetching mid-forehead tan line from my headband.

Just after lunchtime on the day that summer arrived, I ran past Cream o' Galloway, a working dairy farm with a cafe and visitor centre. I went in to get an ice cream and refill my water bottles, when I saw something that filled me with both horror and hope: an invitation to "Meet the cows". After months and months of avoiding cows, taking detours, crying every time I saw one... perhaps this was my chance to come face to face with one. Immersive therapy, wasn't it called? The next tour was at 3 p.m., just over an hour later. Surely a chance to overcome my phobia was worth waiting for, I thought, heading to the counter to book onto the tour. I got my ticket, bought my ice cream and sat down to read my book.

At about 2.45 p.m., one of the cafe staff approached my table.

"I'm afraid nobody else has booked onto the 3 p.m. tour, so we're going to cancel it. I'm sorry about that."

Looking around the cafe, this wasn't surprising. The tour was clearly intended for children and, being midweek during term time, there weren't any about. It might have been a bit awkward to do it by myself, as an adult, I have to admit. But still, I was devastated to be leaving the Cream o' Galloway with my bovinophobia still in tow.

The last few miles of the day took me through woods bursting with bluebells. The sun was shining and I was listening to a new playlist I'd put together the day before. A song by The Wombats came on. The lyrics talked about one person's hobby being moaning, and the other's being making money. I used to listen to that song and think of me and Greg. He was forever telling me that I moaned too much, and making references to how much money he made. I would listen to it and laugh about how apt it seemed, although I'm not sure it was ever actually particularly funny. But when those lyrics came through my headphones as I ran through the bluebells, I wondered if they were still true. Then it occurred to me that perhaps they had never been true. Perhaps, instead, these were just the stories that Greg had told me and that I had chosen to believe.

As far as I could tell, I was more than six months into a 5,000-mile self-supported run, my main objective of which was to enjoy it as a priority above anything else. And, as far as

I knew, Greg was still living with his parents and studying for his undergraduate degree.

Was I moaning? Was he making money?

It didn't seem like it.

What else hadn't been true?

———

With the same speed that winter had become spring, spring became summer – if not officially, then in the weather at least. I ran from Wigtown (known as Scotland's National Book Town, aka a place I would highly recommend visiting) to Whithorn, and all I wrote in my diary was "super hot and great" which just about summed it up.

That night in Whithorn, I sat and thought about what a good day I'd had. The winter had been wonderful in so many ways and I was so glad I hadn't given up, but often it had felt like a slog. It had been something to endure, and the challenge was in trying to enjoy it, at least a bit. This felt like my reward for all those long, cold days. My feet weren't constantly wet any more. I had a ferocious T-shirt tan brewing. I could sit on the beach and eat ice cream when I needed a break. And I was getting stronger – I could run mile after mile after mile, and then get up and do it again the next day.

In some ways, that was all great. In another, it made me want to do more. If running back-to-back 20+ mile days had somehow become normal, what would be next? What could the next iteration of "normal" look like?

From Whithorn, I was running around to the Rhins of Galloway, a hammerhead peninsula that is home to the Mull of Galloway, the southernmost point of Scotland. There are quite a few "mulls" in Scotland. The term comes from the Gaelic word "maol" and just refers to any land formation bare of trees – it could be a hill, summit, mountain, headland, anything really.

Caisie, yet another person who I'd met through the Yes Tribe, had offered up her mum, Suzanne, as a host for the night. Suzanne lived in Ardwell, which was 33.5 miles away from where I was sitting in Whithorn. I was meeting my dad for another of his visits in the next couple of days and really wanted to have made it down to the Mull of Galloway and started heading back up before then. Splitting the section to Suzanne's into two would have put me behind that schedule and knowing how great Caisie was, I really didn't want to miss meeting her mum.

There was only one logical solution for it. I would have to run a 33.5-mile ultramarathon the next day.

One problem: I had never run that far before.

———

A freak May heatwave decided to join me for my impromptu ultra. Scotland was hotter than Ibiza and Istanbul that day. It was nearly 30 degrees and the air was completely still, so it felt hotter. The quiet road closely hugged the shore for most of the morning, making for fairly easy running. I stopped in the shade of a tree to smear face cream all over my body because it had SPF in and I hadn't got any sun cream. At one point, I thought my water bottle must be leaking, only to discover that it was my own sweat dribbling down the back of my legs.

I split the distance into 5-mile chunks in my head and ran along dreaming of ice-cold Fanta and singing along loudly to Queen songs. I passed the half marathon mark at 13.1 miles and felt okay, but was struggling to picture myself running almost twice that distance again. Twenty miles in and things were getting tough – my legs felt okay but it really was very hot. At around the marathon point I was thrilled to pass a corner shop, and surprised the man behind the counter by buying four cold drinks and two ice lollies.

Nearly 30 miles in I reached Sandhead where there was a holiday park. I ran down the long drive, hoping to fill my water bottles up again. Despite the heatwave making it feel like midsummer, it wasn't peak season yet, but the park was still busy with families enjoying the weather. I went into the restaurant to ask for water and saw they had a woodfired pizza menu.

I had already achieved my goal of running an ultramarathon that day. Perhaps I could just stop here, pitch my tent, order a pizza, look out over the bay and pat myself on the back for a job well done.

But Suzanne was waiting for me, and I'd already made my daily video where I clearly told the camera that I was 27 miles down, six to go. It was a silly thing but the thought of re-filming those videos, or admitting I'd failed was always enough to spur me on. Once I'd said something on camera, it was too late to change my mind. Reluctantly, I ran back up the driveway of the holiday park and started making my way to Suzanne's. I tried to call her to say that I was running a little behind schedule, but I didn't have any phone signal.

I was overjoyed when I reached the address Caisie had given me – really, properly relieved that I got to take my pack off and stop running. Nearly 9 hours had passed since I set off that morning, and the combination of the heat and the sweat and the long day meant that I had once again rubbed off most of the skin on my back. The last few miles had been pretty uncomfortable.

I rang the doorbell, and then again, but no answer. I checked the address; this was definitely the right place. I walked around the back of the house but there was no sign of anybody there either, although I did see a tap, so I took the opportunity to refill my water bottle again.

I took my backpack off and sat on a low wall, wondering what to do. Had we got our dates mixed up? When would Suzanne be back? How long should I wait for? I remembered the holiday park again and I could see myself very clearly with my tent pitched overlooking the water, eating a pizza with a cold beer in hand. I tried to push the vision from my mind. This wasn't helpful. The thought of running another 4 miles back there made me want to cry.

Just as I was thinking I might actually cry, I heard the crunch of tyres on gravel and saw a big white car pulling into the driveway, with a woman who looked very much like she could be Caisie's mum behind the wheel. *Hallelujah*. Suzanne stepped out of the car.

"I came to find you because it was getting a bit late, but you must have taken the other road. Anyway, I thought you might like these…"

She handed me a cold bottle of Lucozade Sport and an ice lolly. The sight of condensation running down the sides of the bottle… I'm sure that I heard angels sing. I tried to maintain some sense of decorum as I tore open the wrappers.

Suzanne took me into the house, showed me to a spare room with a shower, and handed me a pair of clean pyjamas of Caisie's that I could borrow for the night, so that we could wash all of my kit. After I'd showered, Suzanne cooked fish with potatoes and vegetables for dinner and showed me around the house, letting me look at the beautiful, intricate ballet costumes she embroidered by hand.

I slept so well that night, the kind of tiredness you only ever feel after a long day outdoors in the sunshine.

I'd done it, I'd run more than 30 miles, and it hadn't even felt that hard. I remembered the version of myself who had felt completely done in after 17 miles on that first day. It was only six months ago, but I barely recognised her.

The next day, I ran down to the Mull of Galloway, at the tip of the peninsula. It was an out-and-back run, but I didn't feel like I could miss the most southerly point of Scotland. I stood by the lighthouse looking out to sea for a moment before turning around.

It was time for the final pull north.

CHAPTER 24

Trying to work out a route around the messy tangle of land that is the west coast of Scotland was difficult. There are so many different peninsulas and lochs and fingers of land with just one path running down the middle. As is hopefully clear by now, I didn't feel too strongly about sticking religiously to the coast. I just wanted to see as much of the country as possible via a route that was safe and pleasant.

When I looked at the map, the route that made most sense to me involved some island hopping. This would let me skirt around some of the craggiest edges of the mainland, while ticking off some of the islands that Scotland is so famous for. It seemed like a win-win solution to me and I felt no qualms whatsoever about not taking in every single nook and cranny of the west coast.

From the Rhins of Galloway, I made my way north again. My dad came to join me for a few days as I ran up the coast towards Ayr. In Ayr, I went to Sports Direct to buy some new running shorts as my ever-growing quad muscles had split my last pair at the seams. Ged, another Yes Triber, picked me up from Ayr and I spent a couple of days in Glasgow with her where she introduced me to famous Scottish delicacies like lorne sausage (just a square sausage, from what I can tell) and haggis, neeps and tatties (haggis, turnip and potato). She then dropped me back to Ayr and I ran up to Adrossan to catch the ferry over to the Isle of Arran and commence my island hopping.

There was a large supermarket near the ferry terminal in Ardrossan and, knowing I was starting to head more into the wild, I stopped there to stock up on some supplies: a plastic camping mug, some porridge oats, a jar of peanut butter and some Vitamin C tablets. I was ready for anything now.

———

As soon as I stepped off the ferry in Arran, I knew that I loved it. There was just a really nice feel to the place. It was early evening on a Friday and there were lots of people milling around the harbour, wearing down jackets and walking boots, clearly ready for a weekend of adventure.

My plan was to skirt around the northeast shoulder of the island, running from where the Ardrossan ferry drops you in Brodick to Lochranza, where I'd take a ferry over to the Mull of Kintyre, back on the mainland. I had originally thought that perhaps I should run the whole Arran Coastal Way, but I didn't really need to and figured I probably wasn't at the stage where I should add miles on. Best to leave that for another time, I thought.

Coasting

On my second night on Arran, I stopped at a hostel, where the owners had offered me a bed for the night. In the bar that evening I got chatting to two couples in their 70s who were walking the whole coast path over a week. They asked what I was doing, and I told them about my trip. They sounded very impressed as I tried to big up what a brave, rugged adventurer I was and left out all the bits about crying on grass verges.

The next morning I set off before the two couples and started making my way up to Lochranza. The coast path took me right down to the shoreline, and I scrambled between rocks, admiring the rugged coastline. The Arran Coastal Way takes you over a boulder field here. It's slow going, but if you're lucky you might spot dolphins and basking sharks. Running anti-clockwise around the northeast shoulder of the island I could see the mainland to my right, sitting across the Firth of Clyde, which separates it from Arran.

I was busy trying to balance watching out for dolphins and avoiding tripping over any boulders when I saw a ram ahead of me. It was standing right in the middle of the path, blocking my way through.

Of course, you already know about my fear of cows. A few weeks earlier, in a bid to overcome this, I had done some research about what I should do if a cow ever chased me. I figured some practical solutions might help put my mind at ease. I ended up in a Google black hole and found myself reading about the best combat techniques to use against a variety of different farmyard animals. One of the articles talked about rams.

Apparently, so this article said, if a ram ever looked like it was going to charge at me, I shouldn't turn away and run.

Instead, I should face it head on and look it in the eyes, asserting dominance. When it ran towards me, which it inevitably still would, I should grab it by the horns, and spin it around. This wouldn't be enough to scare it off though. No, it would almost certainly charge again, perhaps up to 50 times, and I would need to keep repeating this process of grabbing it by the horns and spinning it until it got tired and gave up – 50 times! Rams are stocky things. I didn't have the upper body strength to spin one once, let alone 50 times.

From then on I was terrified – not so much of the ram itself, but of the prospect of having to attempt to grab one by the horns and spin it. It's this fear that paralysed me on the Arran coast path. I didn't dare get any closer, just in case.

Could rams swim? I wondered. If not, maybe I could get into the sea and swim past it instead. Clearly, this was a terrible idea, so I reluctantly turned around and started retracing my steps. Arran is fairly remote in places and I knew that I'd have to run quite a way back before I found a footpath that would take me up to the road. I would have taken any added distance over swinging a ram though.

I hadn't got too far when I saw the two couples I'd met last night coming towards me.

"You're running in the wrong direction!" one of the men shouted when I got close enough.

"Well, erm, there's a ram up ahead..." I explained about the ram, and how I was going back to find an alternative route. I could tell that my being scared of a sheep wasn't doing much for the brave adventurer persona I'd attempted to convey the night before. They very kindly didn't laugh at me too much.

"Come with us, we'll get past it okay," one of them said.

So, I turned around again and was escorted to safety. We sat down for a snack together and then I carried on, nursing my dented ego but feeling very relieved I had managed to live another day without swinging a ram.

———

I was sure that I had read somewhere that the ferry from Arran would drop me in Campbeltown, in the south of the Mull of Kintyre. This turned out to be fake news. The ferry actually dropped me at Claonaig in the north and it took me another three buses to get down to the bottom of the peninsula. When I first decided to run around the country, I had been drawn to the simplicity of it – and there was something very grounding about only having one change of clothes. But, once again, the logistics of it proved to not actually be that simple. There was a lot of being in the wrong place at the wrong time and ferry timetables not quite lining up.

I probably wouldn't have bothered with this epic public transport journey all the way down, just so I could run straight back up – as you know, I wasn't being too strict about seamlessly running every inch. But I was staying with Mary in Campbeltown, who ran a small B&B from her home but also worked at the local primary school, Castlehill. The school had been taking part in the Daily Mile scheme, where all the pupils run or walk a mile around the playground every school day. They'd invited me to come along and join them for their Tuesday run and I really didn't want to miss it. It's such a great scheme and the teachers all reported having seen huge benefits since they started the previous September.

They had been out come rain or shine and said the children seemed healthier, happier and more alert in lessons.

I was glad I made it. If you ever lose your running mojo, I highly recommend going for a run with a bunch of excited nine-year-olds to regain it. Once we'd done our Daily Mile, I sat down with the kids to shed some light on the most important aspects of running adventures, such as "Do you still have all your toenails?" (Yes) and "What happens when you run out of food?" (Cry, normally).

The icing on the cake was that one of the teachers who lived a bit further up the peninsula offered to take my pack and drive it home with her, and I could pick it up later when I passed. Being freed from the shackles of my backpack for the afternoon was such a treat and I ran through 16 miles of scenery and sunshine that afternoon.

By the next day I was starting to run out of ways to say "Scotland is really beautiful". The heatwave had dialled down a bit and it was almost perfect running weather. I spent most of the day gazing back towards Arran, which was perched across the water looking magnificent. I stopped by another primary school to answer some more questions about snacks and toenails and where I went to the toilet (the main thing most children seem to want to know – in answer, the more populated sections of the coast are well-serviced with public toilets, and everywhere else there was always a bush). The school only had 15 pupils, which I thought sounded small until they told me that the one up the road only had three.

I ran through a village later that afternoon and stopped by the corner-shop-cum-cafe. I paid for a slice of cake and a drink and asked the man behind the counter if he would mind filling up my water bottles.

"We're on a water meter, don't you know. You'll have to buy bottles."

This was the first time in nearly seven months that anybody had refused me water. I went to the fridge and looked at the water. They only had tiny bottles for sale. They were £1.50 each and I would need about five to keep me going for the rest of the afternoon. It was such a waste of money and plastic.

"I understand… but I am buying cake and a coffee too, I am a paying customer," I tried to plead.

"I can't just be giving out water for free, I'm sorry."

"How about if I pay a bit extra to cover the water meter costs? I really don't want to buy so many plastic bottles when I have my own. It's such a waste."

"If I let you I'll have to let everybody. The answer is no."

I looked around. There wasn't anybody else in the shop. In fact, I'd barely seen another person all day, let alone hordes of tourists demanding water. It seemed so completely unreasonable and I regretted having already bought the cake and coffee – I didn't want to give this man my custom at all. He clearly had a tap full of perfectly good, clean drinking water – *that I was offering to pay for* – but he was insisting on selling me bottles instead.

I left without any water and the remainder of the afternoon was a thirsty one. Luckily, that was the one and only time anybody refused me water, and I didn't have to try to quench my thirst with my moral high ground again.

CHAPTER 25

There were some days that made all the hard bits feel worthwhile. The 22 miles from Kilberry to Lochgilphead felt like pure running magic. The day started with a bowl of porridge topped with blueberries and Nutella – how far downhill can a day that starts with Nutella really go? I ran along the stony shores of Loch Caolisport, past bobs of seals bathing at the water's edge, through the forests of Argyll and Bute and beside Loch Fyne. It was like running through Narnia – gentle trails leading through dense greenery to these sea lochs with water clearer than I could ever imagine seeing in the UK. It felt more like somewhere I had dreamed up – I couldn't believe it was real.

I reached Lochgilphead much earlier than expected and called Steve, who I was staying with that night.

"I can finish work in about an hour," he told me. "Find somewhere to grab a coffee and I'll come and pick you up then."

I met nice people everywhere I went (water-withholding cafe owners aside). Time and time again, I was blown away by their kindness. Yes, I was raising money for charity, and I'm sure that inspired some people to help me out, but mostly this was just a kind of weird, very self-indulgent thing that I had decided to do on a bit of a whim. The fact that people were going so far out of their way to make it easier for me was very humbling. I was so grateful for every warm bed, hot meal and clean load of laundry. But more than that, I was grateful for all the eye-opening conversations, for the glimpses into people's lives, for the acceptance they showed me.

And every now and again, I would come across a little pocket of people who just seemed extra special. A web of people who showed a real sense of community, who took me in and passed me around and made somewhere completely new feel familiar for a while. The Mid-Argyll Triathlon and Cycle Club, of which Steve and his wife Hazel were members, was one of those pockets.

Steve picked me up once he'd finished work and drove me to his house where he lived with Hazel and their two sons, Callum and Keiran. After I'd showered and put my most horrible kit in the washing machine, we drove over to their friend Rebecca's house for dinner.

Rebecca was also a member of the triathlon club and, after dinner, she got her map out and we started working out the best route for me to take over the next few days up to Oban. It was one of the more complicated sections to figure out. If you look at the map, you'll see that Lochgilphead is on the east of the finger of land that makes up the Kintyre peninsula. It isn't really an option to run along the more obviously "coastal" westerly shore though – there aren't footpaths that follow the edge of the land, and where they do exist it's often just an out and back. It was more a case of hopscotching my way north, sticking to the wiggly western coastline wherever possible, but being fairly relaxed in my approach to it.

So when Steve asked, "How much do you care about sticking to the coast?" I responded truthfully by saying, "Not very much."

To get to Oban following the most coastal route from Lochgilphead, they explained, you had no choice but to run on the busy A816 for at least some of the time. At best it wasn't very nice, and at worst it was dangerous. A much better idea, they suggested, would be to veer inland a little and run beside Loch Awe, before taking a left across to Oban a little further up. This route actually added about 10 miles on, so I certainly wasn't doing myself out of any mileage. I didn't take much convincing.

Steve, Hazel and Rebecca had organised for a relay of runners from the triathlon club to come and join me for various sections of the next day. One of the most exhausting things was the lack of any familiarity with my surroundings and constantly having to think about where I was going, where I needed to be next, how I was going to get there. I was excited both to have some company from the Mid-Argyll runners and for them to take charge of the route for the day.

For the first part of the next day we followed the Crinan Canal, which was pancake flat. Lots of different people from the tri club came to join me for various sections of the first 10 miles, up to Kilmartin where we stopped for coffee and cake. From there, I was carrying on alone for a while until Hazel and Steve caught up with me again a bit later.

"Where are you ending today?" one of the men asked as we finished our coffee and got ready to set off again.

"Dalavich," I told them. There were a few raised eyebrows and some stifled laughter.

Coasting

"Oh, that road's a roller coaster that is."

I was used to being given fairly exaggerated warnings of upcoming terrain, but usually it was from people who didn't run or walk themselves. These guys clearly knew what they were talking about though and I was a little worried.

The first few miles from Kilmartin were only gently undulating and I started to relax. It had been drizzling lightly all morning but the sun came out and the views onto Loch Awe opened out in front of me. Some passing motorcyclists stopped to chat and even offered me a swig of wine from their flask. Hills, I thought, what hills?

Then the roller coaster began, and there were some brutal ups and downs. It was different to the vertical valleys of the coast paths, where you were almost on your hands and knees and had no choice but to walk. Here, the road sloped gently enough to start with that you felt like you should keep running, but then kept going up and up and up, before you plummeted back down.

Steve and Hazel came and found me and took it in turns to run a few miles while the other drove ahead. Their chatting distracted me from my burning quads and soon we were descending into Dalavich. A folk festival was in full swing and our arrival timed perfectly with a round of applause that I happily pretended was for us. We had an ice cream on the grass and watched the band for a while, before driving back to Lochgilphead to spend another night in Steve and Hazel's spare room.

Kieran, Steve and Hazel's son, dropped me back in Dalavich the next morning. It was time to fly the Lochgilphead nest and after several days without it, I strapped my fully loaded pack back on and headed off towards Oban. Oban was 27 miles away and my main aim was to get there before Tesco closed to stock up on supplies and buy some dinner.

I was around 7 miles from Oban when I saw a herd of Highland cows blocking my way. They were on the path, on the grass either side of the path, on the little bridge of a stream, in the stream. There was no way around – I was going to have to go through.

Maybe it was because I had that deadline of arriving before the shops shut, or perhaps it was because I was in such a good mood after the few days I had spent being looked after by Steve and Hazel and everybody else. I'm not sure why but somehow I didn't feel as scared as I normally would. I ran straight through the herd, who didn't pay me a blind bit of notice, and made it out the other side unscathed.

My bravery didn't last but it was nice to experience it, just that once.

My original idea was to run straight up to Fort William from Oban, then head further west from there, towards the Isle of Skye. Rebecca had pointed out that this maybe wasn't a great idea, due to the fact that I'd have no choice but to run along the A82 for the last stretch, which was a notoriously dangerous road. Much better, she suggested, to nip across to the Isle of Mull instead, run halfway around the island and then get a ferry back to the mainland to Kilchoan, on the west coast. I'd be skipping Fort William but, as it's inland anyway, this didn't feel particularly problematic – it was only ever a means to an end.

"And my friend Becky lives on Mull. I'm sure she would put you up. It'll be Monday night, right? Let me just call her."

Coasting

Just like that, my next few days were planned. I spent a night in the hostel in Oban and then took the ferry over to Mull. I ran along the east coast of the island, beside the Sound of Mull, up to Tobermory in the north, where Becky lived.

I knocked on Becky's door after just over 20 miles of running. She handed me a peanut butter sandwich and showed me where the shower was.

"I have choir this evening, would you like to come along?" she asked.

If there's one thing you should know about me it's that I am completely musically illiterate. I'm tone deaf and I can't clap in time. I can't hear notes or beats. When I dance, music plays and I move, but there's absolutely no correlation between the two. A choir, therefore, is not exactly my natural habitat. But when in Rome and all, so I got into Becky's car with her and off we went. I was relieved when, rather than being asked to join in, I was instead shown a seat in the auditorium where I could sit back and watch the choir rehearse for their next show.

A relief for everybody involved, I'm sure.

———

"Elise!"

I was running along trying not to melt in the continuing heatwave when I heard somebody shout my name. This was a surprise: I was in the middle of the Scottish Highlands and I hadn't seen anybody at all so far that day, let alone anybody I knew. I squinted into the bright sun and saw, running towards me, a figure in a bright pink T-shirt with a mop of white hair.

"Simon?!" I called back.

A few weeks earlier, I had received a message from Simon on Facebook. Simon was also attempting to run around the British coast. He had set out from North East Scotland on Easter weekend and was running anti-clockwise, the opposite way to me.

I had only run about 3 miles so far that day and it wasn't really time for a break. I couldn't pass up on the opportunity to compare notes with Simon, though. We found a small patch of shade on the grass verge and spent the next hour laughing about how ridiculous this whole thing was.

We both decided that we should probably get moving again – less because of any time pressure and more because we were being eaten alive by midges – and said goodbye. My brief roadside encounter with Simon had given me a boost though, and I ran away smiling.

Doing a big adventure often feels like living in an alternative reality, one that revolves around frantically topping up on sugar and electrolytes and midge spray and Vaseline at regular intervals. It turns out that just running and eating and sleeping (and trying to remain somewhat cheerful at the same time) takes up a lot of headspace. It was sometimes difficult to explain to people how it was simultaneously the best and worst and most wonderful and hardest thing I'd ever done. Just as I'd found so much comfort in talking to Wayne about the endless soggy paths and wet feet over the winter, it was so relaxing to sit and chat to Simon for a bit and know that he just "got" it. It was during those surreal Jesus-Christ-why-are-we-doing-this conversations that it all felt like it made the most sense.

CHAPTER 26

I only planned to skirt around the corner of the Isle of Skye, just as I had with Arran and Mull. It was meant to just be a way to join the dots between different parts of the mainland. I caught a ferry from Mallaig over to Armadale, in the south of the island. I was planning to only be there for one day, which was as long as it would take to run the 22 miles from Armadale to the Skye Bridge.

The heatwave from earlier in the month was continuing. It had been one of the hottest Mays on record and looked set to carry on into June. It was a Sunday morning when I set out from Armadale into the blazing furnace. There was no shade. I called my mum and all I remember saying is that I was hot, very, very hot. Fifteen miles in, I reached a crossroads. I could either go right to continue the last miles on to Kyleakin, where the bridge back to the mainland is, or I could turn left to Broadford where I knew that a mile up the road there was a shop that would sell me a buffet of cold drinks.

I'm sure you can guess which option won.

I stayed near Broadford that night. The next morning I packed up my bag and headed to Kyleakin, where I booked into a hostel for the night, still on Skye. I finally managed to get myself over the bridge on Tuesday morning – only to inexplicably find myself on a bus travelling back onto the island before I knew it. The bus took me to Portree, Skye's capital, where I ended up staying for three more days.

I'm not sure what happened, I just felt very strongly that I didn't want to leave Skye. It is a beautiful island, sure, and perhaps I really did just want to explore it for a little longer. Perhaps I just needed a rest, I don't know. Either way, it took me until the following Thursday, nearly a week after I'd arrived for my one day on Skye, to get the bus back over the bridge and pick up my running route again. I spent those days sitting by the harbour reading my book, napping in the hostel, wandering around the town and enjoying the freedom of not having to carry all my belongings with me at all times.

———

Three days after my impromptu holiday on Skye, I was crying on the banks of Loch Torridon. My dad had come for his June visit and had met me in Plockton, the so-called "Jewel of the Highlands". We were spending a few days running, camping and eating a lot of locally smoked fish together in one of the most beautiful places I had ever been. I should have been having a great time. These are the kind of father-daughter experiences they make wholesome American made-for-TV movies about.

Coasting

But I wasn't having a great time at all. It seemed to be a trend that I'd end up having a bit of a meltdown of some kind whenever my dad came. Perhaps it was just because I knew I could do that in front of him. As much as I loved meeting so many new people, it was sort of exhausting pretending that you were a nice person *all the time*.

The source of this panic was that I'd run out of money, again. Getting through winter had destroyed my budget and now I had no reserves. It was easier to spend less during the summer when you could hang out outside, rather than whiling away hours by shivering next to heaters in coffee shops. But then that in itself was a problem because camping more meant I didn't have as many opportunities to do the questionable freelance writing jobs I had been topping up my adventure funds with.

I had finally got to the point where I felt like I could do this thing physically – but now I couldn't afford to carry on.

Every now and again, somebody would comment on one of my videos or blogs asking if they could make a donation to me, personally, to virtually buy me a coffee or a beer. I always thanked them and just directed them to my charity fundraising page instead, telling them that I would really prefer it if they donated there instead. Above all else this was just a jolly, a kind of gap year that just happened to sound more virtuous than drinking fishbowls of cocktails on a beach in Thailand.

Although fundraising for charity wasn't the primary reason I was doing this, it seemed that some people actually wanted to give. I was putting time into sharing my journey online and, as I've said, if that inspired people to donate some money to causes I thought were important, then so be it. I wasn't going to complain about that. Of course, I was also benefiting personally from the interest and goodwill generated by this too. Some kit brands had gotten in touch to offer gear and I had been gifted lots of B&B and hotel stays, as well as all the other people who were letting me stay.

But the idea of asking anybody following me for cash? The thought of that made me feel deeply, deeply uncomfortable, even when they did offer. I was so far into the journey now that it would have felt almost like I was guilt-tripping them. *I've come so far, I can't carry on without your help…* I couldn't do it. This was my own fault. I should have planned better, drunk fewer coffees, sucked it up and braved camping over the winter, been more frugal…

These are all the things I was telling my dad as we sat in his car, by the loch, at the end of a long day's running. I'm a failure, I told him, over and over. I can't do anything right. Maybe I should just give up now.

"Do you want to just borrow some money, Elise? You only have to ask."

It isn't very adventurous to get bailed out by your dad though, is it? But I didn't feel like I had another choice. It was that, or quit. A few days later, he had transferred a chunk of cash into my bank account as a loan.

"How did you afford it?" is one of the questions I get asked the most. I want to a) be transparent about how I paid for the adventure, and b) acknowledge that it won't be possible for everybody to do it the same way I did. I've mentioned already what a big part I think privilege plays in adventure and it's something I don't think it's possible to overstate. It's something that I'd like to talk about more but I don't, perhaps because I'm worried that I'll get it wrong, explain something in the wrong way, unwittingly offend somebody. Ultimately though, I am very aware of how enormously privileged I was to have somebody who was able to bail me out when I needed it.

When I do get asked that question, the first thing I say is that despite me failing to complete it as frugally as I hoped, my adventure still wasn't particularly expensive, not when you compare it to rowing across an ocean or going to the South Pole or climbing Everest. I don't think it's helpful to quantify what is a little or a lot of money, because that will vary so much from person to person, but even with all the cafe stops and extra hotel rooms, I'd still say mine was on the more modest end of the spectrum. Certainly, I spent less over that ten months than I would have living my normal life in London over the same period – much less. I wasn't paying rent or hoarding clothes or buying rounds of shots for strangers on nights out. And in some part that's down to the amount of generosity I encountered along the way. I was lucky that, for whatever reason, people seemed to engage with my story. If it wasn't for all the people who put me up, there's no way I could have afforded accommodation throughout the whole winter.

I financed my trip using a combination of money I saved from working full time before I left, winning an adventure grant, some cash sponsorship from my old employer, working freelance on the road and then, eventually, this bailout from my dad. I wildly underestimated how much I would spend and feel very lucky to have somebody who could pick upthat slack for me. Even if my dad did threaten to make me list "D J Downing Gardening Services" (his one-man band gardening business) as the headline sponsor… I don't want anybody to think that I'm either not grateful for that, or that I'm naive enough to think that's an option open to everybody.

———

We camped together for one more night and then I hugged my dad goodbye in a car park in Kinlochewe. I felt a little lighter now that I knew I would be able to finish my lap of the coast without begging for money from the general public.

Twelve miles into what I thought was going to be a 25-mile day I saw a footpath sign shooting off the road. It was pointing to Poolewe, which is where I was heading, and said that it was only 7 miles away. A quick bit of arithmetic told me that this would save me 6 miles. It also looked like it would take me along a nice trail instead of the road. Result, I thought.

I followed the sign down a track headed through some amazing woodland. After a little while I came through a clearing to see Loch Maree right in front of me, shrouded by the surrounding mountains. Definitely an upgrade from the road, I thought.

At that very moment, the heavens opened and I was soaked within seconds. The heatwave had gone, it seemed. Then the lovely trail that I had been having the time of my life prancing along become a slippery, boulder-strewn uphill scramble, as I attempted to spot the cairns disappearing in the mist. There were also a few near misses with some frogs who were lurking on the path and came very close to having a heavy foot land right on top of them. Bracken caught my legs with almost every step, leaving angry red scratches on my skin.

But when I arrived in Poolewe, I was happy. Tired and wet and scratched and filthy – but happy. I felt as though all the tears and panic of the past couple of days had been washed away. I'm not sure that there's a more exhilarating, life-affirming way to spend a Sunday afternoon than running 20 miles though the highlands in the pouring rain.

After changing into dry clothes and warming up, I called my mum to tell her about my afternoon, about how great it had been, how alive I felt.

"Oh Elise, you know how your shortcuts turn out," she said when she picked up the phone, having already seen my Facebook update.

You can always rely on your mum to bring you back down to earth.

It was still raining when I woke up the next day. I had another 25-mile day on the cards, around to Little Loch Broom, where I had a hostel bed waiting for me. I pulled my sopping-wet kit back on and ate a post-breakfast slice of cake for courage before eventually setting off. Outside, it was like running with a tepid power shower suspended above me.

Rain is fun until it stops being fun. I had just about reached that point when I ran past a man who was out in his front garden chopping logs. He called hello and I stopped to chat, relieved to have an excuse to stop running up the huge hill that his house was near the top of.

He introduced himself as Rob and asked where I had come from and where I was going next. When I told him that I had come from London and was heading back there now, he looked surprised and laughed.

"I sailed around the coast of Britain once!" he told me, in a fantastic turn of coincidence. I instantly felt like we were part of the same club.

Standing still to talk is tricky because that's when the midges start feasting, so we couldn't chat for too long. As we were saying our goodbyes, I tried to flick a piece of dirt off the back off my knee but it wasn't budging. I realised, with a mixture of horror and pride, that it was a tick. My very first tick! It felt like an adventure rite of passage.

My dad had been going on at me to buy a tick removal card for months but, as with most of the sensible advice he attempts to give me, I hadn't listened. Not to worry though, Rob assured me that a blunt penknife would do the trick and, lo and behold, he happened to have one in his pocket. He deftly removed the little trespasser from my leg and held it up for me to look at.

"Not quite what I expected to be doing today," he said, which just about summed up my feelings too.

This whole bizarre encounter cheered me up considerably for the remaining 11 miles. The sun even broke through the clouds for some incredible early evening views over Little Loch Broom. All's well that ends well.*

(*But I wouldn't recommend doing what I did. I've since learnt that removing your ticks incorrectly with an old penknife, or allowing a stranger you meet by the side of the road to do so, can actually end quite badly. It's a good idea to carry a tick-removal card with you when you're out and about.)

Coasting

I had mostly been following the NC500 route around the Highlands so far. It's a scenic route intended more for cars and bikes than for feet. It was only June though and the school holidays hadn't yet begun, so there wasn't a huge amount of traffic. If you look at a map of NC500, you'll see that it snakes around a lot and almost doubles back on itself at times. As I'd found trying to plot my route around Oban and Fort William, there was no straightforward way to plan a route around the Scottish Highlands. Even if I had wanted to stick completely to the coastline, it often wasn't an option due to a lack of footpaths, and there were so many ins and outs. You'd think you could go one way, then a huge great loch would appear. I'm not sure it would even be possible to plan the same route twice – if I did it again, I've no doubt it would look completely different.

It was frustrating, at times. The way the route wiggled around, it felt like I wasn't getting anywhere at all. I would sometimes run 30 miles in a day just to end up on the other side of the loch, only a stone's throw from where I'd started. For every decision I made about the route, every new place I got to visit (like the island hopping I'd done around Mull and Skye), it felt like I'd missed somewhere else – it was impossible to go everywhere. But this whole area was so beautiful and, as long as I avoided the main A-roads, everywhere felt quiet and safe. I had to plan my days more carefully, making sure I didn't miss the one place along the way where I could buy food, or refill my water bottles, but I liked the peacefulness that the sparsity brought. I could run for miles and miles and not see another person. I'd often felt scared in some of the more populated sections, but here, in the wilds of Scotland, I mostly just felt calm.

Mostly – but not always.

I'd chosen to head around to Ullapool after staying at the hostel by Little Loch Broom. I was planning to carry on following the NC500 along the main road.

I told the hostel manager this just before I set off. He didn't seem impressed.

"Oh you don't want to go that way," he said and led me over to the wall where there was a map hanging up.

"There's a trail you can take instead, it will save you some distance and mean you skip a chunk of the road. Just turn left at the waterfall and follow the track. You can't miss it."

Turn left at the waterfall and follow the track. He made it sound so simple.

Half an hour later, I had found the waterfall, but the same couldn't be said for the track leading away from it that apparently I couldn't miss. Eventually, after scrambling up a grassy hill and poking my head through various clusters of trees and fences, I saw what I assumed must be the trail.

It was a shortcut and it did skip a section on the road, that much was true. What the man in the hostel had failed to tell me was that this was a full-on mountain trail that took me over two summits. It was so mountainous that I saw mountain goats, which is evidence if nothing else. As we've now mentioned many times, at this point *I still can't read a map*. I felt completely ill-equipped to be up there. I was having terrible visions of having to be saved by Mountain Rescue and the newspaper headlines that would follow.

Luckily, it was a fairly clear day and after god knows how many miles of chewing me up, the trail spat me back out onto the road. The A835 is a busy road and attempting to dodge the oncoming traffic did nothing for my already frazzled nerves. By the time I made it to Ullapool, I felt well and truly done in. Luckily, I had a room in a pub B&B sorted for the night. I'm not sure I was capable of putting my tent up.

There was a bath in my room. This seemed like a better bet than the shower because it didn't involve standing up. As I sat down in the hot water, I was convinced that moles were suddenly popping up all over my body, appearing before my eyes.

I got out of the bath as quickly as possible and called my mum.

"I'm growing moles!" I told her, frantically.

"I think you just need to have something to eat and go to bed. It sounds like you're a bit tired."

I took her advice and, sure enough, when I woke up in the morning there were no new moles to be seen.

It had taken nearly eight months, but it had finally happened: I had actually gone mad.

CHAPTER 27

A campervan slowed beside me.

"Hello, it's very hot, would you like to come inside for some orange juice?" a woman asked, peering out of the door. She was right, it was very hot. It did cross my mind that I was about to be abducted, but it was a chance I was willing to take for some shade and a cold drink. I climbed up into the van, and the lady introduced herself and her husband as Hannie and Markus. They had come over from the Netherlands to spend a few weeks touring around the Highlands. Markus was into cycling, so was doing some rides too.

Hannie handed me a cold carton of juice. It tasted like an elixir. I was very happy.

"Where are you running to?" Hannie asked.

"I'm heading up to Durness today. I camped in Scourie last night."

"Oh, that's a long way." She wasn't wrong.

Coasting

It was already nearly three o' clock in the afternoon and I was still 22 miles away from Durness. I had actually only run 3 miles so far that day. The problem was that I had lost any sense of urgency. It was 18 June, nearly the longest day of the year, and it stayed light until past 10 p.m. Now that I was camping more, I often didn't have an arrival time I needed to meet. I knew that I could just put my tent up whenever I wanted. This had turned me into the most terrible procrastinator – every morning I'd sit around for hours before eventually starting to run around lunchtime. Every day, I'd curse myself for it when it was 8 p.m. and I was still running and swore I'd get up early the next day. The day before, I'd left myself with a full 28 miles to cover in the afternoon and had ended up with a mad dash when I realised I might not make it to Scourie before the chip shop shut.

For somebody who is usually quite uptight, I was getting awfully relaxed.

I couldn't complain too much, though. If it wasn't for my procrastination, my path wouldn't have crossed with Hannie and Markus's and I wouldn't have been sitting in their lovely, cool van drinking orange juice.

It was swings and roundabouts, I suppose.

———

I had another long day on the cards the next day, 30 miles from Durness to Tongue. I'm not sure why I suddenly decided to start running such big miles, day in day out. Perhaps it was because I was so close to John o' Groats, just a few days away, and I just had it in my head that I was on the home straight from there.

I did learn my lesson from the previous day and set off from Durness at a much more reasonable time, well before lunch. The day got off to a bad start when I ran past a gift-shop-cum-cafe, intended for all the NC500 traffic. I went inside and bought some fudge. I was very excited until I stopped for a break a couple of miles later, opened said fudge and discovered that I had accidentally bought whisky flavour. I hate any kind of alcohol-flavoured confectionery and I especially hate whisky. The disappointment was almost unbearable. I'm sort of joking but also sort of not – it's these little things that keep you going, and when they don't live up to expectation it can feel crushing.

Then it started raining. As the rain fell harder, I got slower. I was trying to play games with myself to move faster – run until the end of this song, run until the next tree, that kind of thing – but it wasn't really working. It was a Sunday afternoon and the chances of me getting to Tongue while anything was still open were getting slimmer by the minute.

In my pack I had some oats and a sachet of hot chocolate that I'd stolen from a hotel a few weeks ago. I tried to get myself excited about eating cold oats, water and a hot chocolate sachet for dinner, but with the rain pouring down and nearly 90 miles in my legs over the past three days, it wasn't quite hitting the spot.

I must have looked fairly miserable trudging along because every car that passed slowed down to offer me a lift. Each time, I wanted nothing more than to say yes, but instead I plastered on a grin and said "No thank you" and tried to make it look like I wasn't actually having the worst time ever.

There was a campsite about a mile this side of Tongue where I had planned to stay. With every step I became more tempted to just stick my tent up where I was standing and wild camp instead, but for a long stretch there had just been bog either side of the road, no firm ground to pitch on. The filter in my water bottle also really needed replacing, and the thought of making my cold oats and hot chocolate special with not-quite-clean puddle water made it even less appetising.

Finally, I saw some lights up ahead. I remembered, with a jolt of searing hope, that the campsite had a hostel attached. I tried not to get too excited but the thought of going to sleep in a bed that night was almost more than I could bear. You had to walk through the camping field to get to the main building and, as I did so, I saw tents being battered by the wind.

A rush of hot air hit me as I opened the door.

"Hello love, how can I help?" asked a cheerful woman at the front desk.

"I was going to camp but actually," I gestured to the door and the wind howling outside it, "I don't suppose you have any beds left?"

"You're in luck. I have one bed left in a female dorm. You're just in time, I was about to clock off."

I'm not really a hugger, but I nearly hugged her. Then, just as I thought things couldn't get any better, out of the corner of my eye, I saw a price list for different types of hot meals stuck up against the glass.

"Are you still serving those at all?" I asked, holding my breath and barely daring to hope.

"Yes, they just come as a frozen meal for you to pop in the microwave. We only have a Thai Green Curry left though, is that okay?"

Anything that wasn't cold oats and puddle water sounded fantastic, like the biggest luxury I could imagine. I handed over the cash for the one night's accommodation and the curry and then, at the last minute, asked for a family-sized bag of chocolate buttons and a beer too. I can say, hand on heart, that it was the best £30 I have ever spent.

I walked into the communal kitchen a little later, clutching my microwave curry like it was a valuable heirloom. It probably was the most precious thing I owned right then, in fairness. Somebody cheered.

"You made it! We weren't sure if you would."

I looked around and recognised several faces from the cars that had stopped to offer me lifts. It turned out they'd all been chatting about the miserable runner they had passed in the rain while they cooked their dinner.

They were right. I had made it.

I've never enjoyed a ready meal or a bed in a hostel dorm so much.

———

I made it to John o' Groats on 22 June, the second longest day of the year. I ran 20 miles from Thurso under stormy Scottish skies to get there – plus the nearly 4,000 more miles preceding that.

I snatched a glimpse of sunshine between rain showers to have my picture taken by the famous signpost. It's free to have your picture taken in John o' Groats, unlike Land's End where you have to pay £10 for the privilege. At the signpost I started chatting to an Australian couple who were touring around Europe, and a man around my age who was starting his length-of-Britain cycle down to Land's End from there. They commented on my tan and asked what I was doing there.

"Well, you've stolen my thunder a bit then haven't you," the man on the bike complained. "Before you arrived these guys were well impressed with my challenge!"

We stood there laughing for a while and it all felt very surreal. The man cycled off to start his own adventure and I said goodbye to the couple and went to find an ice cream and a beer to celebrate.

Whilst drinking that beer, cheers-ing myself because there was nobody else around, I looked at the pictures that the Australian woman had taken of me by the sign. My legs looked strong, I noticed for maybe the first time. I had muscles – who knew? I looked healthy and happy, like somebody who had spent a lot of time outside in the sun.

It still felt fairly unbelievable that my legs had carried me that far. I had another two months left and 1,000 or so miles to run before I finished. In any other circumstance, that in itself would be a fair old feat. But sitting there in John o' Groats it really did feel like I was on the home straight, just as I had hoped it would. Unless I got swept out to sea or a cow ate my leg or something else equally awful, I knew that I was going to make it now. It was in the bag, so to speak.

———

I took a rest day in John o' Groats. I'd put in quite a shift to get there, running 145 miles over the last six days, travelling all the way from the west coast to the east, traversing the whole width of the country. I was tired.

During my day off, I went to the visitor centre to claim my Land's End to John o' Groats certificate.

"When did you start?" the woman asked who was filling it out. I pulled up my camera roll so I could see the date on the picture I'd taken at Land's End.

"January 15th," I told her. She looked understandably confused. I attempted to explain my convoluted route and she looked even more confused. Also understandable – it is quite a weird thing to do.

I managed to meet up with yet another Round the Coaster (answers on a postcard for a snappier title for our collective crew). Tim was cycling around and happened to be passing through John o' Groats that day. Over coffee and cake we debated the pros and cons of cycling vs running, my verdict being that cycling might be a more sensible mode of transport but I still liked running more.

I camped at the John o' Groats campsite that night. I woke up the next morning to a text from my dad saying "We're out! ☹"

It was June 25th. The EU referendum had taken place the day before and the votes had been counted. Britain was leaving the EU. I felt deeply saddened by the news and it proved what an echo chamber I lived in. From the conversations I had been having with my friends and family, and the opinions being shared on my Twitter feed, it really hadn't occurred to me that this could be the result, yet here we were.

I had spent the last eight months running around Great Britain. I'd witnessed its beauty and its vastness. How the landscape doesn't just look different from part to part, but *feels* different too. I had seen the best in people over that time too, experiencing overwhelming kindness. The people I had met were good people. They were generous and open and interesting. I couldn't marry up the country I had spent these past months exploring with the one I was seeing on the news. It didn't make any sense to me. All the hostility, blame throwing and fearmongering.

As I packed up my tent, a timely fog descended over John o' Groats. I started running, beginning the long journey south, singing along to Taylor Swift as I went – what else is there to do in a crisis?

I just had to keep believing that the goodness I had witnessed first-hand over the past year would eventually overcome the concerning political trends that were emerging. (As I sit writing this now in 2020, in the midst of the coronavirus pandemic, Democrat candidate Joe Biden has just beaten Donald Trump in the US election. It gives me hope that the tide is turning.)

———

The first stop on my journey south was Wick, 16 miles south of John o' Groats. I was just putting up my tent at the Wick campsite when I saw a black and white van on the other side of the campsite with "401" emblazoned on the side.

I couldn't believe it. It was Ben.

Ben Smith was in the process of running 401 marathons in 401 days at the time. He was touring around the country, completing each marathon in a different town and mobilising hundreds of runners in local communities to join him. We had exchanged a few messages on Facebook to see if we might be able to meet up at any point, but it had proven difficult to coordinate his schedule with my lack of schedule. We'd just about given up hope when, suddenly, there he was.

I finished putting my tent up and went and knocked on his van door. I felt quite nervous. Would he recognise me?

"Ben, it's Elise!" I said when the door opened.

He looked a bit shocked but then hugged me.

"What a coincidence!"

I suddenly felt very aware that I hadn't washed my hair for 11 days. I had literally no excuse for this as, for most of those nights, I'd either been staying at someone's house or on a campsite with readily available showers. It's not normally the way I like to introduce myself to strangers, with hair so full of sweat and grease and dirt that it doesn't move when you touch it, but there we go.

"We're just about to start a barbecue, do you want to have dinner with us?" Ben asked.

Back in my tent I had a pouch of microwavable rice and a tin of salmon that I was planning to eat cold. The rice packet didn't explicitly say you *couldn't* eat it unheated, but it still wasn't the most appetising of meals. I very much wanted to have dinner with them instead. Kyle, Ben's partner, poked his head out of the door too.

"Cider?" he asked.

After a gloomy start to the day, this felt like a sign of some kind.

CHAPTER 28

The coastline around the Scottish Highlands is spectacular. White sandy beaches as unspoiled as any you'll find anywhere. Sparkling blue water. Backdrops of mountains and forests. Idyllic fishing villages with picturesque harbours. A goldmine of wildlife – seals, whales, birds of prey, deer cantering through the woods.

Sadly, in lots of areas, nobody has considered the plight of the long-distance runner or walker and these spots aren't connected by passable coastal trails. It's frustrating at times because you know that you're so close to somewhere incredible, a feast for the eyes, but instead you have no choice but to travel along the main road that runs parallel. And this experience isn't just down to my lack of map-reading abilities – I've since checked, and for the most part those coastal trails simply don't exist.

The stretch heading down south from Wick is one example of this. You can either take a huge detour inland or you have to run alongside the A9. I took the latter option because, to be fair, even if you head inland there aren't any particularly obvious routes.

Which is how I found myself crying on the side of the road in Helmsdale. I'd been running for about 4 hours – 16 miles of avoiding cars flying around bends and trying to flatten myself against walls and hedges. It was pouring with rain, and I was soaked and couldn't stop shivering. I'd found that you couldn't cry and sing at the same time though and so had spent a large portion of the morning belting out Amy Studt lyrics to distract myself. That strategy worked until it didn't – and the point where it stopped working was when I learned that the hostel in Helmsdale, the one I'd been pinning all of my hopes on staying at – was closed for refurbishment. I felt crushed. I couldn't bear the thought of ever running on the A9 ever again, especially not again today. This wasn't what I had come on an adventure for. It was stupid and dangerous and no fun whatsoever.

A car pulled over to see if I was okay, which is probably reasonable given that I was standing in the pouring rain sobbing by the side of a road.

"Do you need a lift anywhere?" the man asked. "I'm heading down to Brora."

Brora was about 10 miles further south than Helmsdale. It looked like there were some quieter roads heading inland from there and I could maybe piece together a different route. There was also a campsite I could stay at for the night.

I don't usually get in cars with strangers, but I figured that this seemingly genuine man murdering me was probably statistically much less likely than me being killed by one of the lorries hurtling down the A9. It was a risk I was willing to take, so I said "Yes please" and hopped in.

Coasting

He dropped me at the campsite in Brora and I felt no remorse whatsoever at having skipped 10 miles of the A9. I paid for a pitch and then went to the toilet block, just to be somewhere dry for a few minutes. Sheltering in the doorway, I peering out into the rain and saw everybody else in their caravans looking very warm and dry. I couldn't really think of many things I wanted to do less than go back out into the deluge and pitch my tent.

There was one other tent in the camping field. I eventually left the toilet block and managed to get mine up without getting the inside too wet. I crouched inside the tiny porch to strip my sodden kit off, blew up my mat and got into my sleeping bag. Once I was inside and dry, everything felt a lot less bleak. I was grateful for the tiny waterproof home I was carrying on my back.

So grateful, in fact, that when I woke up the next morning to the sound of rain beating against the tent once again, I wondered if I could perhaps just live in it forever. I could call off the rest of the run – hadn't I made it far enough already? – and spend the rest of my life in this one-man tent in Brora, never going outside or getting wet again.

Unfortunately there were some logistical question marks hanging over this plan, not least that I only had 15 per cent phone battery, a bag of Haribo and one clean pair of socks to sustain me for the rest of eternity. I decided I should probably just get on with it, and hoped that a better eternity would be waiting for me somewhere else.

I pieced together a route going south that mostly avoided the A9, via a place called Rogart, which is inland a little, packed up my tent and set off. Surprisingly, I actually had quite a good day, running along a lovely quiet lane around the hills. In Rogart, there was a stationary first-class train that had been converted into a hostel, and I treated myself to a night there.

I was glad of my decision to head inland. My life and my sanity were worth more than running a perfect coastal loop.

———

I carried on heading south, down through the Tarbat and Black Isle Peninsulas to Inverness, and then started travelling east from there. As June became July and I was into my last few days in the Highlands, I had some visitors.

First, my friend Paddy came to visit. Paddy is a train conductor and discounted train travel is one of the main perks of the job. You can therefore pretty much always rely on him to come and visit you wherever you are. I'd already seen him in Brighton, but I think he was excited to have an excuse to get the sleeper up to Scotland.

I met Paddy in Lossiemouth. A few weeks earlier, I'd received an email from a man called Craig. Craig had a self-contained holiday apartment joined onto his home in Lossiemouth that he usually rented out for Airbnb, which he offered me for a night or two when I ran through. Given that it was peak season by this point, this was super generous of him, and felt like such a treat after all the long days, no hair washing and damp camping experiences of the past few weeks. Just having somewhere warm and dry to stay was enough, and the fact that this coincided with Paddy's visit was perfect timing. What I didn't expect was for Craig to organise my best rest day so far.

Coasting

It was the first day of the school holidays and Craig had taken the day off work to hang out with his kids – and with Paddy and me, it turned out. We woke up to the sun shining and Craig standing in the front drive wearing a wetsuit.

"Fancy going out on the water?" he asked, opening the garage door to reveal a jet ski.

He found some wetsuits for Paddy and me to borrow and we headed down to the beach. I think I scared Craig a bit when, within the first 10 seconds of my turn, I had nearly crashed the jet ski into the harbour wall, but I'd like to think that I improved after that.

It was great fun. I started to wonder if I'd chosen the wrong mode of transport. Jet skiing suddenly seemed like a much better way of travelling 5,000 miles around the coast.

———

Paddy left and my parents arrived. They had booked a cottage in Elgin for a week for their summer holiday. We did some running together along the Moray Coastal Trail but mostly it was just a chance to relax. I felt like I'd raced around the Highlands a bit, so it was nice to just sit down and eat biscuits for a week. I also got my mum to dye my hair, which felt like an essential maintenance task given that I had eight months of roots growing through at this stage.

Mum and dad headed home and I carried on running east. I'd always intended to take some days off while they were there, but maybe not quite as many as I had. Combined with Paddy's visit, I had slipped behind the schedule I had in my head. I was meeting up with some more friends on the Monday after my parents' visit and I really wanted to have made it down to Aberdeen by then. That was looking less and less likely when, by Saturday, I had only made it as far as Fraserburgh on the northeast shoulder of Aberdeenshire.

I had just about given up when I looked at the map (still just Google of course) and saw the Formartime and Buchan Way. It's a 40-mile converted railway line that runs from Fraserburgh all the way down to Dyce, just above Aberdeen. The train line itself had stopped operating in the 1960s and was turned into a cycleway and footpath in the early 1990s thanks to the Buchan Countryside Group.

I had never run anywhere near that far in one day, my longest distance so far still being the 33-mile day back at the beginning of May in the south of Scotland. It would be a long day, but it would allow me to meet my self-imposed deadline of getting to Aberdeen by Monday. And wouldn't it just be kind of cool to be able to answer with "40 miles" when people asked what the furthest I'd run in a day was (something they did ask, often)?

Like most of these schemes, I thought about it for approximately 30 seconds before deciding it was a great idea and committing to it.

By 7 a.m. the next morning, I was on the move. I had written myself a timetable for the day that included a scheduled lunch stop in Ellon. I didn't need to move at any kind of pace to make it to Dyce – I just needed to keep moving. I always find that a very motivating thought. I use it a lot in races with cut-offs. If I bank enough time at the beginning, I tell myself, *you can walk from here and you'll still make it, just don't stop.*

Coasting

I would describe my experience of running 40 miles carrying a tent on my back as approximately 70 per cent fun and 30 per cent miserable. I ran and ran and ran and then I ran some more. About 20 miles in, just as my legs were starting to feel quite tired and constant rain was starting to get to me, a man came cycling up behind me and slowed as he passed.

"Hello, I'm Chris," the man introduced himself. He was 78, from New Zealand, and was over here visiting his daughter for a few weeks and, now, cycling around Scotland. For the next 7 miles Chris entertained me by singing Scottish folk songs and telling tales of being a dentist on the Shetland Isles (which he apparently had been, some years ago). My legs were screaming at me to start walking, but having Chris cycling along steadily beside me kept me moving. I was too embarrassed to tell somebody all about how I was running a lap of the country, and then immediately start walking.

I didn't have much energy to contribute to the conversation and I was worried Chris would think that I was rude, or that I didn't want him there. This couldn't have been further from the truth – having him next to me singing away was really lifting me out of a dark spot. Luckily, he didn't seem to mind too much about my radio silence, and carried on chuntering away calmly.

We parted ways in Ellon, where I'd scheduled my lunch break. I'd even looked up a cafe I liked the sound of. All morning I had been daydreaming about a sandwich and a cake and a hot cup of tea. What I failed to realise was that the Formartine and Buchan Way actually skirts around the edge of Ellon and you have to divert about three-quarters of a mile off the path to get to the town centre. On any normal day I wouldn't think anything of adding another 1.5 miles to my journey for a nice lunch. On this day, however, I felt certain that the extra distance would break me.

Luckily, there was a Co-op almost on the route. Instead of sitting in a nice warm cafe eating the lovely lunch I had planned, I found myself on the floor of a car park, sheltering from the rain by some shopping trolleys, eating three pains au chocolat and drinking an entire carton of apple juice. Not quite what I'd had in mind.

It was mid-afternoon and I still had another half marathon left to run. I walked for a few miles after lunch, but this section of path seemed to be a hotspot for flies, and every time I slowed down they were all over me. It took less energy to just run than it did to keep batting them away. I started running again, but every step felt like I was being massaged with sandpaper. I clearly hadn't been thorough enough with my Vaseline application and all the rain and wet shorts had created a fairly unpleasant chafing situation.

Finally, after nearly 12 hours on the move, I made it to Dyce, a suburb that sits around 5 miles to the north of Aberdeen and is home to the city's airport. It's not the most scenic of places, but I'm not sure I've ever been so happy to see anywhere.

I'd like to say that I slept well that night. Actually, the combination of adrenaline rushing around my system and the burning sensation all over my body from the extreme chafing made for a terrible night's sleep, but I felt accomplished at least.

CHAPTER 29

My reward for meeting my self-imposed deadline was spending a few days with my friends Daniel and Mimi. I had worked with them both in London, but Daniel was from Scotland. A family wedding had coincided with me running past, and Mimi had flown up to visit for the weekend to join us. I told Daniel that I might be quite tired so it would be best not to plan anything too strenuous. He chose strawberry picking which sounded like a sedate enough activity until you remember how much bending down it involves, and which was a challenge on my post-40-miler legs.

After seeing Daniel and Mimi, I then had a few days alone running down the east coast, through Stonehaven and Montrose and Arbroath, before some more friends arrived. This time it was Sophie and Georgia, both of whom you've met already (Sophie in the race where I pulled out in a graveyard, Georgia after *that* night in Bristol). Sophie ran the 18 miles from Dundee to St Andrews with me (which was much more successful than the last time we had run together – see aforementioned graveyard incident) but mostly we just roamed around eating a lot and hanging out at the beach.

There was the odd day of downpours here and there, but mostly the Scottish heatwave just kept going and going. With all the visits over the past few weeks I just felt like I was on holiday, albeit a holiday that involved quite a lot of running. It was a bit of a crash when I had to say goodbye to Sophie and Georgia and knew I'd be going it alone for a while.

Sophie ran 5 miles with me the morning they left, and then we found a cafe to have breakfast in with Georgia before they headed off. It was especially hot that day and they were facing 8 hours or more in a car with no air con. This made me feel much better about the 21 miles I still had left to run, rounding it up to a marathon for the day.

My Vaseline, Starburst and emergency chocolate all melted, as did I, and I had "Donald Where's Yer Trousers" stuck in my head all day. It made for a fairly grating backing track but luckily the scenery more than made up for it. I ran through postcard-pretty fishing villages including Crail, which is apparently the most photographed harbour in Scotland. I'm not sure quite how this accolade is quantified, but I dutifully took a picture of the scenic harbour as I ran through.

———

I couldn't quite believe that it was my last week in Scotland. It made me laugh to think how terrified I'd been of this leg of the journey when, in reality, everything had actually started to feel a lot simpler. It's much easier to have an adventure, I discovered, in a place that's actually geared up for adventures. Scotland felt like somewhere you were just meant to be outdoors, in a way that the more populated places I had run through didn't.

I was still being hosted by so many amazing people, and even still being offered the occasional B&B room or hostel bed free of charge despite the fact it was peak season now. But just knowing that I had my tent in my bag and that I could put it up anywhere if needed (and legally, thanks to the Scottish 2003 Land Reform Act that made wild camping legal in Scotland, unlike in most of England and Wales), made everything feel a lot less stressful. And after a stint of camping, getting to sleep in a bed and do my laundry would feel like such a treat. I felt like I deserved those kindnesses a little more then, I suppose, than I had before.

I'd spent so much time during those first few months worrying that I wasn't doing this properly. I thought that if I wasn't suffering as many hardships as physically possible and doing it on as much of a shoestring as possible then I was doing it wrong, somehow. I'm not sure why I thought this. I only ever said I was going to run around the country – I hadn't at any point specified that I was going to do that by only spending a certain amount of money, or that I was going to sleep under canvas for at least a certain amount of nights. These were just estimations I'd made, mostly out of necessity. I don't know why I thought anybody else would even care about those things, and I don't know why I cared either.

But I did care, and it was something I'd spent so much time puzzling over – was I doing this right? And it was in Scotland that it started to play out like I thought it should and that I started to feel like maybe I *was* doing it right. Running back-to-back 30-mile days, camping night after night in downpours, eating cold rice and raw oats from a camping mug.

Nobody could say I wasn't having an authentic, bona fide Adventure-with-a-capital-A then, could they?

———

My main priority during that last week in Scotland was to eat as many macaroni cheese pies as possible. The scenery and the communities and the weather had all been great, but if you forced me to tell you my absolute favourite thing about Scotland, I'd have to say that it was the macaroni cheese pies. It's what it says on the tin, really: macaroni cheese in an open top pastry case. A simple, strange concoction but really bloody good. You can buy them in the supermarket to cook at home but the best ones come hot from the bakery. As I ran along the Fife coast, I was proving fairly successful in my mission to eat one at every opportunity. If nothing else, I had this achievement to cling onto.

I crossed the Forth Bridge and ran into Edinburgh. I ran along the main road into the city centre, which was a bit of an assault on the senses after so long in the wilds of the Highlands. The main thing I noticed was the pollution, which felt heavy in the air as cars sat in traffic with their motors running, heading home for the weekend.

I met Lucja Leonard for dinner. Lucja is a runner herself and she was just a few weeks away from heading over to Holland where she would be attempting to run 500 km in 5 days. People kept telling me that what I was doing sounded ridiculous, but then I would meet somebody like Lucja and just think, *what*

Coasting

I'm doing is nothing. I had felt so broken after my 40-mile day. The thought of doing one and a half times that, five times in a row... I could not wrap my head around it.

Lucja joined me for the next day's running, to show me the best route out of the city, and then I headed east along the East Lothian coast. I only had three days of running left in Scotland.

I finished my penultimate day in Scotland in Dunbar, birthplace of John Muir. Known as "John of the Mountains", he wrote numerous books, letters and essays describing his adventures in nature and his activism helped to preserve many wilderness areas in America. A legend of the outdoors.

I finished running fairly early that afternoon and stopped in a cafe to get some lunch. I made my coffee last as long as possible and then, when I thought I'd really outstayed my welcome, I headed off to the supermarket to stock up on supplies and wandered the couple of miles down the road to the Dunbar campsite. I paid for my pitch and went to put my tent up.

This proved difficult because, I soon realised, I didn't have my tent. I had a sudden vision of where I must have left it in the cafe, sitting on the spare chair at my table after I took it out to get to my book.

It was just gone half three. The cafe shut at 4 p.m.

I ran into the campsite reception, breathlessly explained, asked if they could mind my bag for a while and went sprinting back up the road. It was the fastest I had moved for months. I arrived at the cafe at 3.58, out of breath and very sweaty having not had time to stop and take my jumper off.

"Looking for this, are you?" smiled the waitress who had served me earlier. I breathed a heavy sigh of relief. *Thank god.*

An hour later I was back at the campsite, tent up and settling down with my favourite no-cooker camping meal of cold rice and tinned salmon. Losing my tent in a cafe: reason number #192728 why I needed to stop eating so much cake.

————

I had 28 miles to run on my final day in Scotland. There's a very straightforward route over the border, following a cycle route out of Dunbar and then picking up the Berwickshire Coastal Path. I've heard that the Berwickshire Coastal Path is pretty spectacular with winding trails, sea views, rolling fields, crumbling castles, picturesque fishing villages, extensive birdlife... I've complained a lot about the lack of dedicated coast paths in Scotland but here's a stellar example of how beautiful they can be.

Sadly, all of the above is just hearsay, because this straightforward route is not the one I took. Footpaths like these only appeared on the OS map, which I still wasn't using. Instead, I referred to my old friend Google, which told me to just run straight down the A1. Yes, the A1, as in the whopping great dual carriageway that connects Edinburgh with London, the longest road in Britain, the one with lorries flying up and down it at 70 mph and no footway. Clearly, Google wanted to kill me, once again.

I wasn't stupid enough to attempt to run alongside the A1 (I had learned *something* in the past nine months) and thought I was being clever by taking myself inland to follow a roundabout route of quieter country roads instead. This was all well and good until, about a mile from the end, one of those country roads threw me out onto the A1 anyway. I stepped towards the hard shoulder. It looked wide enough – maybe I could just run alongside it? It was only for a few hundred metres.

The rush of air from a passing lorry before I even got onto the hard shoulder told me that this was the worst idea I had ever had. I absolutely could not run on the A1. There was only one thing for it. I was going to have to do some trespassing. I squeezed through the hedge by the roadside.

I had spent most of the 27 miles I had run so far that day planning my "Welcome to England" sign selfie. I could remember taking the "Welcome to Scotland" one so vividly, nearly three months ago, and this felt like a big moment. Unfortunately, at the moment I crossed the border I was actually knee-deep in a cornfield and missed the sign altogether. It wasn't quite how I'd planned it – but then, nothing else had been either.

I crawled back through the hedge, crossed the dual carriageway (at a designated crossing point) and took a left onto a quiet lane to run the last few hundred metres to Marshall Meadows Bay, just north of Berwick.

I'd done it. I had made it through 84 days in Scotland without being eaten by a Highland cow or consuming a single can of Irn-Bru.

I was on the home straight now.

CHAPTER 30

It was the end of July when I embarked on my final leg of the journey, down the east coast of England back to London, and it really did feel like the home straight. I had around 500 miles left to run and I hoped it would take me around a month. I'd heard that sometimes the wheels fall off a bit towards the end of a big journey, as if your body knows that it doesn't need to hold on much longer. I felt optimistic though. I could still remember all those hard days at the beginning, with all the uncertainty and tears and heartbreak. Throughout, this had been so much more of a mental challenge than a physical one. Now, the sun was shining and my legs felt strong and I didn't have anybody telling me that I couldn't do it. I felt like perhaps it was all going to be okay.

Claire joined me for my first full day back on English soil. She had driven past me the day before and pulled over, apparently recognising my headband and plaits, to ask if I wanted some company the next day. I met her in Berwick-upon-Tweed that morning where, before the day even started, we had stopped for a coffee-and-biscuits break at her house.

When we eventually got running, we started by following the Northumberland Coast Path. It was fairly straightforward to begin with until the point where it vanished. We carried on forging forward, following what was looking less and less like an actual trail.

"Do you think we might be lost?" I asked Claire.

"It's definitely a possibility," she responded, taking a map out of her back pocket and peering at it, brow furrowed.

Claire was serving in the British army. This meant that she was not only prepared by having a map with her, but she also knew how to read it.

"The good news is that I know where we are," she informed me after staring at the map for a while. "The bad news is that it's definitely not where we should be. We're here."

I looked at the spot on the map Claire was pointing to. Whereas the coast path had headed inland, we had somehow strayed into the swampy area connecting the solid land to the mud flats. I could see the "mud and sand" warnings on the map, printed right next to where we were standing.

"So how do we get out of here?" I asked her.

"We carry on heading in this direction" – she indicated that she meant roughly south – "and eventually we should hit one of these footpaths that will take us back up to the road."

With that, Clare took an impressive running jump over a particularly swampy looking bit of swamp. Clearly map reading wasn't the only thing they taught you in the army.

Getting back to the road wasn't quite as simple as the map made it look but after more than 20 miles of battling waist-deep stinging nettles, sinking into bogs and climbing through barbed-wire fences, we made it to Budle where I was staying that night. I said goodbye to Claire and vowed to finally learn to read a map.

————

Sometimes the miles fly by and sometimes they don't.

Maybe I'd become too blasé about scheduling in long days running big miles and just expecting my legs to go along with it. It always looks so easy on paper. Then I'd remember times like the ultra I had attempted to run with Sophie in the September before setting off around the coast where I'd crumbled after 20 miles. Here I was less than a year later, expecting to run further than that day after day without a second thought. It's no wonder sometimes it felt hard. I'm not sure why I expected it not to.

I continued following the Northumberland Coast Path from Budle, past Bamburgh and its famous castle, through village after village – Beadnell and Alnmouth and Amble and then Cresswell. In Cresswell, I stayed with Bob and Mary. Their daughter was a runner and she'd been following my journey via the videos I was posting on Facebook. Deciding I looked fairly trustworthy, she had offered up her parents to host me for the night, which I was very grateful for.

Bob and Mary were going to a wedding the day after I stayed and had to set off first thing, which meant an early start for me too. This was no bad thing – I had 30 miles to run down to Sunderland, and we all know by now about my tendencies to procrastinate. I was excited to get going at a reasonable time for once, to hopefully have a big chunk of the distance covered by lunchtime and maybe stop for a leisurely lunch somewhere, read my book on the beach, enjoy a relaxing evening.

That didn't happen.

Instead, imagine the slowest thing you can think of, then slow it down a bit more, and then some more, and you'll have an accurate idea of the pace I was moving at. It took me nearly 9 hours to cover the first 15 miles, which I think beat my own record for slowness, and on fairly flat, runnable ground nonetheless. That was an achievement in itself, I guess. Thank god for the early start.

About 22 miles in I had to take a ferry over the River Tyne, from North to South Shields. The crossing takes 7 minutes. I sat down, peeled a banana and gave myself a talking to.

Just get on with it.

It was late afternoon already. I had booked a hotel for the night, not fancying my chances wild camping in the suburbs of Sunderland and unable to find any campsites near my route. I really wanted to get there before dark.

Just get on with it.

I stepped off the ferry and started running. I had a new rule: I could only stop once every mile. And I had to actually try and run. No more dithering.

Eight miles to go, stop for a snack, seven, think about getting a taxi, six, five, four, wonder if I could hire a bike, just a parkrun to go, two, question why I hadn't booked a hotel at the nearer end of the seafront, half a parkrun to go, one mile...

I was there. The never-ending day was over. It had taken me longer to get through those 30 miles than it had to do 40 a few weeks earlier.

A wedding reception was taking place in the function room beneath my room in the hotel. I could feel the vibrations from the bass as I got ready for bed, and hear the screeching of drunk guests singing along. It didn't bother me at all: I was asleep within seconds. I had nothing left.

———

The difference a day makes.

After a long sleep and a great breakfast, I set off towards Middlesborough. I had another long day ahead, another 32 miles to cover, but I actually felt like I was running again rather than walking very slowly pulling lead weights along behind me. It was a big improvement.

This was 2016 and the English Coast Path was in the process of being built at the time. They had recently opened the section through Middlesbrough and I was absolutely overjoyed to be reunited with those friendly yellow acorns that were used as waymarkers for all the National Trails. Since my day with Claire I had kept to my promise of attempting to learn to read a map. At least, I'd downloaded the OS maps app to my phone and I now knew which lines meant footpaths and which meant train tracks (useful to be able to distinguish between). It was a big leap forward from where my navigation had been before, but still not exactly a skill I could rely upon.

The past few months had been relatively flat. Although Scotland is, of course, notoriously mountainous in parts, the gradients on my route around the coast had been fairly gentle and largely on roads – a different experience entirely to the roller-coaster sections of coast path I had experienced earlier on where you were constantly ascending and descending into and out of valleys. It was terrain more like the latter that I was now being reunited with. My legs didn't know what had hit them and grumbled a bit, but I was having the time of my life scrambling around on proper trails again.

The entirety of that run took an hour and a half less than the first 15 miles of the previous day. I was increasingly finding that I just had to wake up in the morning and decide that I was going to have a good day. It was the crucial first step. I had to say to myself: I'm going to run a long way today and I'm going to enjoy it. Invariably, it then happened that way. If I let the doubt creep in, then it was a lost cause. I could never get it back again.

With the exception of encountering some alarmingly aggressive seagulls in Hartlepool, I enjoyed every single moment of the 32 miles I ran that Sunday, and I believe it's because I woke up and promised myself that I was going to. It doesn't work every day, but the bad days are exhausting. You can't have too many of them, or you'd never be able to carry on. I had to do whatever I could to keep them at bay.

I didn't know it at the time, but that would be the last 30+ mile run of the trip.

———

I woke up the next morning feeling excited for two reasons.

Firstly, it being the first day of August meant that I was officially into my last month of the adventure (fingers crossed, if nothing went wrong). I still couldn't quite believe that I had made it this far. Part of me thought I might wake up any moment and find that this had all been a dream, that actually I was still in Devon, trudging through mud, with months and months still ahead of me.

I had put up an announcement on my Facebook page a couple of days earlier telling people that I was planning to finish on August 27th, all being well, and inviting them to join me for a celebratory picnic in Greenwich Park. I kept going back and forth about whether this was a good idea or not. I'm the sort of person who hates their own birthday party – the idea of organising a whole event all about me made me feel very uncomfortable. Half of me thought it might be better to just finish myself, get the train home, turn up at my parents' door unannounced and ask what time dinner was. But then another part of me thought perhaps it would be quite nice to have people there clapping and saying nice things about me. I'm only human, after all. And having a fixed date gave me something to aim for – if I said I was finishing then, I would.

The other thing that I was excited about was the fact that 1st August marks the well-known and much celebrated national holiday: Yorkshire Day. I discovered this scrolling through Twitter in bed and then, when I looked at the map, realised that lo and behold, this would actually be my first day running in Yorkshire, with the county border running through Middlesbrough. What are the chances?

I had stayed with Mandy the night before. She'd instantly made me feel at home and when I headed downstairs for breakfast that morning, feeling smug about my excellently timed celebration of Yorkshire Day, I was thrilled to see her brewing a pot of Yorkshire Tea.

Sometimes the stars just align.

Mandy dropped me in Redcar, stocked up with her homemade rocky road (which I proceeded to eat within the first 2 miles) and I carried on heading south. In Saltburn-by-the-Sea I picked up the Cleveland Way and spent the rest of the day running along the dreamiest coastal trails, views out to sea for miles, my legs slowly adjusting again.

My peace was interrupted when I started climbing up a huge hill.

"Nearly there!" called a couple coming back down – at a point when I was absolutely nowhere near being nearly there. I later learned that this "hill" was Boulby Cliff, the highest cliff on England's east coast, measuring 203 metres. No wonder it had got my legs burning a little.

———

Yorkshire carried on bringing the goods. I ran through Whitby where I stopped at the Magpie Cafe to try supposedly some of the best fish and chips in the world (I'll admit they were pretty good). Then it as round to Scarborough and Filey and Bridlington, all quintessential British seaside towns. The sun shone and the trails were perfect and, honestly, I was just having a really nice time.

Before I set off on this adventure, all my daydreams of it involved long summer days, bounding effortlessly along nice gentle coast paths. Although some part of me knew that I was taking on a big endurance challenge, mostly I just imagined myself having ice cream breaks and picnics on the beach and eating fish and chips for tea. I took all of my favourite childhood seaside memories, peppered them with the more fun aspects of running, and dreamed up a combination that I couldn't imagine being anything less than magical.

It probably goes without saying that, for the most part, those daydreams were pretty far off the mark. The reality was a lot muddier and windier and just, well, harder than I had pictured.

Sometimes, though, it was exactly how I imagined it to be. On those days, memories of all the cold, hard, lonely bits faded away and I couldn't understand why I'd ever want to spend a day doing anything different. The many, many existential crises I'd suffered on various grass verges around the country paled into insignificance.

The day I ran from Scarborough towards Bridlington, 29 miles along the Yorkshire coast, was one of those days. I started making a video, one that I hoped would capture some of that effortless bounding, when I tripped, did a rolly-polly in mid air and landed on my back with a thud. The camera was still rolling.

"… until you fall over, that is," I finished.

It turned out to be one of my most-watched videos. My niece apparently requested it be played every morning before school for several months and Frank Bruno retweeted it, which still stands as my biggest claim to fame.

That night I stayed at a hotel in Bridlington, where the owner had kindly organised for me to have a sports massage in one of the empty rooms. It was the first one I'd had in over six months and I was a little worried what the masseur's feedback was going to be. More than 4,500 miles in and I felt fine, miraculously, but was I about to find out that, actually, I had caused some sort of permanent damage without realising?

It turned out that I was in quite good nick, surprisingly.

"What sort of stretching have you been doing pre- and post-run?"

"Erm…" I fluffed a bit, making some vague references to those dubious shin stretches back in Margate, nearly nine months ago now. She interrupted me halfway through a sentence.

"I think it's probably best if I don't know. Well, whatever you're doing it seems to be working. Keep going, you're nearly there now."

She was right. I was nearly there.

CHAPTER 31

"Where are you?!" I asked when my dad finally answered the phone.

This was the 17th time I had tried to call him that morning. My dad is usually fairly reliable at answering the phone so I probably should have been concerned when he didn't pick up, but instead I just felt very, very irritated. He was meant to meet me in Bridlington that morning to run 20 more miles down the coast of Yorkshire together. He had told me that he couldn't set off too early because he needed to go and do something with his beehives, but that he would let me know when he was on his way.

He hadn't let me know.

"I've been in A&E, like a proper ill person."

"What?!" In the nearly 30 years I have now known my dad I have never known him seek any medical attention whatsoever. It must be bad.

"I'll tell you when I see you. I'm setting off now – I'll be about three hours. Start running and I'll find you."

Coasting

At about four o' clock, my dad did indeed find me – sitting on the beach near Hornsea, feeling very sorry for myself. After the fantastic day I'd had the day before, my mood had plummeted. I suddenly felt very, very tired. The kind of tiredness that a good night's sleep can't fix. It had come on so suddenly but now I couldn't imagine ever not feeling tired.

As my dad walked towards me, I noticed how puffy his face was. Maybe I wasn't the one who should be feeling sorry for themselves...

My dad had recently taken up beekeeping. "If you're going to do something, you may as well do it properly" is Dave Downing's motto in life (that and his "weed your patio" classic, of course). He isn't one to do things by halves and so, when he embarked on his beekeeping journey, he bought every book he could find, attended an eight-week college course and even built his own hive. He was the most well-prepared amateur beekeeper you will ever meet.

There was one thing the books and the courses couldn't prepare him for: that he is, in fact, highly allergic to bee venom.

He had been tending to his bees that morning when one had stung him on the back of the head. He realised his face was swelling up and decided that he should probably get himself to the chemist for some antihistamines. When it swelled up even more and a red rash started to develop, he thought that the chemist perhaps wouldn't cut it and drove himself to the minor injuries unit. This had actually closed down but was luckily only over the road from A&E.

"I thought they'd just laugh at me for coming in with a bee sting, sit me in the corner, give me some antihistamines and then send me home," he told me.

What actually happened was he got rushed through to the resuscitation unit and put on a drip. The doctor had come around a little later to see how he was doing, and asked if he had any questions.

"Can I drive a hundred and fifty miles to Hull and run twenty miles this afternoon?" had been dad's question. The doctor looked a little alarmed but apparently more because he couldn't see why anybody would *want* to do that, rather than because of any real medical concerns. They gave him permission to drive, but not to run until tomorrow and now here he was – recovered but still looking quite puffy.

Hearing about my dad's morning helped put my own wobble into perspective a little. We headed to the campsite we'd booked for that night and, after a campstove dinner and a mug of wine, my spirits improved significantly.

There's nothing like somebody else having a really bad day to make you feel better, is there?

———

Once his face was back to a normal size, dad ran with me for a couple of days. Luckily we didn't come across any bees along the way. We did, however, discover the "Doughnut Whippy Sharer", a highly nutritious snack involving a platter of deep-fried doughnuts and soft-serve ice cream, plus sauce and sprinkles. When people question traditional English cuisine, I'm just not sure what point they're trying to make.

It wasn't too sad a goodbye when he headed home as I would actually be seeing him again in less than two weeks. It probably would have been better to get my dad to write this book, given what a starring role he played.

Dad left me in Cleethorpes, where I made probably my biggest mistake of the whole trip. I applied some Vaseline between my legs to help stave off the dreaded chafe, then immediately sat down on the beach to take a picture. The sand stuck to my skin, turning my inner thighs into two pieces of actual sandpaper. The next few miles were some of the least comfortable of the entire nine and a half months so far, which is really saying a lot.

The Greenwich Meridian Line runs through Cleethorpes, which felt fitting given that I was on my way back to Greenwich. Apparently, at the moment I ran over the line I was only 143 miles from London, but it was going to take me quite a few more than that before I made it home. (In case you are interested, I was also 2,517 miles from the North Pole, 3,481 from New York and 10,483 from Sydney. At least it was only London I was running to.)

I was running down to Mablethorpe from Cleethorpes, giving me 27 miles to cover that day. Things obviously hadn't got off to a fantastic start, what with the sandpaper thighs and all, but after all of the industry of the past few days, through Hull and Immingham and Grimsby, I was enjoying plodding along flood banks.

Then suddenly it got very hot and very sandy and I was very lost, hopelessly attempting to navigate the featureless mud flats. There wasn't enough sun cream in the world to protect me from what felt like running on the surface of the actual sun. I hadn't realised that Lincolnshire was home to a desert but here I was, running through it. I'd drained my water supplies within the first 10 miles, which was fairly bleak given that I had no idea where I might be able to refill.

After several long, thirsty hours, using a combination of the OS map I had downloaded after my run with Claire, and my blue GPS dot on Google Maps, plus a little bit of light trespassing through somebody's back garden (it was a big back garden, to be fair), I found myself in Saltfleet, a coastal village.

I staggered into the village pub where I immediately downed three pints of water, refilling my glass at rapid speed from the jug left out on the bar, then ordered a pint of coke, a pint of soda water, then another pint of tap water (having now emptied the jug). The barman would just pause for breath and then there I was again, back at the bar, ordering yet another drink.

I felt like I could have drunk an entire bathtub.

The many pints of liquid revived me a bit and I felt like I might be able to run the remaining 10 miles, something that had seemed completely out of the question 10 minutes earlier. This was good as Sally, who I was staying with that night, was coming to meet me for a few miles. I suppose it might have put a bit of a downer on her afternoon if she'd found me collapsed from dehydration on the floor and had to deal with the mess of that.

———

I had an overdue rest day pencilled in the following day, which felt needed after my afternoon in the desert. My brother, sister-in-law, niece and nephew drove up to visit and we spent the afternoon on the beach. The next morning Chris, my brother, joined me for a half marathon into Skegness.

Coasting

Chris is the original runner in our family. He was probably more surprised than anybody else when I told him I was going to run a lap of the UK and, over the course of the past nine months, had continued to express this surprise repeatedly. I suspected part of the reason he had come to run with me was to get some concrete proof that I wasn't secretly just running up and down the living room and photoshopping coastal scenery in behind me. To be fair, if this was the case, and I'd managed to pull it off, I would argue that would have actually been more impressive than doing the run.

He carried my pack for me, which meant he was welcome back any time, and when we got to Skegness we immediately ran into the sea for what would still only be my third swim of the trip.

Chris ran with me again the next day, another 23 miles. Coming into Skegness had been a straightforward jaunt along the seafront. Heading south out of Skegness was a different story. I spent a good hour sitting down with the maps – both Google and OS, having kept true to the promise I made myself after running with Claire in Berwick – to try to work out the best route down to Boston. The options seemed to boil down to either 22 miles along the A52, or 23 miles of trails featuring a spot of mild trespassing.

I'm worried that this book portrays me as a rampant trespasser. This isn't the case, of course, but needs must and all...

We chose the latter option, obviously.

About 3 miles in, we came to a bridge we needed to cross that was blocked off by a heavily padlocked gate with large metal spikes on top. It probably tells you everything you need to know about Chris that he has competed in the Obstacle Course Racing World Championships three times. Whereas I see padlocks, spikes and a body of water standing in my way as a reason to turn back, Chris just sees a challenge.

"Come on, we can get around that," he said, and immediately climbed over the railings and started traversing the bridge from the outside. Within a matter of seconds he'd hopped back over the railing and was safely on the other side of the gate.

I didn't have much faith in my ability to replicate this move, mainly due to my own lack of upper body strength, but it didn't seem like I had much choice except to try, as Chris definitely wasn't going to come back for me. Just as I was suspended above the river, one leg on either side of the gate and my hands gripped around the railings for dear life, a man approached us. He was wearing a lanyard around his neck, jangling a bunch of keys and all-round looking very official. *Oh no.*

"Would you like me to just open that gate for you?" he asked, laughing.

By this point I'd managed to haul myself over the other side so it was a little too late, but I was just relieved we weren't getting arrested.

We had finally made it onto an official right of way when I saw the trail snaking through a field of cows. There was absolutely no way I was going through. As if we hadn't done enough scrambling up, over and through things already, I made Chris climb across several ditches and through a cornfield until we safely rejoined the trail, this time with a nice sturdy gate standing between the cows and us.

Terrifying wildlife encounters didn't stop there: over the next few miles we had our path blocked by "Bull in Field" signs, were chased by several tiny angry dogs and followed by manic horses.

Just another day of lovely family bonding.

CHAPTER 32

The flags were cracking in Lincolnshire over the next few days, or so David kept saying. Kate and I had absolutely no idea what he meant.

"You know, when it's really hot, and the flags crack!" he kept saying.

"What flags?! Where are the flags?!" we kept asking in return. No matter how many times he said it, we still didn't understand.

"Is this a Northern thing?" I asked, as David was from near Manchester.

"I'm from the North too and I've never heard of it!" Kate adamantly responded.

We eventually got out of him that he meant the flag*stones,* and that it was a way of saying that it was really bloody hot.

Kate and David were yet more friends I had met through the Yes Tribe. Having not seen either of them for the best part of a year, I was thrilled when they suggested coming to run with me for a couple of days to catch up. And there was a lot to catch up on: since we'd last seen each other David had met the woman he would go on to marry and Kate had spent four months stand-up paddleboarding nearly 2,000 miles down the Danube River.

On day one of their visit we ticked off 22 miles, from Boston to Long Sutton. You have to come inland here as there isn't a way to run around the Holborn Marshes. As a result, Kate and David got to experience one of the most un-coastal stretches of the English coast. I took them on a roundabout tour of Lincolnshire villages and hoped they wouldn't mind not actually seeing the sea at any point.

It took us a while to get anywhere because I had to stop approximately every 50 metres to eat another handful of blackberries and because the skin was falling off Kate's feet. Literally, falling off. Having spent so many months submerged in water from the ankle down, the skin on her feet had softened considerably, and this was the first time she'd attempted to wear shoes for any length of time. Thwarted by blisters, we were mostly walking. I was happy with this as it meant more opportunities for blackberry eating.

As we pitched our tents at a campsite in Long Sutton, we reflected on two key observations from the day:

1) Lincolnshire really is very flat, isn't it?

2) The number of absurdly large guard dogs we had run past and been barked at. What were they hiding in Lincolnshire, exactly?

Kate and David carried on to King's Lynn with me the next day before heading home. I was sad to see them go, which felt a bit silly when I was so close to the end.

Coasting

I took myself out for lunch to cheer myself up and spend the last of the chicken cheques that Travis had given me way back in the second week, the day after my credit card debt catastrophe in Folkestone. It genuinely felt like a lifetime ago.

I ran from King's Lynn to Sandringham, where I was camping that night. I had just started pitching my tent when I heard the sound of jangling metal. I looked up to see a man on a bike pulling a trailer. On the trailer was what looked like the entire contents of a one-man band.

"Hi, I'm James, a cycling one-man band," the cyclist told me. It *was* the contents of a one-man band.

Just when I thought things couldn't get any weirder, they always managed to.

From Sandringham, I ran to Hunstanton to be reunited with the sea. Here, I picked up the Norfolk Coast Path, another of the National Trails, which would carry me for the next 45 miles.

I had been lucky enough to run on quite a few National Trails over the past few months. Some in their entirety, like the South West Coast Path and the Pembrokeshire Coast Path. Others I just dipped in and out of: the North Downs Way, the Cleveland Way, Hadrian's Wall Path and, now, the Norfolk Coast Path.

These paths are some of Britain's best-kept treasures. They're well maintained, perfectly waymarked (useful given how long it had taken me to pick up a proper map) and offer something for everyone, whether you're looking for rolling countryside, expansive sea views or big days in the mountains.

A huge amount of volunteer time goes into maintaining and developing these trails – including the longest of them all, the England Coast Path, which now traverses the entire English coastline. I can't help but feel a little hard done by that this path wasn't open five years earlier. It would have made my life a lot simpler.

These trails are able to exist because of the unique access to open country we have in the UK and our enormous web of public rights of way. It's easy to take for granted this access to land in the UK but it's something our predecessors fought vehemently for. In 1932, hundreds of people took part in the Kinder Scout mass trespass to highlight the lack of public access to areas of open country in England and Wales. It was only in 2005, after more than 100 years of campaigning, that walkers were finally given a new right of access to most areas of open countryside – mountain, moor, heath, down and common land. This is called the "right to roam" and it's something we need to carry on defending.

I was thrilled to be reunited with these little acorns. They felt safe and familiar, something I could trust.

The Norfolk Coast Path took me as far as Cromer, where it merged into the England Coast Path. This was the first stretch of the new National Trail to open, and was, at the time, open as far as Sea Palling. Here, after a few days of acorn following, I would say goodbye to them again, knowing that the next time I saw them would be on the Thames Path as I headed back into London.

Back into London. What a funny thing to think about.

———

Coasting

It was Monday 15th August, which meant that in less than two weeks, I would be done. I could officially say that I was finishing "next week". It felt like madness, after all those days and weeks and months of trying to never think about anything further away than tomorrow. I had less than 300 miles left to run.

I nearly cried at how perfect Norfolk was on that penultimate Monday. Perfect blue skies, a gentle stripe of white clouds, soft golden sands, still air, hot-but-not-too-hot. This was everything I had dreamed of. It was incomparable to some of those wet and wild earlier experiences and made it hard to believe that I was still on the same adventure, let alone still in the same country. For a relatively small island, Great Britain has a lot going on. I felt lucky that I had been able to spend so much time getting to know it.

I ran from Cromer to Waxham that night and stayed at Breathing Space, a holistic retreat centre for women. It was maybe the most peaceful place I had ever been. The thatched cottage overlooks a lake, there is a wooden cabin in the grounds and if you stay for longer you can book onto all sorts of different treatments, from reflexology to art therapy. I had dinner with the other guests that night and over a feta and spinach pie, I learned about their lives and how they'd found themselves there. Almost everybody was a returning guest.

I felt relaxed heading to bed that night. I turned on my phone to check my messages before going to sleep, and saw one from Greg. It was the first time I had heard from him for months and months. Just as the British coastline was unrecognisable compared to earlier in the year, I felt certain that I wasn't the same person either in so many ways.

I had spent a lot of time by myself over the past few months – lots of thinking time, lots of time in my own head. I knew that the way Greg had treated me, and in turn the way that had made me treat myself, hadn't been okay. I knew that's not how somebody who cared about you behaved. I knew that the things he had told me about myself, especially, weren't true at all. I knew that I wasn't the person he had said I was.

But, still – still – there was a part of me that was happy to hear from him.

"I'm sorry I can't make it to your finishing party," he wrote. "Good luck with the last week."

Technically, of course, I had publicly posted about the finish with an open invite to come along, but I thought Greg would have had enough common sense to know that didn't include him. Of course he couldn't come. It would be a disaster. Why did he think he could muscle in at the last minute and make this about him again?

But then there was another part of me that had half-hoped he would be there, hoped he'd show up and prove me wrong about all the rest of it. Then the old self-loathing started to creep in, hating myself for even entertaining that thought.

I tossed and turned all night; an old wound reopened.

———

I decided to take the beach route across the Norfolk-Suffolk border. We were down to single digits in how many days of running I had left and I wanted to make the most of being so close to the sea. I ate my breakfast on Great Yarmouth beach, sitting among all the windbreaks and sandcastles of families who had come out early. I had images of myself running effortlessly beside the water, waves lapping at my feet and cooling me down, sea air tousling my hair.

The first few hundred metres were fun, when I was still running on the concrete prom. Then the prom ran out and I remembered why, despite having chosen to spend a year of my life running near them, I didn't actually like beaches very much: sand. So much sand. Sand in my shoes, in my sandwiches, in my bra and somehow, I discovered later that night, even in my sleeping bag. Sand bloody everywhere.

I made it to Southwold and swore I would never run near a beach again.

It was mid-August, peak tourist season, and Southwold was heaving, people pouring off the pavements and out of every bar and shop. I headed to the campsite where I had pre-booked a pitch and chatted to the man at the reception for a while. I told him all about my very sandy day.

"Did you know," he asked me, "that there are ten times more stars in the night sky than there are grains of sand in all of the world's deserts and beaches?"

I didn't know that, I had to admit. If stars get between your toes in the same way that sand does, I never want to be an astronaut.

———

Every morning, as I ate my breakfast and packed up my bag and got dressed in my increasingly scruffy running kit, a little bit of fear would creep in. I still get it now, even if I'm just heading out for an easy 5 km around the park. The fact that I've done this hundreds and thousands of times before flies out of my brain and I can't imagine how I am possibly going to run even one mile, let alone more. That first step would feel so unutterably heavy. I could never fathom how I was going to take it.

But as I had been learning, the only way to have a good day was to decide to have one. I had to lace up my shoes and get outside and move before the fear grew. Because once it took hold fully, it was almost impossible to shake. It would stick around all day and every single step would feel as heavy as I initially imagined that first one would.

If I just got myself out the door and told myself it was going to be a good day then, inevitably, after a few miles the fear would fade away and I would remember, *oh hey, this running lark is pretty fun, isn't it? You like doing this, don't you?*

I made the mistake of dithering around a bit that morning when I woke up in Southwold. I nearly let the fear take hold but I couldn't, for one important reason: there were 18 miles standing between me and my grandma, who would be waiting for me in Aldeburgh with an ice cream. And you can't let your grandma down.

I laced up and got going. I caught the tiny rowing boat ferry from Southwold over the estuary to Walberswick, where I ran past all the fishing huts lined up by the water. The Suffolk Coast Path took me up onto Dunwich Heath, over the heathery tops, alive with colour at that time of year, and then through RSPB Minsmere. I ran over the sand dunes (not even hating the sand so much today), past Sizewell nuclear power station, through seaside village Thorpeness, and then I saw Aldeburgh ahead of me. The coast path is dead flat for the last couple of miles and I picked up some speed – a rarity.

Coasting

There, sitting in front of a beach hut on a hodgepodge of different chairs, were my grandparents, and my mum and dad too. Grandad was asleep in his chair, his hat tipped forward over his eyes, and Grandma was examining a shell she had found. I was so happy to see them. It had been worth squashing the fear for.

The next day, my aunt and uncle and cousins arrived to join the party. I took a rest day to spend with them. The weather had turned but we persevered with having fish and chips on the seafront. As we sheltered from the rain near the public toilets, my grandma with her gloves on and her hood tightened around her face, my dad turned to me.

"Fancy a swim, Elise?"

Let's remember how many times my dad had visited at this stage. We were into double figures and plenty of those times had been during the summer, during blazing heatwaves where we had run past numerous idyllic, secluded beaches with sparkling clear water. He hadn't suggested we swim on any one of those occasions yet here we were, in the rain, staring out at the murky North Sea and *now* he wanted to go in?

I will never understand that man. But still, the answer was a yes, of course. There was no way I could let him outdo me.

We went back to the hotel, got our swimming stuff (well, he got his swimming stuff, I got some running shorts and a sports bra) and headed out to sea while the rest of our family stood ashore laughing at us. We were the only people on the beach not wearing coats and an untrustworthy seagull circled overhead the whole time, but we got in. Another swim ticked off, bringing me up to the grand total of four.

CHAPTER 33

I had one final slice of cake with my family the next morning, waved goodbye and headed down a dirt track... right into a pig farm. The smell was terrible and the pigs were very noisy. I made a mental note to add pigs to my ever-growing list of farmyard animals I didn't like.

This was it. I only had a week to go. Seven more days of running and I could get back to my normal life... whatever that was. It was a bit daunting, in a way, to think about stopping. For so long now, running around the coast had been all-consuming. It was everything I did, everything I thought about... it had become who I was. I definitely felt like I'd changed over the past ten months but, without the coast, I had no idea who I actually was.

But I had a few more days until I needed to start worrying about that properly, so I shelved that thought for a while.

From Aldeburgh I ran towards Bawdsey, where you wave a wooden bat to hail a ferry to take you over the River Deben.

Coasting

The ferry captain asked why I was running with such a big pack, told me I was mad, and let me on for free. I was met on the other side of the river by Adrian and his dog Jasper. Adrian had been following me on Facebook and invited me to stay with his family that night. Him and Jasper ran into the last stretch of Felixstowe with me.

Sunday morning started with a ferry too, this time from Felixstowe over to Harwich where I met Andy. Andy had been one of my number-one supporters on Facebook throughout the entire journey and I was excited to finally put a face to the name.

There were so many days when everything ran smoothly, the route was straightforward and barbed wire didn't feature too highly. Unfortunately, those days always seemed to happen when I was on my own, and never coincided with when somebody had taken the time to come and run with me. That day – my final Sunday – Andy fell victim to the running companion curse.

It was the same old story: in a bid to avoid the main roads and also take some shortcuts, I led Andy through a complicated maze of footpaths, stinging nettles and barbed wire. Eventually we emerged from the little-known jungle of Essex onto a track. We took this as the perfect opportunity to sit down and eat the lemon drizzle cake that Andy's sister had kindly made for us. Unfortunately, we had unknowingly wandered into some kind of restricted grounds and a car soon pulled over to quiz us, looking for any suspect motives for being there.

We managed to play the lost-runners-eating-cake role rather convincingly and were allowed to continue on. The next stop on our magical mystery tour was a tiny village where we found sinister messages printed out and pasted onto every lamp post and bus stop. The person who had written them was apparently "in utter moral outrage at this disgusting society".

Our legs moved a bit quicker after that and we soon made it to Clacton-on-Sea where the bright lights of the arcade made for a welcome sign of civilisation.

Mixed reviews all round on the first 22 miles of Essex, but I was extremely glad to have had Andy with me.

———

That final week felt bittersweet. I was both very ready to finish, and a little nervous for what came after. I was determined to enjoy it though, to squeeze those last drops out of the adventure.

It was a shame, then, when my Monday ended up being a complete and utter write-off. I had some ferry-related dramas, cried a lot and faced the terrifying prospect of being stranded on Mersea Island after messing up my timings and nearly getting cut off by the tide.

This wasn't the footing I wanted my last week to get off on. When I woke up on Tuesday morning I decided to scrub Monday out altogether and call that the start of the week. Thankfully, it was a much better day. In fact, it was one of the best I'd had.

I ran from Maldon to Burnham-on-Crouch, took the ferry over to Wallasea Island and then headed down to Southend-on-Sea. Here I swung a right and began what would be my final journey west, into London. For all intents and purposes I'd actually finished the lap of the coast that I had first proposed to do. This last section along the Thames was just an add-on really.

Coasting

As David would have said, it was really cracking the flags that day and people were packed onto the beach in Southend like sardines. I managed to make it to Leigh-on-Sea without drowning in my own sweat, which felt like an achievement.

From Leigh-on-Sea, if you walk a couple more miles to the west, you reach Hadleigh Castle. I'd camped here once before, the previous summer, and remembered waking up in my bivvy bag to sunset creeping over the Thames Estuary and through the castle ruins. It had been beautiful and, from the very beginning, I'd been excited for another night like that.

What I hadn't expected was to be sharing that night with 45 members of the Yes Tribe who descended on Leigh-on-Sea to join me for the last night I'd be sleeping outdoors. I met them in the pub, we had fish and chips for dinner and then wandered up the hill. We slept under the stars and I felt so content. I wished that this could be the final night – it felt like I'd come full circle, to be here with so many people who had come into my life just as this journey was beginning.

But it wasn't the end. We weren't quite there yet.

———

I woke up the next morning in my bivvy bag, stretched out and checked my phone. There was a message from my dad. This wasn't unusual – he has sent me a good morning text every single day since I left for university in 2010 (sometimes he forgets and it arrives at about 8 p.m.). Today's was a little longer though.

"Take plenty of water. Gravesend is the hottest place in the country today." Gravesend being where I was running to that day.

It wasn't even 7 a.m. yet and it already felt pretty warm. I shook my water bottle, which was worryingly empty. Hopefully I would pass somewhere to fill up fairly soon.

Laura was one of the people who had camped with me the previous night. In a few months' time, Laura was planning to run "from Rome to home" – the trip that Lawrence who ran with me in Cornwall would end up joining – and she'd asked if she could join me for a day's running to get a taste of what adventure running was really like.

We packed our kit up, said goodbye to the remaining campers who hadn't already dashed off to catch the first train into London for work, and set off. We started running down the hill away from Hadleigh Castle. We had probably run about 100 metres when I had to stop.

"Laura, I'm sorry, but I think we might have to just walk today."

"Oh no, what's wrong? Are you injured?"

I took my pack off and turned around to show her my back. I had been wearing the same red T-shirt for nearly six months now, day in, day out. There was a specific patch in the centre of my back where the fabric had rubbed against the metal clasp of my sports bra and worn away. This meant that my pack was now rubbing directly against my skin and this friction had essentially created a hole in my back, the same as it had in the T-shirt. This hole was now essentially an open wound, oozing some rather revolting gooey stuff. It didn't exactly make for a comfortable running experience.

Of course, there was an easy solution to this problem: buy a new T-shirt. In fact, I even had a spare in my bag that I usually designated as my "clean" top. It seems completely unfathomable to me now that I didn't just stop and change.

But I had become weirdly superstitious about the one I was wearing and I really wanted to keep it on for my final few days – even if that meant walking instead of running, apparently.

It's probably one of the most ridiculous ideas I had. I can't explain myself.

Laura looked fairly horrified by the sight of my oozing back and was kind enough not to point out the obvious solution. She patiently walked 20 miles that day, beside a series of uninspiring main roads.

As we marched along one of these roads, sweating profusely, we passed a builder standing by a kebab van. He was, surprisingly, wearing denim hot pants.

"You girls look hot! Do you want some water?" I could see the fridge behind the counter, full of cold drinks. I really did want some. "And what are you doing out here today with those big packs?"

Reluctantly, prompted by Laura, I told him that it was one of the last days of a ten-month adventure.

"Well I'm definitely buying you some water then!" I tried to refuse but the next thing we knew we had two bottles of ice-cold water in our hands, condensation dribbling deliciously down them. He pressed a £20 note into my hand too, "for your charity collection."

Confirmation, as if I needed more, of how many incredible people there are in the world and how serendipitously they tend to appear. Just as you think you might melt into a soggy heap somewhere near the Essex-Kent border, along comes a builder in hot pants to save you.

Buoyed by our chance encounter, Laura and I made it around to Tilbury. Laura was heading home and I was taking the ferry over the Thames to Gravesend to meet my mum. I was worried that I might have put Laura off adventuring for life, but I'm happy to report that she did indeed manage to run from Rome to home a few months later (and, even better, my parents were coincidentally in Rome when she started and went to wave her off).

When I stepped off the boat in Gravesend, I can confirm that it felt like not only the hottest place in the country but the hottest place in the universe. The last time I had been here was the previous November, on the second day of my adventure. It felt surreal to be back again having completed a loop around the coast. I even ended up sleeping in the very same bed again, thanks to the Clarendon Royal Hotel who kindly put me up for a second time.

————

The next morning, I went to Gravesend Asda, which was open earlier than the sports shops, and bought a new top from their activewear line. It was a pretty unattractive item of clothing but had the one feature I was looking for: a complete back. I'd clung onto my other one until the bitter end, but I really felt like I should run the last two days and that was only possible with a T-shirt that covered the hole in my back.

Mum and I ran together back to Dartford, taking the same route we had ten months earlier. I'm sure that I had heard her say she was never going back to Dartford again as long as she lived the first time around, but here we were again. Clearly she had enjoyed running around the outskirts of town so much that she couldn't resist revisiting the route again.

Coasting

Mum left me in Dartford and headed home while I carried on to Erith. I wasn't actually finishing until Saturday, two days away, but this was my penultimate day of running. When I'd first been working out my finish date, more than a month ago, I had built some buffer days into the schedule. I hadn't quite dared to believe that my legs would get me there in time and I wanted to have some extra time just in case.

Now that they had carried me here, I still couldn't quite believe it. Part of me just wanted to carry on from Erith, run the last 14 miles now, just get it done. But I felt too guilty about letting down all the people who had said they would come and wave me in. Instead, I holed up at my friend Daniel's flat until it was time to finally – finally – finish.

It was weird having a rest day right before the end. Daniel went to work and left me to amuse myself. In the end, at a loss as to what else to do, I went for a run.

CHAPTER 34

On my final morning, I left Daniel's flat and made my way back to where I'd stopped running in Erith two days earlier. I bought a takeaway coffee and a croissant on the way and sat on a bench to eat it.

This was it, the last day.

I downed the dregs of my coffee, dusted pastry crumbs from my legs, strapped on my pack and started running.

I had some friends meeting me for the very final stretch back into Greenwich, but I wanted to do a few miles alone first. Running on the flat, paved ground of the Thames Path, the miles flew by. I still had that gungy hole in my back, skin worn away by day after day of chafing, but my pack was lighter today having left most of my stuff at Daniel's and, combined with my new T-shirt, it was bearable. I was moving quicker than I had for months and before long I'd run the 9 miles to Pontoon Dock, an obscure station on the DLR near London City Airport, where I had arranged to meet the others.

Coasting

I arrived there about an hour ahead of schedule – it had been ten months, but I still didn't fully trust my legs to get me to where they needed to be. I probably needed to start giving them more credit. They'd got me here on time, just like they'd got me around the other 5,000 miles. My legs were never really the problem – it was my head that always gave up first.

I went into a hotel to use the toilet, buy a can of Coke and fill up my bottle with lukewarm water from the bathroom sink, then found a concrete step outside the station to sit and wait. At 1 p.m., the others started to arrive. We laughed for a while at how desolate Pontoon Dock felt. After all the dramatic scenery of the past ten months, it felt a strange place to be ending things.

There were nine of us in total, and we had just five more miles to go. The streets were empty as we ran through the financial district, the tower blocks of offices closed for the weekend. We stopped at a corner shop mid-way through (I've got absolutely no idea why this was necessary on a 5-mile run) and I bought some chocolate milk. When I peered into the carton it looked curdled – I threw it in the bin, not wanting the end of my adventure to be thwarted by some sour milk.

I'd spent so long thinking about how it would feel to finish but now we were approaching that moment it just felt quite… normal. Just as that very first day had, ten months earlier, I felt like I was on a normal weekend run with friends. We chatted, laughed, talked about which pub to go to later. It was just your regular Saturday afternoon.

We crossed the river at the Greenwich Foot Tunnel. Our footsteps echoed as we ran through, the sound of our voices bouncing off the walls. I felt weirdly aware of the hundreds of thousands of litres of water surrounding us. When we emerged on the south side of the river, it felt like we were in a different city altogether. There were big crowds gathering around the Cutty Sark, spilling out of pub gardens, enjoying the bank holiday sunshine. After a lot of tourist dodging, we reached Greenwich Park, where my family and more friends were waiting.

This was it, my finish line.

Except, I didn't actually know exactly where the finish line was. I just knew that it was in this section of the park somewhere. My mum had told me to look out for a group of people with balloons, but it was busy and there were lots of groups scattered across the grass, enjoying the sunshine. I heard my name being called and ran towards the nearest cluster of people but when I got closer, I realised I didn't recognise any of them.

It turned out my dad had just told some random people in the park to cheer for me, and this group happened to be celebrating a birthday and also have some balloons. They were, in fact, complete strangers.

I turned around and saw a bigger group of people at the top of the hill. I could see my mum now. Why had they put the finish line at the top of the hill? What kind of sadists were they? The general rule of ultrarunning is to always walk the uphills, but I didn't think I could get away with strolling to the finish line. I started running again. We might have been in a park in the middle of London, but for me these were the last few steps of the British coast.

Through all those hard moments – the wet feet and the self-doubt and the tears – I'd just kept telling myself that if I just ran one more mile, and then another, I'd get here eventually. And now that moment I'd been dreaming of was here, it was happening, right now.

At the top of the hill, I ran through a tunnel of human hands and... that was it. That moment I'd dreamed of wasn't happening any more – it had happened, past tense. It was over.

We took some photos. I ate a slice of the cake that one of the charities had brought down, getting more icing in my hair than in my mouth. My dad handed me a warm can of Foster's and we cheersed.

I had so badly wanted to be the kind of person who ran around the coast of Britain and now I was.

I'd done it.

———

I spent that night with my best friends. After the picnic, when everybody else had drifted home, we went out for a curry, then to a bar. There was a sticky dance floor and a DJ playing drum and bass in the corner. I climbed the steps to his booth to make a request.

"Will you play Anastasia, 'Left Outside Alone'?" I screamed in his ear, asking for my favourite karaoke song, the one that had been on every playlist over the past ten months.

The DJ looked at me as if I was mad and gestured around us. Admittedly, it perhaps wasn't quite the crowd for Anastasia.

"I've just run around the country! Five-thousand miles!"

He stared at me blankly for a second before shaking his head and turning back to the decks.

"Please?! I've been running for ten months!"

"I don't care what you did – I'm not playing Anastasia."

I had crossed the finish line of the biggest adventure of my life less than 12 hours earlier – the thing I'll probably forever be most proud of myself for – and it still wasn't enough to convince a DJ to play my song.

EPILOGUE

"You are under no obligation to be the same person you were five minutes ago."

Alan Watts

It was a running joke in my family that I changed my mind a lot as a kid. One minute I wanted orange juice, the next it was lemonade. One day I hated baked potatoes, the next they were my favorite food. *Just make up your mind*, they'd laugh, *don't be so fickle.*

But I'm okay being a bit fickle if it means having the freedom to try something new, if it means being able to grow and change. What's the alternative? Being shackled to one idea of ourselves forever, regardless of whether it still serves us or not?

Life isn't linear. I spent so much of the time I was running worrying that, by making the occasional mistake, I somehow invalidated everything that had come before. But it isn't like that – you've still run a long way even if you then go and have an absolute shocker of a night out, or your bank card gets declined, or you end up sucked into yet another conversation with a man who makes you cry (I know, *I know*).

Those first few months – or years, even – after finishing were hard. Totally broke and not sure what else to do, I found a new job that paid well and that I tried to kid myself I felt some passion for, and moved back to London for it. I was barely running, having no motivation to do any exercise. I started dating somebody who didn't like the outdoors at all, and I happily spent that next year just hanging out with my friends, going to the pub and buying clothes that weren't made from Lycra.

I mostly avoided talking about the whole running-around-the-coast thing. Occasionally somebody would ask me to go and give a talk and I'd suffer the worst imposter syndrome. They'd ask for tips about long-distance running and I'd just stand there feeling very aware that I hadn't been for a run for weeks and I'd gained some weight and I probably wouldn't be able to keep up on a run around the block with them.

It took a while but slowly I started to find some balance. I hired a running coach and by virtue of the fact I was paying him, I religiously stuck to the plan he wrote. Running became a part of my life again – more so than it ever had been before the coast. It became – and continues to be – my favourite way to spend my weekends, the focal point of my social life, the thing that I do to feel better when I'm sad and to celebrate when I'm happy.

And it wasn't just running. I started a new job at a charity (doing something I actually cared about, at last) and in a bid to win a team step-count challenge, I became obsessed with walking everywhere. With every walk, I felt like I was coming out of that post-adventure fog. In a way that I struggle to fully explain, but which remains very true, the more time I spent outside and the more I moved, the more the world made sense to me. Eventually, after talking about it non-stop for years, I left London and moved to Bristol, where I'm about one hundred times happier for being just a couple of miles away from the countryside and never having to get on a rush-hour tube.

It's so easy to think that everybody you follow online has it all figured out. Trust me, they don't. Sometimes I meet people and they're still surprised to hear I have a day job, that I'm not a "full-time adventurer". But the truth is that while I love running and being outside and exploring and occasionally tiring myself out on stupidly long challenges, I actually have no desire whatsoever to go on another ten-month long adventure. Never say never, but I like having a home, and friends, and being able to go and see my family without feeling wracked with guilt that I'm "cheating" at something.

And that's okay. I wasted so much time trying to reconcile all the parts of me that felt contradictory, but I didn't need to. You can do something completely new, a total U-turn from anything you've enjoyed before, and decide that you love it and to carry on doing it for the rest of your life. Or you can try something once and then never do it again. Or you can do a bit of both. You can run around a country then decide you're happy just being a weekend-and-holidays runner.

It's all fine. You are under no obligation to be the same person you were five minutes ago.

If you do decide you want to try something new that you-of-five-minutes-ago wouldn't have, then I can highly recommend planning an adventure here in the UK, even if just for a day or a weekend. There's so much to discover on our own doorsteps. As I write this, we're coming to the end (hopefully) of the coronavirus pandemic, and I'm sure this is something we've all learnt to some extent over the past year. How many different 3-mile loops can you walk from your front door? More than we ever could have imagined. Britain has so much to offer – you can climb up mountains, hike across moors, run along coast paths, or you can just walk around the block a few hundred times.

And more than the incredible landscapes, there are all the people who live on this island, the ones who were happy to throw their doors wide open for a total stranger covered in mud. Experiencing this sort of kindness seems to be the universal story of travel all over the world and I can certainly vouch for it here in the UK. I consider it a huge privilege to have been able to spend so much time becoming intimately acquainted with the country I call home (or the edges of it, at least). My favourite party trick is to ask people where they've been on holiday, if they mentioned they've visited the coast.

"Oh, it was just a tiny place," they reply, "you won't know it."

"Try me," I say.

AUTHOR'S NOTE

I've told this story to the best of my ability, as honestly as I could. I have swapped around some locations, changed names and occasionally amalgamated encounters in order to protect people's identities but, beyond that, everything you have read is true. Human memory is notoriously fallible, but this is a portrayal of the journey I went on, of the people I met and of the experiences I had, as I now perceive them. These are memories I'll cherish forever.

ACKNOWLEDGEMENTS

Writing a book is a lot like going for a long run, mainly in that they both involve lots of snacks and spending way too much time in your own head (you don't realise *quite* how irritating you are until you've written 80,000 words about yourself). Another similarity is that although they are technically solo endeavours, in reality both take a village. Ergo, I have a lot of thank yous to say.

Firstly, thanks to the entire adventure community for their unwavering support and enthusiasm from the very beginning, when I came from nowhere, looking distinctly un-outdoorsy I'm sure, and started talking about this idea I had to run around a country. Special thanks to Anna McNuff and Dave Cornthwaite for their incredible generosity and gentle coaxing in those first few months and beyond. And to the Yes Tribe, without whom my whole trip would have been an awful lot lonelier (as hopefully evidenced by the number of mentions they get in this book).

Thanks to Tim Moss and all those who contributed to The Next Challenge Grant in 2015. The email saying I'd won came at the height of my pre-trip panic and, as much as the financial support was very much appreciated, it was the confidence boost that came from knowing that other people believed in my plan that was the real prize.

Next is the big one, and the one I'm not sure I'll ever quite do justice to: thank you to everybody who was a part of the journey itself, who made it both infinitely more comfortable and more enjoyable than it would have been otherwise. From beds for the night to homes for a week, miles and miles of company, countless home-cooked meals, cake deliveries, dogs to befriend, loads of laundry done, pub-quiz winnings donated to my chosen charities, hundreds and thousands of encouraging messages and emails and "likes" on my Facebook posts... The kindness of strangers knows no bounds, it seems – even right on your own doorstep, where you least expect it. I wish I could have included every single person, but I'm not sure anybody would want to read a book that long. Just know that for every interaction I've written about, there were so many more. Without these people I wouldn't have made it to the start line, let alone the finish. Hopefully it goes without saying how grateful I am.

Thanks too to the brands who supported me with kit and supplies along the way: Newton Running, La Sportiva, Bounce Ball, BAM Clothing, Alpkit, Lyon Equipment, Berghaus, Rude Health, Crosstown Doughnuts, Trail Cook, Oi Fiti, Panache Sport, Om Bar and Water-to-Go.

On to the writing part! Thank you to the whole team at Summersdale for bringing this book to life, and especially to

Debbie Chapman, my editor. Debbie first got in touch when I was midway through the run, and somehow didn't lose patience when it took me another five years to actually put pen to paper. I received her email offering me a book deal right in the midst of the first Coronavirus lockdown, two days after getting dumped and shortly before being made redundant. It was a roller-coaster few weeks and I think it's safe to say that I needed *Coasting* more than *Coasting* needed me. I've wanted to write a book for as long as I can remember, since long before I wanted to go on an adventure, and I can't thank Debbie enough for making that dream come true, and for helping me turn my words into something people might actually want to read.

Thanks to my friends who, after listening to me talk about running around the country for five years, then had to put up with me banging on about writing a book about it, and yet have still been kind enough to sound excited about it. In particular, thanks to Georgia for listening to the endless voice notes I've sent her over the past year narrating every high and low of the book-writing process. To Ange, for the daily deliveries of chocolate buttons and cans of Coke Zero to my desk when I was a week away from my first draft deadline and I still had 40,000 words left to write. To Sarah, first for all the long walks where we talked about writing books (which helped remind me this was actually a thing I wanted to do), and then for being my first reader. And to Oscar, for coming up with the title of this book.

Last but absolutely not least, thanks to my family. We aren't typically the most demonstrative but I know that I'm very lucky to have them (even if they are all really bloody weird). My brother Chris deserves a special mention as, without him being my number one cheerleader and sharing my Facebook page all over the internet when I was too shy to do it myself, I doubt anybody would have even known the run happened and you probably wouldn't be reading this book.

And thanks, of course, to Julie and Dave, my mum and dad. Without hesitation, they gave up ten months of their life to visit me in various obscure places around the coast of Britain, listen to me whinge on the phone several times a day and then put up with the post-adventure blues playing out in their spare room once I finished. Almost everybody who meets my mum and dad ends up liking them more than they like me but I can't really argue with that. They're pretty good, as parents go.

ABOUT THE ILLUSTRATOR

Laurie King is an illustrator and graphic designer living in Swanage Bay who takes his inspiration from the outdoors. Through his love of cycling and running, he finds beautiful landscapes and routes that he captures with his distinctive use of line work and detail.

Start with a squiggle.

www.laurieking.co.uk
Instagram: @iamlaurie

Have you enjoyed this book?
If so, why not write a review on your favourite website?

If you're interested in finding out more about our books, find us on Facebook at **Summersdale Publishers,** on Twitter at **@Summersdale** and on Instagram at **@summersdalebooks.**

Thanks very much for buying this Summersdale book.

www.summersdale.com